ON SOCIAL ORGANIZATION
AND SOCIAL CONTROL

THE HERITAGE OF SOCIOLOGY

A Series Edited by Donald N. Levine

Morris Janowitz, *Founding Editor*

MORRIS JANOWITZ

ON SOCIAL ORGANIZATION AND SOCIAL CONTROL

Edited and with an Introduction by
JAMES BURK

THE UNIVERSITY OF CHICAGO PRESS
Chicago and London

MORRIS JANOWITZ taught sociology at the University of Chicago for twenty-six years. He founded and then served for twenty years as editor of the Heritage of Sociology series.

JAMES BURK is associate professor of sociology at Texas A&M University.

The University of Chicago Press, Chicago 60637

The University of Chicago Press, Ltd., London
© 1991 by The University of Chicago
All rights reserved. Published 1991
Printed in the United States of America
00 99 98 97 96 95 94 93 92 91 5 4 3 2 1

Library of Congress Cataloging-in-Publication Data
Janowitz, Morris.
    On social organization and social control / Morris Janowitz : edited and with an introduction by James Burk.
        p.   cm. — (The Heritage of sociology)
    Includes bibliographical references and index.
    ISBN 0-226-39301-1.   —   ISBN 0-226-39303-8
(pbk.)
    1. Social control. 2. Social structure. I. Burk, James, 1948– . II. Title. III. Series.
HM73.J37   1991
303.3'3—dc20   90-48229
                                                          CIP

⊗The paper used in this publication meets the minimum requirements of the American National Standard for Information Sciences—Permanence of Paper for Printed Library Materials, ANSI Z39.48–1984.

Contents

Acknowledgments

Many debts were incurred in the making of this volume. The Department of Sociology and the College of Liberal Arts of Texas A&M University generously provided material support to defray some of the expenses of this project. Gayle Janowitz supplied large quantities of materials for my use, patiently answered what must have seemed an unending stream of questions, and opened her home to me as I conducted my work. She and her family welcomed me as kin. In no small way, this volume owes its existence to them.

I corresponded with and interviewed many friends, colleagues, and former students of Morris Janowitz, too many to name in this place. How much I owe to their insights is only suggested by the footnotes in the Introduction. I am especially grateful to Douglas Mitchell, of the University of Chicago Press, Donald Levine, and Edward Shils, for encouraging me to undertake this project, and to Donald Levine, for his close reading of, and helpful comments on, my introductory essay. The staff of the Department of Special Collections in the Regenstein Library of the University of Chicago were also forthcoming to aid me as I worked through the Janowitz Papers on deposit there. The good atmosphere they provided for scholarly work and the good cheer with which they performed their jobs belies the stereotype that hospitality is a trait confined to the South. Jaime Vinas and Anne Smith made the tasks of research and editing much easier by the high quality of their work as my research assistants.

There is perhaps no better place for me to thank Professor R. Guy Sedlack, who first introduced me to the "Chicago school" of sociology. His critical, but irrepressible, enthusiasm for that approach was largely responsible for my decision to undertake graduate training at the University of Chicago, where I first met and studied under Morris Janowitz.

Introduction: A Pragmatic Sociology

Morris Janowitz's reputation as a sociologist stands, for many, upon his extraordinary achievements as a student of armed forces in modern societies, and for good reason. His studies of the military—most notably his study *The Professional Soldier*—opened up systematic study of the institutionalization of legitimate coercion, which was a serious yet neglected problem for modern societies. By defining key variables and exploring their connections, he brought order to an inchoate field with ideas that continue to guide the best sociological research on the subject. Moreover, at a time when this field possessed few resources, Janowitz generously created mechanisms to support the research of other scholars studying the military establishment and its role in society. Nevertheless, it would be an error to suppose his contributions to sociology were limited to study of the armed forces. He was no specialist of that kind, narrowly defined.

On the contrary, Morris Janowitz's scholarly career displayed substantial diversity. Over the course of five decades, from the 1940s to the 1980s, he published studies on race and ethnic prejudice, collective behavior, propaganda and mass communications, voting and macropolitical organization, urban community, schools, and social stratification, all in addition to his work on armed forces and society. This list omits the work he did for twenty years as editor of the Heritage of Sociology series, a series designed to recover the enduring contributions of past sociologists. No simple statement adequately summarizes such a varied achievement. Unlike his older contemporary, Talcott Parsons, Janowitz offered no grand theoretical scheme to organize his various empirical accomplishments. One might suppose, then, that his work exhibits a fragmented quality, which some would take to indicate a crisis in sociological theory, the demise of sociology as a unified discipline.[1] Yet this too would be an error, a more misleading error perhaps than the first.

In retrospect, Morris Janowitz's career reveals a coherent set of thematic concerns and a common logic of inquiry. In broadest terms, Janowitz focused his research, first, on the complex relationships between advancing industrialism and novel trends in social organization, and, second, on the consequences of these relationships for maintaining the strength of parliamentary democracies. As his thought on the subject matured, he came to believe that advanced industrial societies demanded higher levels of personal and social control than earlier industrial societies in order to retain the same degree of democratic governance. In his massive study of American society, *The Last Half-Century,* he argued that the developing social organization of advanced industrial societies created conditions of institutional disarticulation, made it more difficult to accommodate societal strains, and so promoted a crisis of political legitimacy. To meet the crisis, social institutions had to be rationally adapted to improve their capacity to raise the level of social and personal control on which a democratic society depends. While social science could not prescribe precisely how such social reconstruction was to be done, it could clarify the issues which institutional leaders had to resolve.

These themes built upon the core concepts of social organization, social control, and institution building, which are identified with the Chicago school of sociology. Janowitz was a bearer of the intellectual traditions of that school, especially as they are found in the writings of W. I. Thomas and Robert E. Park. The observation is neither novel nor surprising.[2] Janowitz, after all, did his graduate work in the Department of Sociology at the University of Chicago and, apart from ten years spent at the University of Michigan during the 1950s, taught there until his retirement in 1987. He chaired the department from 1967 to 1972 and during that period restored it to a position of preeminence not enjoyed since Thomas and Park were its major figures. He edited a volume of Thomas's papers and the famous introductory text by Park and Ernest W. Burgess for inclusion in the Heritage of Sociology series. As Edward Shils observed, "he felt himself to be the heir of the great Chicago sociologists."[3]

One must beware not to treat the Chicago school as though it were only one tradition. "In fact," Morris Janowitz wrote, "at the time of its most intensive activity the Chicago school contained theoretical viewpoints and substantive interests which were extremely variegated."[4] Steady tolerance of varied approaches to understanding the objects of sociological study helped establish the Chicago department as a center for creative research early in the twentieth century.[5] Nevertheless, there were common tendencies in outlook and mode of inquiry which characterized the Chicago school, and the sources of these can be linked historically with the development of philosophical pragmatism.[6] To assert that Morris Janowitz was an heir of the great Chicago sociologists points to the crucial role his career and writings played in carrying on and extending the logic of a pragmatic approach to the study of modern society.

This essay has two purposes, to indicate the personal and institutional contexts which shaped Morris Janowitz's intellectual development and to review the major categories and themes of his sociological research. Both are united by a common pursuit of these main ideas: that Janowitz's scholarly research is marked by a coherence of theoretical, methodological, and substantive concerns, that underlying this coherence is primarily, though not exclusively, the influence of philosophical pragmatism (especially as it was exerted through the work of John Dewey), and that Janowitz's main contribution to sociology— separate from the particular findings of his empirical research and the building of institutions to carry on similar work—has been to demonstrate the continuing value of a pragmatic approach for macrosocial theory and research.

Formative Years

Morris Janowitz was born on 22 October 1919 in Paterson, New Jersey, the second son of Jewish parents who had immigrated to the United States from different parts of Poland before the First World War.[7] His father, Samuel, had no formal education but was trained as a silk-weaver in his native Lodz. Like many fellow Jews who were fleeing from the Russian Czar's oppressive regime in Poland, he was drawn to Paterson, which was known for its silk industry. He worked in the textile factories until he was able to establish his own silk business. Janowitz's mother, Rose Meyers (née Rachel Meyerovich), was originally from Bialystok, the daughter of a Russian tailor. She had some formal education, and like most Eastern Europeans spoke several languages. Before emigrating in 1905, she had been active in the Bund, the Polish branch of the Socialist revolution. Janowitz would say of her that she was a "terrorist" and a "gun-runner," and associated with Leon Trotsky. Yet she was disillusioned with revolutionary activity. After escorting her niece to the United States, she decided to remain, working as a hatmaker until she met and married Samuel.

Neither prosperous nor poor materially, the family and the urban community in which it lived nevertheless provided a rich environment within which to grow intellectually. There was an appropriate balance among the forces of security and nurturance, challenge and confrontation.

The family and local neighborhood allowed a gentle way of life, less common now in urban settings. A rhythm was maintained by the ice-man and milkman, the ragman and scissors man, who, along with the policeman, made regular rounds through the neighborhood; by trips to markets where fresh produce, chickens and fish, beef and rabbits could be bought; by outings to one of the parks on either end of town or hikes up High Mountain; and by Saturday afternoons spent in the movie theaters. In the summer, the Janowitzes traveled with close friends for a drive to Brighton Beach or to a state park for a picnic and swimming. In the winter, friends gathered at the Janowitz house on Saturday nights, to eat cold cuts, play pinochle, drink tea, and talk.[8] Within the family, Janowitz's intellectual abilities were recognized early on and deferred to: When the Great Depression and the invention of rayon ruined his father's silk business, Janowitz (still in high school) conducted what he called his first community survey and determined that his father would be well advised to open a liquor store to earn his living, advice his father followed. Janowitz was also popular among his friends, who respected his intelligence, his capacity for leadership, and his concern for serious things, who enjoyed his subtle and quick sense of humor, and who appreciated the good sense he displayed by not taking himself too seriously. He was an excellent student at Paterson's Eastside High School, taking a classical course of instruction which included intensive study of Latin and German as well as mathematics, science, and English. He was active in extracurricular affairs, displaying in youth the energy which would characterize his academic career, editing the high school newspaper (fashioned after the *New York Times*), organizing an informal reading club (which attempted to read Joyce's *Ulysses*), and establishing a science club (which referred to itself as *Discipuli Scientiae*).[9]

However gentle this primary-group circle, Paterson was yet a rough industrial city. The poet William Carlos Williams described its violent character in graphic terms: "And the guys from Paterson / beat up / the guys from Newark and told / them to stay the hell out / of their territory and then / socked you one / across the nose . . ."[10] Before the First World War, Paterson had been the scene of intense and bloody labor quarrels, which had not altogether subsided after the war. When a boy of seven, Janowitz witnessed strikebreaking troops crush a Communist-led demonstration in nearby Passaic. He recalled Polish immigrants who beat up Jews in school, an experience which prompted him while an undergraduate to read W. I. Thomas and Florian Znaniecki's book *The Polish Peasant in Europe and America* for insight into the sources of their hostility. He was sensitive to the shame of poverty brought on by economic depression, and in high school planned with his classmates to begin a cooperative farm for broken-down souls.[11] And he experienced ethnic prejudice firsthand when, despite his excellent high school record, he was discouraged from applying to Princeton University because he was a Jew. These local experiences of sociopolitical strain in industrial society occurred within a global context which threatened large-scale war. Janowitz was fully aware of the threat and closely followed the unfolding civil war in Spain.[12] His mother's revolutionary past and subsequent disillusionment made her an avid but critical observer of political events in Europe; she taught her son about the dangers of radicalism while sustaining his hope that some political change for the better was possible.[13]

In 1937, Janowitz entered the Washington Square College of New York University, from which he would graduate four years later with honors, having majored in economics.[14] He continued to be involved with journalism, editing the college newspaper, an accomplishment in which he took some pride. Yet he had no clear vocational direction, beyond a vague sense that he might work after graduation in Washington, D.C., for a federal government agency. He took no courses in sociology, but became acquainted with the Chicago school of social science through his close association with Bruce Lannes Smith, and was exposed to the serious study of pragmatism and the major movements of macrosocial thought under the tutelage of Sidney Hook. Smith taught economics at the time as a general social science which included materials from anthropology, psychoanalysis, and political science.[15] Taking Janowitz under his wing, he arranged for Janowitz to collect tickets for public lectures in which current policy issues were contested and to meet one of the lecturers, Harold D. Lasswell, who was Smith's former teacher from the University of Chicago.[16] This led Janowitz to study Lasswell's written work—which he greatly admired—and to discover how psychoanalytic theories might be used to enrich an empirical social science of institutional processes.[17]

Sidney Hook, the distinguished philosopher and student of John Dewey, was a center of controversy during the late 1930s because he was avowedly anticommunist when communism was thought by many to be a "world-saving" doctrine needed to counter economic depression and fascist oppression. His course on the philosophy of history and civilization, taken over from Morris Cohen, critically reviewed not only the Marxist theory of economic determinism, but physicalist, racial, heroic, and idealist theories of determinism as well. So against the temper of the times, Professor Hook recalls, "it took some courage to take this course from me and they called those who did 'Hook-worms.'"[18] They were among the better students and Janowitz was in their number, unusual only for not having taken any other course from Hook. The exact influence it had on Janowitz's intellectual outlook is difficult to trace, but was profoundly important. Reflecting on the experience in his preface to *The Last Half-Century,* Janowitz wrote that Hook's teaching of pragmatism "saved me from the burdens of both materialism and idealism." [19] Elsewhere he claimed that the course laid the basis for his own teaching about theories of social organization and that it made "a powerful impact" on him.[20]

The connection with Harold Lasswell, however, proved a more immediate and practical influence. After graduating from college in 1941, Janowitz worked for a short while in the Library of Congress as a research assistant in Lasswell's "War Time Communications" project. He hauled large volumes of bound newspapers published throughout Europe and North America to the project's offices for content analysis that was done by others.[21] Three months later he went to work for the Department of Justice's Special War Policies Unit, a unit created by Attorney General Francis Biddle.[22] Its purpose was to prevent the closure of foreign-language presses and persecution of ethnic minorities which occurred in the United States during the First World War. Standing against those in government who followed a more conservative course less respectful of civil liberties, Biddle assured President Roosevelt that the unit would carefully monitor publications of the presses and that the Justice Department would take quick action should anything dangerous appear in them.[23] Janowitz's own responsibility was to follow the native fascist press, beginning his systematic study of mass communications and propaganda. Though young, he supervised an increasingly larger number of the staff, and took part in the trial of at least one native fascist.[24] By working in Washington, he also met many good sociologists—Edward Shils, Herbert Marcuse (before he became a radical), and Barrington Moore among them—who, like him, were mobilized for the war effort.[25]

In 1943, Morris Janowitz was drafted into the Army. He relished the opportunity of closer contact with the "real war." Following preliminary training, in the winter of 1943–44, Janowitz joined the Research and Analysis Branch of the Office of Strategic Services (OSS) in London. He was detailed by the OSS to the Psychological Warfare Division of the Supreme Headquarters, Allied Expeditionary Forces (SHAEF), where he continued his work on mass communications and propaganda by analyzing the content of German radio broadcasts. There he worked closely with W. Phillips Davison, Alexander George, Felix Gilbert, Leonard Krieger, Val Lorwin, and Edward Shils, among others. The urgency of wartime conditions encouraged serious discussions among them about how the theories and methods of social science might be used to fulfill the duties they had to perform.[26] After the invasion of Europe, Janowitz left London for the Continent and began directly to interview German prisoners of war, gathering data which he and Edward Shils would later analyze in their famous article on "Cohesion and Disintegration in the Wehrmacht in World War II."[27]

Janowitz was deeply affected by the war, and aware of the special insight into its complexity which he gained despite his youth and low rank: "I think the terror of the war was more visual to me since I was an observer, a sociological observer. I could see the war at the lowest levels of operation and at the highest levels, and I was unique in that sense . . . and I think that's what made my education. I don't recommend having a war in order to educate a sociologist, but that was what happened in my case."[28] This experience with war, with the research that war required of him and with other social scientists engaged in the war effort, crystallized Janowitz's self-identification as a social scientist. It taught him how to do research and it provided him with opportunities to report the results of his research in scholarly journals. While in government service, he published articles on the reliability of content analysis methods, the propaganda technique of the native fascist Gerald L. K. Smith, trends in Wehrmacht morale, and the democratic political attitudes of German youth immediately after the war was concluded.[29] After his discharge from the Army in 1945, Janowitz worked in Washington, D.C., as an intelligence analyst for the Department of State, but had no thought of making government service a permanent career. He was prepared to return to school, to undertake graduate studies in sociology.

In sum, the years from early childhood through the end of the Second World War brought Janowitz into direct contact with the substantive problems and institutional settings he would study during his scholarly career: the military, the community press and mass media, collective violence and urban riots, ethnic prejudice and hostility, and the social conditions for maintaining a democratic society. They also brought him into contact with the major intellectual traditions which would influence his thought: the Chicago school of empirical social research, psychoanalysis, and philosophical pragmatism. And they oriented him toward sociology as a career. They describe a pattern of critical formative influences, the exact operation of which would require more extensive research and documentation to reveal. There is no evidence, however, that these influences had congealed to form a relatively explicit and coherent theoretical outlook. This came later in his life.

Academic Career and Intellectual Development

The main lines of Morris Janowitz's academic career are easily traced. He began graduate study in sociology at the University of Chicago in January 1946 and graduated two years later in June 1948. He was hired as an instructor in the College of the University of Chicago in 1947, before he completed his Ph.D. degree, and was promoted to assistant professor in the College in 1948. Yet there was no hope for an appointment in the Department of Sociology at Chicago. In 1951, Janowitz accepted a position as an assistant professor in the Department of Sociology at the University of Michigan. He taught there until 1961, being promoted rapidly to associate professor in 1953 and to full professor in 1957. After spending the academic year 1961–62 as a Ford Foundation Visiting Professor at the Graduate School of Business of the University of Chicago, Janowitz returned to Chicago in 1962 with an appointment in the Department of Sociology, where he remained until his retirement in 1987. On 7 November 1988 he died from Parkinson's disease, which had afflicted him for over a decade. More than these sparse facts are needed, however, to provide a full picture of the man.

Janowitz's career can be divided into three phases. The first phase begins with his decision to enter Chicago's graduate program in 1946 and concludes with the publication of *The Professional Soldier* in 1960. During this period, Janowitz published prolifically to establish his reputation for critical and original research in the various subfields he would study. He also showed himself to be an unusually capable instructor of graduate students, a creative builder of institutions to facilitate the conduct of research, and an able adviser (and sometime participant) in public affairs.

The second period begins with Janowitz's return to the University of Chicago in 1961 and ends in 1972, when he concluded his five-year chairmanship of the Department of Sociology. In this period, Janowitz's creative energies were directed rather more to building institutions to facilitate research by others than to opening new avenues of research for himself. During this decade Janowitz put the Inter-University Seminar on Armed Forces and Society on a comparatively sound financial footing, allowing its growth into a worldwide association to assist social scientific study of the military; he founded the Center for Social Organization Studies as a vehicle to promote the Chicago tradition of field research by faculty and graduate students; with Lloyd Fallers, Clifford Geertz, and Edward Shils, he helped establish at Chicago the influential Committee for the Comparative Study of New Nations, which focused research of faculty and graduate students on the problems of building nations from former colonial possessions; he also founded the Heritage of Sociology book series published by the University of Chicago Press; and as chairman of the department, after 1967, he strengthened faculty appointments and guided the department through the crisis which arose over the student disturbances of 1969. It was a period of great activity, for in addition to these professional enterprises, Janowitz worked arduously (most often without pay) to improve the local housing stock, schools, and police, and as an occasional adviser for the federal government. Not less important, however, it was a time during which Janowitz mulled over the assumptions and significance of his previous work.

The third period extends from 1972, when Janowitz spent a year in England as a visiting Pitt Professor at Cambridge University, to his retirement in 1987. During this period, when Janowitz was relieved somewhat of administrative responsibilities, his work bore the fruit of his long reflection about democratic social control and the transition from early to advanced industrial society. Nowhere was this focus clearer than in his books *Social Control of the Welfare State* (1976), *The Last Half-Century* (1978), and *The Reconstruction of Patriotism* (1983). In these, Janowitz attempted, with partial success, to codify his prior research and the findings of a vast social science literature around substantive themes based on postulates drawn explicitly from philosophical pragmatism.

From Chicago to Ann Arbor

The first period of Janowitz's career carried him from the University of Chicago, where he did his graduate work and began his teaching and research, to the University of Michigan, where his reputation as one of the nation's foremost sociologists was established by publication of his book *The Professional Soldier*.

Janowitz's decision to study sociology at the University of Chicago was influenced by his early contact with the traditions of the Chicago school while an undergraduate student of Bruce Lannes Smith, by his subsequent association with Harold D. Lasswell and Edward Shils,[30] and by the presence on the faculty there of Bruno Bettelheim.[31] Although the Department of Sociology at Chicago in the late 1940s was not as eminent as it had been, it remained an outstanding institution with a distinguished faculty.[32] And it attracted an excellent cohort of students to its program. When Janowitz arrived on campus in January 1946, with a Social Science Research Council Demobilization Fellowship to defray his expenses, he recalled that

the tradition of the Chicago school—a strong pressure for fieldwork in-
fused with a theoretical orientation—was already being carried on as much
by graduate students as by the faculty. The presence of an active generation
of older students who were veterans of World War II produced a ferment
that lasted about half a decade. They experienced a collective intellectual
existence which was a mixture of the older style plus a search for emerging
sociological directions.[33]

One imagines that Janowitz welcomed the opportunities and stimulation of such an environment.[34] Energetic as always, he was immediately involved in significant research projects quite apart from the
requirements imposed by taking courses. By the summer of 1946, he
presented a draft of his paper "Cohesion and Disintegration in the
Wehrmacht in World War II" at the twenty-fifth annual Institute of the
Society for Social Research. He continued work on this study with Edward Shils through 1947 while also engaged in his dissertation research. In conversation, Janowitz sometimes claimed that the article
was rejected for publication "by every major journal." But there is no
substantiation for this claim in his correspondence. While some letters
suggest that the paper was rejected by a few journals for being too
long, to emphasize this misses a more important point. Janowitz was
already concerned with preventing isolation of the military from communication with university-based social scientists. He hoped the Army
would publish the study in book form, use it for instructional purposes
at the Military Academy in West Point, and distribute it widely among
the officer corps. Janowitz feared the article "would not receive much
attention in military circles" if it were published in an academic journal.[35] Only after the breakdown of negotiations with the *Infantry
Journal* to publish the study as a pamphlet did Janowitz send it to the
Public Opinion Quarterly, where it was quickly accepted, published,
and much read, even by those in military circles.[36]

At the same time Janowitz worked on this study of Wehrmacht morale, he also began work with Bruno Bettelheim on a study of prejudice
among returning war veterans.[37] This was one of a series of research
projects on prejudice—*The Authoritarian Personality* was perhaps the
best-known one—commissioned by the American Jewish Committee.
The data collected for it supplied the basis for Janowitz's dissertation,
Mobility, Subjective Deprivation, and Ethnic Hostility, and for his
serving as a consultant to the Commission on Civil Rights appointed
by President Harry S. Truman. Most important, under Bettelheim's
guidance, Janowitz began to study psychoanalytic thought systematically and in depth. He was deeply influenced by this study, as is evident

from the theoretical framework adopted in *The Dynamics of Prejudice* (1950), which he wrote with Bettelheim. He was not and never would become a doctrinaire Freudian who held to a deterministic orthodoxy or a psychologistic reductionism. But he accepted dynamic ego psychology as a fundamentally true theory of human nature. His understanding of personal and social control as a realistic limitation on the pursuit of self-interest by higher collective principles plainly bears a psychoanalytic stamp.

The practice of working simultaneously and productively on multiple research projects was a well-formed habit by the time Janowitz completed his degree in 1948. While teaching at Chicago after finishing his degree, he completed his work on prejudice with Bettelheim and began research for *The Community Press in the Urban Setting* (1952). Following up on the leads of W. I. Thomas and Robert E. Park, he used techniques of content analysis in this study to show how local newspapers contributed to the maintenance and integration of local urban communities. Here was an important empirically based argument against the "gemeinschaft-gesellschaft" tradition, which forecast the wholesale replacement of local communities by mass societies. And he also collaborated with Bernard Berelson to edit a *Reader in Public Opinion and Mass Communication* (1950), which is still in print in its third edition, co-edited with Paul Hirsch.

Despite his record of achievement, Janowitz was not offered an appointment in the Department of Sociology. Although he continued to teach in the College, doing so was a source of strain. Robert Maynard Hutchins insisted that students in the College at Chicago read "great books." Janowitz found the approach too constraining, especially for instruction in a sociology concerned with the organization of contemporary society.[38] Under these circumstances, in 1951 Janowitz accepted an appointment as an assistant professor in the Department of Sociology at the University of Michigan.

Although he was a junior member of the faculty at Michigan, Janowitz played a substantial role in directing the department's development through the early 1950s. Unlike the situation at Chicago, sociology at Michigan did not enjoy high prestige. The department was noted for its program in social psychology, led by Theodore Newcomb, Dorian Cartwright, Daniel Katz, and J. R. P. French. These were distinguished figures in their field, but their ambition was to establish social psychology as a separate discipline of the social sciences. The task for Janowitz—and other junior faculty in the department in that decade, who included Guy Swanson, Gerhard Lenski, Hubert

Blalock, and Harold Wilensky—was to strengthen the program in "mainstream" sociology, the study of social organization and social change.[39]

Janowitz was effective in the role. He offered a graduate seminar on social organization with Guy Swanson which provided an occasion to reflect on what he had learned from Sidney Hook's course on the philosophy of history and civilization.[40] The course focused on the major collectivities and institutions of society and the properties of organizations; it adopted a comparative-historical approach, emphasizing collective behavior as crucial for understanding organizational growth and functioning; and it was a popular offering, frequently oversubscribed by the graduate students. The reason for the course's popularity, in part, was the charismatic quality of Janowitz's teaching. Janowitz was not a good classroom teacher in formal terms. As Guy Swanson remembers, "He often rambled, his formal formulations were often vague, he was given to outrageous overstatements (and to good-natured retraction when challenged). But the problems he addressed were central in scientific and societal terms and the half-explicit, half-implicit frameworks through which he analyzed them were so original, penetrating, and promising that nothing else mattered."[41] Janowitz sought to push and to challenge his students, not to direct them; he expected them to have the courage of their convictions and to be ready to defend them.[42] It was an effective method to prod creative learning, although it cowed passive students.

For Janowitz, teaching and research were complementary and compatible activities, not competing specialisms which stood in the way of one another. While at Michigan, he published more than twenty articles and ten books, following lines of inquiry which he began to pursue at Chicago and opening new lines of inquiry as well. The facilities of the Survey Research Center and the periodic large-scale surveys of Detroit (the Detroit Area Study) provided means for Janowitz to conduct research on the processes of democratic consent formed through national presidential elections and on the relationship between the public and local and national governmental bureaucracies. In this work, he began to formulate the conditions which elections had to fulfill to maintain a democratic society, and to identify the difficulties citizens sometimes had in relating their self-interest to the administration of public programs.

By far his most important research during this period was his study *The Professional Soldier*. When and why Janowitz decided to undertake the study cannot be said with certainty. He had not thought of it before entering graduate school.[43] He did have what he called "a powerful interest" in continuing his work on military organizations. But he believed that sociologists viewed the study of the military "with suspicion and reservation." And so, while he was at Chicago in the late 1940s, he kept his research interest in the military "rather quiet." The situation at Michigan, in his mind, was not very different: "I had strong assistance from my colleagues at the University of Michigan in other topics where our work overlapped. But they were not interested in research and writing on the military, and had little substantive knowledge on which I could draw." [44] Nevertheless, the record shows that Janowitz was at work on *The Professional Soldier* shortly after he arrived at Michigan, and that he was not without institutional support in completing the project.

In the summer of 1953, Janowitz had money to bring together a group of scholars—including Samuel Huntington, Maury Feld, Albert Biderman, and Kurt Lang—for two days in Ann Arbor to discuss the social scientific study of the military. [45] Shortly after this summer seminar, Janowitz wrote his first working paper on the professional soldier. If few people at Michigan were interested in the topic, others elsewhere made up for the lack, knew about the working paper, and were interested in reading it. [46] The following year Janowitz received a Fulbright Fellowship to spend the academic year 1954–55 in Frankfurt at the Institute for Social Research, where he would pursue his interests in social organization research, to include collecting comparative data for his research on "the professional soldier and political power." [47] Further support, from the Russell Sage Foundation, enabled him to prepare a short monograph reviewing sociological research on the military which was published in 1959 as *Sociology and the Military Establishment*. Janowitz then spent the academic year 1958–59 as a Fellow at the Center for Advanced Study in the Behavioral Sciences, where he wrote *The Professional Soldier*.

Sociological study of the military was not then—nor is it now—as well institutionalized or accepted as (say) the study of religious, educational, political, or business institutions. Nevertheless, there was support for and a high level of interest in Janowitz's work on the subject. His book supplied a social and political portrait of the military officer as an emerging profession from the turn of the century through the 1950s. Its central argument was that the boundaries separating the military from civilian society had progressively weakened since the turn of the century. It described a military organization in which authoritarian domination gave way to greater reliance on persuasion and manipulation; skill requirements more nearly reflected civilian skill structures; the social base for recruiting officers broadened, creating a more socially representative officer corps; innovative career patterns were increasingly rewarded; and a pragmatic outlook toward war supplanted an absolutist outlook, making military officers more responsive to the demands of domestic politics and more considerate of the political consequences of military actions on foreign affairs. The book was pioneering in its concept and execution. It began an important dialogue in the social sciences and in the military about the nature of civilian and professional control over military officers in democratic societies.

But the importance of this accomplishment should not overshadow the varied nature of Janowitz's intellectual development in this first period of his academic career. His broad research agenda, organized loosely under the theme of social organization and by a concern for politics, established his reputation as a specialist in organizational analysis, political sociology, urban sociology, and mass communications. And the results of his empirical studies led him to important general conclusions about strategies of social research, the nature of democratic industrial society, and the role of social science. The most important of these can be summarized as follows:

First, Janowitz rejected psychological and sociological reductionism. It was not possible to explain why Germans fought in terms of a fanatical cultural commitment to Nazi ideology. One had to examine the complex interplay among psychological dispositions, primary-group relations, bureaucratic leadership, and attachments to the secondary symbols of the nation. Following the same logic, one could not explain why people expressed prejudice only in terms of psychological dispositions. Movement through social structures was critical to take into account. Psychological responses of prejudice were most likely to show under conditions of rapid social mobility.

Second, Janowitz recognized the inadequacy of the "gemeinschaft-gesellschaft" perspective. In a period of American sociology that was much taken by the image of modern society as "mass society" and by the eclipse of community, Janowitz's own study of the local urban community made clear that industrialization did not replace primary with secondary group relations. The question, rather, was how local urban neighborhoods were transformed, and what the consequences of these transformations were for the larger society.

Third, Janowitz discerned a broad transformation of social structure in the process of industrialization as it affected the military. In sharp contrast to C. Wright Mills's formulations about a unified power elite, Janowitz perceived that the progressive division of labor made it more difficult to organize the military's various functional and ceremonial roles within a single hierarchical order. The result undermined traditional bases of authority and led to a dispersion (not concentration) of power and control.

Fourth, Janowitz rejected the idea that competition among political parties was sufficient to maintain a democratic society. He argued that if competition was to build democratic consent then it had to stimulate effective political deliberation on the candidates and issues, preclude excessive reliance on influence exercised by the mass media, and encourage high levels of effective participation among all social groups. Participation was effective to the degree it was motivated by predispositions of high political self-confidence as well as self-interest.

Finally, Janowitz asserted an important and forceful role for the social sciences to play in the maintenance of democratic society. In an article critical of the ideology of professional psychologists, Janowitz contended that social science research is bound to rest on value assumptions, and that a professional ideology which attempts to deny this under the banner of "value free" science supports a distorted and exaggerated belief in the potentialities of social science to guide social practice. Social science is not capable of "manipulating" human conduct. But realistically conceived, it may "enhance the dignity of mankind by clarifying the fundamental nature of human nature," and limit human exploitation and manipulation.[48]

Return to Chicago

In the summer of 1960, Morris Janowitz negotiated to return to the Department of Sociology at Chicago.[49] The reasons for seeking a move were personal as well as professional. Ann Arbor's attractions were limited for both Janowitz and his wife, Gayle—whom he married after moving to Michigan, but first met in Chicago. They preferred to live in an urban center, and to have a broader social life than could be found within an academic community alone. And both were drawn to the University of Chicago, where his intellectual roots reached deep and she had worked at the Orthogenic School and done a master's degree in education.[50] When Janowitz was offered a Ford Foundation Visiting Professorship at Chicago's Graduate School of Business for 1961 and a permanent appointment as professor in the Department of Sociology in 1962, it was "a great fulfillment for him. . . . At Chicago he always acted as if he had long dreamed of becoming a professor at the University and now that he had done so, the reality turned out to be even better than the dream."[51] This was so even though the department had many weaknesses.

The 1950s was a rancorous period for sociology at Chicago as faculty fought bitterly about what the department should be like, and the wounds from that rancor had not yet healed entirely when Janowitz rejoined the department in 1961.[52] Janowitz recalled:

> When I returned to the University of Chicago in 1961 after a decade's absence, the intellectual ghosts continued to walk the floors and corridors of the third floor of the Social Science Research Building. There was no working definition of what was past and what was present. There was even a strange denial of the past in some quarters. The collected papers of many of the major figures had not been published nor were there plans to do this. Some of the irreplaceable archives of these men had been destroyed or discarded. . . . The past did not come to an end; it was simply fractured and suspended.[53]

Implicitly, he was comparing it to the department he knew in the late 1940s with many on the faculty who had been members of the department (often as students) during its height in the 1920s and 1930s and for whom the intellectual ghosts walking the corridors evoked lively memories. Comparatively speaking, the department in the early 1960s was at a low ebb: it lacked leadership; it was racked by personal conflicts; and it had poor morale.[54]

The second period of Janowitz's academic career was characterized by his efforts to improve this situation, to rebuild the department at Chicago. Rather than argue over what the department should be like, Janowitz's approach was to facilitate and focus faculty and student research by establishing two overlapping research organizations, the Center for Social Organization Studies and the Inter-University Seminar on Armed Forces and Society.[55] Both were creations born of his experience at the University of Michigan.

To encourage social organization studies in the Department of Sociology at Michigan, Janowitz wangled resources—a little space, some old furniture, and a few dollars—to create a Center for Social Organization. It provided little more than a place for graduate students and faculty to meet periodically to discuss current research, and was no more formal than a brown-bag seminar. But the center successfully channeled graduate student training and research.[56]

Building on this model, Janowitz devised plans for a similar center at Chicago, different only in its scale of operation. The primary purpose of the center was to facilitate graduate student training. Students appointed as fellows received financial support to pursue their research. In addition, special research projects, directed by faculty, were organized to study the Chicago Public School system, military organization, delinquency control, and business organization. Graduate fellows were also actively involved in the conduct of these studies.[57] Such a center, of course, required material support. The university provided space for the graduate students to work, but money was needed to fund fellowships and defray research expenses. A long-term commitment from the Russell Sage Foundation (with other funds from the Ford Foundation) allowed the center to begin operation in the fall of 1962 with no fewer than nine graduate student fellows and seven faculty members involved in its activities.[58]

The Inter-University Seminar on Armed Forces and Society (IUS) was organized during Janowitz's last year at Michigan.[59] In February 1961, a small group of university-based social scientists gathered in Ann Arbor for two days to review the present state of, and problems connected with, military sociology.[60] The meeting clarified research plans which members of the seminar would pursue, and agreement was reached about the objectives of the IUS: to support development of sociological analyses of military organization; to prepare a series of specific research papers on internal military organization; and to serve as a focal point for long-term training in and for the development of a relationship between sociology and the military establishment.[61] The following year, after Janowitz moved to the University of Chicago, these objectives began to be fulfilled.

Like that of the Center for Social Organization Studies, establishment of the IUS was assured when the Russell Sage Foundation provided long-term grants in excess of $268,000 for the years 1963–72. These grants allowed the IUS to award graduate fellowships, to pay research and travel expenses of associated faculty, to sponsor periodic conferences, and to establish an executive secretariat to administer seminar operations.[62] But the IUS was unlike the Center for Social Organization Studies in being an interdisciplinary association that reached beyond the University of Chicago worldwide to include social scientists interested in the scholarly study of the military and members of the military interested in social science research.

The capacity of the center and the seminar to help restore a sense of mission and morale in the Department of Sociology at Chicago depended on the quality of the substantive research accomplished by the faculty and students who were associated with them. In fact, members of both organizations (many memberships were overlapping) were highly productive throughout the 1960s and early 1970s. The first fruits of the IUS were published in 1964 by the Russell Sage Foundation in a volume titled *The New Military,* which extended research about the military along lines opened by Janowitz's previous work.[63] The following year saw papers on armed forces and society published in a special issue of the *European Journal of Sociology;* these papers were presented at a conference held in London in July 1964 under the joint sponsorship of the International Sociological Association and the IUS. Similar volumes appeared in subsequent years, along with the publication of research monographs on various aspects of military organization and a comprehensive *Handbook of Military Institutions.*[64]

The Center for Social Organization Studies was more devoted to graduate training than the IUS, and in this capacity was equally productive. No comprehensive list of the fellows of the center is available, but their number included many—Thomas Guterbock, Albert Hunter, William Kornblum, Harvey Molotch, and Anthony Orum, to name a few—who are leading figures in the discipline at the present time. Morris Janowitz, David Street, Gerald Suttles, and William Hodge together formed a core of faculty who worked with center fellows to encourage the efflorescence of participant observation studies, especially in urban communities, which helped define what has been called the "Chicago Renaissance" of the 1960s.[65] The leadership Janowitz exerted in the Department of Sociology in these and other ways made an important contribution to bringing the department out of the malaise into which it had fallen.

In 1967, Janowitz was appointed chairman of the department, a position he held until 1972.[66] In that capacity, Janowitz worked directly "to rebuild the department by attracting outstanding scholars and promising students."[67] Despite his great attachment to the research traditions of W. I. Thomas and Robert Park, which were reflected in his approach to social organization and military studies, he did not restrict faculty appointments to those who shared his methodological and theoretical views. For Janowitz, sociology was not a profession with a single cognitive core that had to be mastered by its students and refined by research. Rather, it was a point of view and a "repository" for diverse methods of analysis and ideas about human society.[68] So Janowitz sought to hire the best representatives of new theoretical outlooks and alternative methodological approaches. He also tried to overcome tendencies in the discipline toward overspecialization. He encouraged faculty from other departments—anthropology, education, economics—to accept joint appointments in the sociology department, and was actively involved with the cross-disciplinary Committee for the Comparative Study of New Nations. As a result, Janowitz was able to create "a department of great distinction."[69]

We cannot overlook, however, that the University of Chicago in the late 1960s found itself at a vortex of conflicting social pressures, as did many other universities in that period. Unlike student protesters at Columbia University or the University of California at Berkeley, where "student revolts" in the spring of 1968 were aimed against the school administration, student radicals at Chicago directed their protest in the winter of 1969 against the faculty.[70] The students protested in particular against the Department of Sociology and Morris Janowitz when the contract of a junior member of the department, Marlene Dixon, was not renewed for a second three-year term. They contended that Dixon was dismissed unfairly because she was female and a self-professed radical, and they argued that faculty were wrong to make decisions about academic appointments without consulting them, that the appointment process should give students an "equal voice" with faculty.[71] Attempts to discuss the matter quickly broke down, and several hundred students—with encouragement from a small number of radical faculty members—occupied the university's administration building for sixteen days. The reasons for the breakdown are too many and complex for treatment here.[72] But it led to much acrimony, with students contemptuously denouncing Morris Janowitz, Bruno Bettelheim, Edward Shils, and others with false charges about their motives and past activities.

Despite being an object of personal attack by the protesting students, Janowitz never relaxed in his efforts to resolve the conflict, and to moderate its worst effects.[73] He continually sought to create forums and vehicles for rational discussion between faculty and students about the matters which separated them. When students broke into the office of the dean of the Social Science Division, Janowitz attempted to dissuade them from their course; when the administration building was occupied, he went into the building to observe firsthand what was going on inside; and when a group of unruly students ran through the faculty's Quadrangle Club stealing food from the plates of diners, he went to the club at the manager's request to try to restore order. He was an unflagging proponent of the virtue of free and reasoned discussion as the method for dealing with the crisis, and an opponent of any resort to force or police powers.

Janowitz claimed that a "full year" was "lost" because of the disturbances.[74] In fact, though he actively defended the faculty's decision in the Dixon case, under his leadership the department carried on with its normal business.[75] No classes were canceled. Janowitz worked and met with students in his office, though protesters camped noisily outside his door. The department's annual Spring Institute for presenting graduate student papers was held as scheduled, with a special evening lecture given by George Homans, and eighteen students completed

their Ph.D. degrees. Janowitz was able to accomplish this because the
faculty were not divided on the issues at stake, and many graduate
students were not in favor of the protesters. Nevertheless, one cannot
underestimate the leadership and courage which he displayed during
this period or their importance for maintaining the department's program of teaching and research.

No doubt Janowitz's own research was slowed by his heavy administrative responsibilities and by his many efforts to rebuild the department. While he continued to be productive in terms of the number of
his publications, this was not the period of his greatest creativity.
Breaking little new ground, his writings elaborated themes he had previously pursued.[76] As Janowitz noted at the time, "I have been living
on accumulated intellectual capital. I need more time to read in depth
and organize my thoughts."[77] In 1966, he received a grant from the
Carnegie Corporation for funds "to do some quiet, undisturbed
work" over a full academic year. But he could not accept it. The university was unable to hire someone to assume his responsibilities for
the year 1966–67, and plans to postpone the award until the following year were canceled when he was made chairman of the department
in June 1967. Janowitz had no year free until after he gave up his
chairmanship in 1972. Nonetheless, Janowitz did find time after his
return to Chicago for serious reflection about the course of sociological thought and his own.

Reconstruction of the department required deliberate efforts to recover the "intellectual ghosts" of the past. To accomplish this, Janowitz founded the Heritage of Sociology series with the University of
Chicago Press.[78] Early volumes in the series focused on contributors to
the Chicago school—George Herbert Mead, W. I. Thomas, Robert E.
Park—but the focus was soon broadened to include volumes of papers
by leading American and European sociologists of the past and by
their precursors. The series was well received and would grow under
Janowitz's editorship to include nearly forty volumes. Editing the series, and contributing volumes of his own on the work of W. I. Thomas
and Robert Park, required that Janowitz reflect on what the heritage
of sociology was and how his work fit within it. "It is amazing . . .,"
he wrote in a letter to Vernon Dibble, "[that] in this period of frantic
research, there is a rediscovery of the classics and of the efforts to
maintain some wholeness in the span of sociology."[79] We may safely
regard this general observation as a personal one as well.

Reflection on past sociological accomplishments led Janowitz increasingly to discern the importance of philosophical pragmatism in
his intellectual development. His correspondence, silent on the subject

beforehand, provides strong evidence of his self-understanding as "an incorrigible pragmatist" after the mid-1960s.[80] "Each of us . . . [is] captured," he wrote Milton Rosenberg, "in our own theoretical heritage. I am more of a George Herbert Mead-Martin Buber type." [81] He took some pride in accepting Anselm Strauss's claim that his study of urbanism was "an expression of symbolic interaction." [82] Nevertheless, he thought the work of W. I. Thomas, Sidney Hook, and John Dewey was most important to his own intellectual development, especially the work of Dewey.[83] "I think neither you nor I," he wrote to David Street, "give John Dewey sufficient credit for his impact on us and on Sociology." [84] He had hoped to correct this insufficiency in part by including Dewey's work in the Heritage series, but the projected volume was never completed.[85]

In sum, the decade following Janowitz's return to Chicago was filled with activity and accomplishment: creating an important center for graduate training, establishing an international learned society to promote social scientific studies of the military, rebuilding the Department of Sociology at Chicago, and founding the Heritage of Sociology series. Each became a vehicle for Janowitz to exert influence on the direction of sociological thought. For the student of Janowitz's own intellectual development, however, his work on the Heritage series is singularly important because it shaped Janowitz's self-identification as a "pragmatic" sociologist. That led him in the next and last period of his career to write more explicitly than he had done before about the pragmatic logic of sociological inquiry, and provided him a way to integrate the various strands of his empirical research into a comprehensive view of advanced industrial societies.

Macrosocial Analysis of Advanced Industrial Societies

The last period of Morris Janowitz's academic career was characterized by more intensive research and less extensive commitments to administrative affairs, both in matters of faculty governance at Chicago and in the affairs of the Center for Social Organization Studies and the IUS. Janowitz remained active in all these areas, until slowed by disease in the 1980s. Notably, in 1974 he founded the journal *Armed Forces and Society* under the sponsorship of the IUS and edited it until 1983, turning it into a major outlet for the publication of empirical studies by social scientists on military subjects. And he continued to chair the IUS until 1981. Yet, with the exception of the IUS, the part he played in these organizations after 1972 was of a man behind the scenes, still highly influential in affecting the outcome of events, but not on center stage.

Much of his writing during this period dealt with the military. His work on this subject developed the idea, now widely accepted, that military organization in the West was undergoing a fundamental and permanent change, away from a citizen-based toward a professional armed force. He was concerned with tracing the consequences of this development for professional controls within the military, for the diminishing utility of military interventions, and for the link between these and democratic government. But his major accomplishment in this period was to complete a comprehensive investigation of social control, societal change, and democratic political participation in the United States, which was published in three volumes between 1976 and 1983.

Janowitz began work on the main volume in the series, *The Last Half-Century*, when he was Pitt Professor at Cambridge University in 1972–73, and wrote the initial text as a Guggenheim fellow in the summer and fall of 1975. The book was published in 1978. It examined the transformation of the United States from an early industrial society in the 1920s into an advanced industrial society following the Second World War. Although this distinction is vague—operationally defined, an "advanced" industrial nation has less than 10 percent of its labor force employed in the primary sector—the terms were carefully chosen. Janowitz rejected the formulation of Daniel Bell that American society was becoming a "post-industrial society," because Bell's argument understated the continuities of contemporary occupational structure with the past, overstated technology's part in determining social structure, and presumed too large a role in politics for scientists and men of knowledge.[86] The central problem of advanced industrialism, at least for liberal democratic societies, was not the emergence of a new ruling elite that based its power on control over knowledge. It was rather the classic problem of social control, of maintaining the capacity for self-regulation and minimizing reliance on coercive controls under conditions of increasing social strain. Janowitz believed that expansion of welfare state allocations along with technological changes vastly complicated the social structures of industrial societies, dispersing power and making it more difficult to aggregate political interests. As a result, political participation necessary to maintain democratic polity and a critical consensus has suffered.

The other two volumes—*Social Control of the Welfare State* and *The Reconstruction of Patriotism*—were direct outgrowths of these concerns. *Social Control of the Welfare State* was published in 1976. It prefigured the major themes dealt with in far greater depth by *The Last Half-Century*. Unlike *The Last Half-Century*, which focused on the American experience, *Social Control* had a limited but still explicitly comparative focus. Relying implicitly on Mill's method of agreement, Janowitz argued that growth of weak political regimes among the advanced industrial nations of the West reflected the influence of the welfare state policies on political parties and political behavior, and on social structure. Unfortunately, the scope of his argument was so broad that it received only the most general statement in this volume. Whoever was unpersuaded by its logic would not be converted by the evidence. (It was *The Last Half-Century* which provided the fullest statement of the case and the evidence available to support it.) Despite this difficulty, in retrospect, we can say that *Social Control* strengthens the argument of *The Last Half-Century* about the United States by showing that the developments Janowitz refers to apply generally to the parliamentary democracies of Western Europe. They are not copied in detail anywhere, but neither are they an example of American exceptionalism.

The Reconstruction of Patriotism, published in 1983, dealt with the problem of political participation. This work located the arguments of *The Last Half-Century* in a broader historical context. In it, Janowitz surveyed the history of civic education in American society from participation in the American Revolution to current debates over bilingual education in the public schools and over the value of a national service system. Its major theme was that the balance between the rights and duties of citizenship had tilted over time too far toward rights, and that the balance could be redressed and social control strengthened by increased voluntary participation in projects of national and community service, to include military service. The argument reflects Janowitz's belief that democratic society is maintained, and competitive elections are made more effective, through the elaboration of realistic forms of communal and organizational participation.

The significance of these works is learned only partly from a summary statement of their substantive concerns. Janowitz looked upon *The Last Half-Century* as an exercise in codification of the results of empirical research in sociology and as a form of intellectual autobiography. Janowitz rejected the idea, current in the 1970s, that sociology was a discipline in crisis. If there was a crisis, it resided in "the real world" of advanced industrial nations, not within sociology as an intellectual discipline.[87] He knew that much sociological scholarship was mediocre, but thought that the vitality of the discipline could be maintained even by the efforts of a few. The task was to synthesize available research, and hopefully to demonstrate "that an enduring intellectual core of sociology exists and that this core cannot be separated from its substantive achievements." [88] For him, it was as important to conserve "the effective heritage of sociology" as it was to generate new knowledge. [89]

With any exercise of codification, the method employed to organize the data is frequently as important as the data themselves. As Janowitz knew well, the categories and interrelationships he used to synthesize his research and the research of others would reveal his intellectual inheritance. His core concepts of social control, social organization, and social reconstruction (or institution building) came to him by direct descent from the early Chicago school of sociology and from philosophical pragmatism. But he also modified his inheritance. He augmented the social psychology of pragmatism with the dynamic ego psychology he learned under Bettelheim. And he added to the early Chicago school an explicit concern for macropolitical structure, the management of violence, and the conditions for maintaining liberal democratic societies. To appreciate how he did so, we may turn from this discussion of his intellectual development to a critical review of his substantive work, beginning with the logic of inquiry which organized his research.

The Logic of Sociological Inquiry

Morris Janowitz's writings do not display great patience with metatheoretical issues in the social sciences. The number of occasions on which he took such matters under consideration is relatively small. Most of his writing on the logic of sociological inquiry occurred during the transition from the second to the third period of his academic career. That is significant, of course. It means we are dealing with the outcome of his reflections about his own intellectual heritage and its significance for the organization of substantive research. In these essays we find spelled out most clearly what it means to say that Janowitz's methodology is linked with philosophical pragmatism.

The historical connection between pragmatism and American sociology, especially at the University of Chicago, is often recognized. [90] Yet there are at least two difficulties with appreciating the fact among contemporary theorists. First, since 1945, the influence of pragmatism on sociology has been associated more or less exclusively with the paradigm of symbolic interaction and focused on controversies about the influence of George Herbert Mead. [91] This approach is too narrow. As Janowitz argued in his review of Neil Coughlan's *Young John Dewey,* "the impact of philosophical pragmatism on sociology is multifaceted and profound and not the result of a single concept or a single figure."[92] The issue is complicated because pragmatism itself is a highly differentiated movement within philosophy rather than a clearly stated single doctrine.[93] Nevertheless, a pragmatic sociology may be only weakly tied to a Meadian-based theory of symbolic interaction and yet be strongly guided by pragmatic postulates in its style of theory construction, the formulation of its central hypotheses, and the conduct of research. Failure to acknowledge the fact has created the wrong impression that a pragmatic sociology necessarily entails a microsocial outlook.[94] As a result Morris Janowitz's work has been characterized by Ralph Turner as exemplifying a "forgotten paradigm" in macrosocial research.[95]

Second, no pragmatic sociology has been systematically elaborated. Its primary adherents—Janowitz included—preferred to rely on "exemplary research and oral transmission" rather than on "explicit self-grounding."[96] When Janowitz did write about "metatheory," as the essays in this volume illustrate, he did not develop a rigorous logical argument. Implicitly, he accepted Dewey's theory of inquiry. His style was to discuss the history of theory as it informed empirical research about a particular problem, and to render an evaluation of the consequences of various hypotheses for clarifying the character of the problem and suggesting how it might be resolved. It was a style that indicated critical continuities and discontinuities in the development of sociological thought, but often left difficult questions unasked and unanswered.

Nevertheless, Janowitz's approach to sociological inquiry is clearly marked by pragmatic themes and concerns. He rejected idealist or grand theoretical conceptions which treated the social world as if it were a unified whole or could be neatly contained within formal dichotomies defined outside experience. For Janowitz, social relations and contexts were always overlapping and interpenetrating, leading empirically to a dynamic social organization which was never more than partially integrated or relatively autonomous. Society was characteristically an unsettled affair, creating problems of social control. While absolute knowledge about it was not to be expected, the significance of sociological hypotheses rested on how they altered or clarified understanding of problems in the "real world." And that could only be known as the hypotheses were publicly tested within a community of inquirers.[97] Sociological inquiry, like all pragmatic inquiries, was thus part of a larger community of discourse. Its validation and its proper role depended on its contribution to public enlightenment about the problems societies have to face.

Commitment to this philosophical tradition of inquiry affected the categories and hypotheses Janowitz relied on in the conduct of research. Though oversimplifying somewhat, three postulates rooted in pragmatism may usefully serve to show how it did so.[98]

First, reality is in a state of flux. This postulate highlights the partially integrated character of social organization and emphasizes its changing character, and it has consequences, of course, for evaluating the appropriateness of various styles of theory construction. Building on early formulations by Harold Lasswell, Janowitz argued for the strategy of systemic analysis.[99] The strategy recognizes no sharp distinction between static and dynamic analysis. Although it prefers "developmental analysis," it remains concerned with the conditions for social stability. In fact, systemic analysis collapses many formal dichotomies distinguishing between general and middle-range theory, interdependent and autonomous social structures, social and material worlds. All testable hypotheses are delimited in scope, but have significance only within a larger theoretical framework. As opposed to an equilibrium perspective, which assumes a "high degree of effective interdependence" among the elements of social organization, systemic analysis takes for granted "a considerable degree of actual and potential autonomy between elements." Rejecting either a materialist or normative determinism, systemic analysis focuses on the interplay between material conditions and norms "to incorporate the environment into the boundaries of social organization."

This is not to imply a strategy of moderation between extremes. If the world is in flux, then no realistic social theory can arrive at a single body of propositions to form a unified theoretical perspective. Excessively general tendencies—for example, to specify one basic unit for sociological analysis like a "social role" or a "network"—are misleading. Instead, systemic analysis relies on overlapping hypotheses about differentiated, concrete objects of analysis embedded in a larger social setting. These hypotheses are given "a degree of coherence" by their shared assumptions and location within a set of master trends which describe the historical context.

Second, social structures are symbolically mediated products of collective action, a postulate which assumes the importance of voluntarism as a key element shaping social life. Once again, the position rejects formal dualisms, in this instance, between subject versus object and freedom versus determinism, and between their particular sociological variants, especially as found in the gemeinschaft-gesellschaft model of societal transformation.[100] Janowitz was much influenced by John Dewey's early attempt to grapple with these issues in his classic essay "The Reflex Arc Concept in Psychology."[101] The central argument of that essay was that such dualisms—Dewey's particular reference was to the stimulus-response model—rely on teleological or functional distinctions, not distinctions which are found in the conditions of existence. One must look at these terms as different phases in a common process of coordination. In sociological terms, social actors and social objects are mutually determining, and while preexisting social structures may constrain, they are not perfectly or all-constraining. For that reason, Janowitz regarded social control as a central problem for sociological analysis.

Social control organizes the cleavages, strains, and tensions of society with the aim (but not the certainty) of maintaining social order while social change occurs.[102] For Janowitz, social control is not a mechanism for obtaining social conformity. It refers rather to "the capacity of a society to regulate itself according to desired principles and values." This concept undergirds a perspective that rejects simple theories of economic self-interest or of an all-powerful ruling elite. It recognizes an element of voluntarism in social relations, but "takes into consideration the realities of social constraints, whether they have their origins in ecological, economic, or normative factors."[103] It also assumes a value orientation to reduce (without eliminating) coercion, to minimize (without abolishing) human misery, and to enhance (without exaggerating) the role of rationality in guiding conduct.

Third, sociological practice involves a commitment to social reconstruction. In fact, all social science, from John Dewey's point of view all critical inquiry, presupposes a community of shared experience with norms and procedures to evaluate, clarify, test, and modify the practices through which community members organize their common life.[104] Social science research contributes to the amelioration of societal strains and helps to strengthen social control by defining realistic alternative courses of action and by clarifying their consequences. This exaggerates neither the predictive nor the prescriptive powers of sociologists, which Janowitz believed were limited. But it suggests a purpose for the discipline and supplies a criterion for choosing fundamental problems for research.

Holding to what may today seem an austere standard, Janowitz argued that it was "self-indulgent" to pursue sociological research which had no clear relation to pressing issues presently affecting contemporary society.[105] Not that sociology was an "applied" science. Janowitz distinguished between what he called the "engineering" model of sociology, which makes a sharp distinction between basic research and applied research, and the "enlightenment" model, which does not.[106] While acknowledging that good research can be done following either model, Janowitz clearly believed the enlightenment model was a more appropriate guide for sociological practice. The engineering model presumes it is possible (through "basic" research) to identify specific cause-effect relationships, knowledge of which provides definite answers to particular questions to be "applied" in solving problems. The approach suggests a degree of stability and a level of determinism at work in social organization that is incompatible with a pragmatic point of view. In contrast, "the enlightenment model assumes the overriding importance of social context, and focuses on developing different types of knowledge which can be utilized by policy-makers and professions. While it seeks specific answers, its emphasis is on creating the intellectual conditions for problem solving. Its goal is a contribution to institution-building." [107] Sociology, following this model, is paradigmatically a teaching profession, or, to use the language of bureaucracies, it has a staff rather than a line function to perform. Whether through classroom instruction or through the dissemination of the results of empirical research, its contribution is made by clarifying the central issues underlying a particular problem and by suggesting how modifying institutions might affect the problem's development over time. The faith, which Janowitz shared with Dewey, is that institution building to accommodate social change will be improved when guided by a pragmatic institutional analysis, as opposed to common sense knowledge or mechanical extrapolation of past trends into the future.

The concepts of social organization, social control, and institution building gain significance when they are placed within this particular intellectual tradition.[108] But in keeping with his pragmatic distrust of dualisms which tended artificially to separate thought and action, Janowitz believed there was a close link between theory and data. While these categories, and the logic of inquiry they sustained, had roots in the soil of pragmatism, they bore fruit through their use in empirical research.

Social Organization: Institutional Development in Advanced Industrial Society

Morris Janowitz was drawn to study social organization by his fascination with the diversity of contemporary society, his reluctance to accept overspecialization in the discipline, and his regard for democratic society. For Janowitz, social organization referred to "the subject matter of sociology . . . the patterns of influence in a population of social groups." [109] This definition is not very satisfactory except to indicate how broadly Janowitz believed the net was cast. Social organization was an all-encompassing term. It spanned all levels of analysis, from primary groups to nation-states, and a wide range of institutions, from political parties and armed forces to local schools and the community press.

Undergirding Janowitz's study of social organization is the substantive proposition that transition from early industrial to advanced industrial society has led to institutional disarticulation (a lack of institutional unity or integration) and weakened social control in the liberal democratic nation-states of North America and Europe. While transition from early to advanced industrial society may be indexed by changes in the occupational structure, it was not simply a matter of labor-force transformation described by the growth of service-sector employment and the decline of agricultural employment. Janowitz accorded a certain priority to technological, ecological, and economic factors when accounting for social change. But he also took political and normative factors into account as they were manifested after the Second World War by growth of the welfare state.

Technological factors are particularly important for understanding the changing role of military elites in advanced industrial societies. Obviously, the introduction of nuclear weapons altered the calculus of war-making among the major powers, for they could no longer assume that fighting a total war would be to their advantage.[110] Quite different from what was required to fight world wars, military organization now prepared to deter the outbreak of conflict or to engage in limited conflicts, to employ the least amount of force, and to seek negotiated political settlements.[111]

Industrial technologies of war-making, Janowitz clearly saw, professionalized military elites and increased the size of permanent military establishments. Traditional assumptions of the democratic model for regulating political-military relations were strained because the functions of politicians and soldiers were no longer sharply differentiated.[112] Politicians increasingly had to consider the advice of military elites to perform their job. Moreover, long-term trends suggested tendencies toward civilianization of the armed forces: As officers became trained specialists, recruiting into the military elite became more socially representative. Despite the military's reputation as an authoritarian institution, reliance on industrial technologies required substantial decentralization of authority and dependence on individual initiative with its concomitant necessity for high morale. Skill differentials between military and civilian elites narrowed. The trend toward civilianization was not absolute; it modified, without eliminating, civil-military differences. Nevertheless, for democratic states, blurring the distinction between civilian and military ran "the risk of creating new forms of hostility and unanticipated militarism." [113]

Local urban communities were no less profoundly changed by advancing industrialism. In the late 1940s until the 1960s, gemeinschaftgesellschaft formulations depicted modern urban society as an alienated and rootless "mass society" where individuals were directly connected to "major agencies of concentrated social and political power" with few intermediary primary-group ties. Janowitz never accepted these formulations even when they were fashionable. His study of the community press supplied early evidence for the proposition, now widely accepted, that "counter-trends to large-scale organization continually develop which modify the impact of technological impersonalization and make possible the gratification of individual needs in the local community." [114] He did not deny, however, that there were important changes taking place.

Ecological separation of one's place of work from the place of residence had wide-ranging implications for Janowitz's understanding of urban social and political organization. For the local urban community, it meant assuming a more specialized but still important role in social life, as "the locus within which the life cycle is given its moral and symbolic meaning." [115] It also meant that local orientations were embedded in a larger societal context. Strong attachment to local community was compatible with, and in fact, seemed to facilitate, development of effective political ties within the metropolitan and national arenas. Yet local urban community was not a community of fate within which one's whole life had to be lived. It was, in Janowitz's coinage, a community of "limited liability." [116] Attachments to local communities were limited in terms of their social and psychological investments. Should the community fail to serve people's needs, they could withdraw from it. The strength of urban communities, in short, was not an automatic result of the need for a place to live, but was a problematic product of the capacity of community leaders to adapt local institutions to changing circumstances to supply the needs of their neighbors.

Given these important changes in social organization outside of the industrial sphere, Janowitz was reluctant to characterize advanced industrial society solely in terms of its occupational structure. He acknowledged the centrality of the economic sector and the division of labor. But he believed it was misleading to follow the customary procedure of sociologists who used these factors to divide society into mutually exclusive and hierarchically ordered social strata.[117] It was misleading for a variety of reasons. First, empirically, trends in the occupational structure documented a process of increasing differentiation in which it becomes harder to distinguish between particular strata. That is true even when one relies on such broad distinctions as "blue collar" versus "white collar" employment or on correlations, say, between income and education. The boundaries are less clear-cut under advanced industrialism. Second, historically, the language of social class, on which the stratigraphic image of society rests, was a political invention of the Western nations to define who would count as a citizen during the period of transition from aristocratic feudal to mass democratic regimes. One's occupational status became a key characteristic for the extension of political and social rights. Nevertheless, the relevance of this terminology for social analysis decreases as we move further away from the nineteenth century. Finally, the notion of social strata fails to account for the expansion of the welfare state after the first and second world wars. Government expenditures for social welfare have increased faster than the gross national product, with pervasive effects on the pattern of social inequality. Normatively, the goal of welfare is to assist those at the bottom of the social structure. In fact a wider view is required, especially to include welfare expenditures which subsidize home ownership, provide higher education, and insure health and retirement benefits. One's position in the social structure is determined by occupation, but only partly so once the spread and weight of social welfare claims are considered. As a result, political conflicts now entail a more complex and sometimes contradictory balancing of interests rooted in both the market-oriented occupational structure and the community-oriented institutions of social welfare.

Democratic political institutions have been adversely affected by the transition from early industrial to advanced industrial society. Professionalization of military elites has strained civil-military relations, separation of work from place of residence has made the tasks of local government more difficult to coordinate and control, and the growth of the welfare state has complicated the calculation of political interests. Together, they contribute to what Janowitz along with others writing in the 1970s perceived as a crisis of political legitimacy among the Western parliamentary democracies.

For Janowitz the crisis was manifest by the emergence of "weak regimes."[118] A regime is weak when no political party can rely on a stable electoral majority that enables it to rule. Empirically, the focus is put narrowly on voting. When the outcomes of elections are indecisive, as they have been in the United States since 1952, Janowitz takes it as evidence of weakening social control. The proximate causes for the emergence of weak political regimes in the American case are a decline in voter participation; the absence of stable voter blocs, which has increased the magnitude of shifts in voting patterns from one election to the next; the growth in numbers of voters who consider themselves to be "independents" instead of allied with a particular political party; and, since 1964, the marked reduction in trust and confidence in the electoral system.

This conceptualization of the problem is not without difficulties. To speak of the weakness of political regimes implies a closer concern for the structures of government than Janowitz's argument ever displays. How the argument applies within centralized parliamentary states, as opposed to the federal American system, for example, is not addressed. Nor is the argument carefully reconciled with the fact, which Janowitz recognizes, of the continuing expansion of the state's administrative powers. These matters are left unaddressed, perhaps because the central issue for Janowitz was not the organization of a democratic government, but the character of its relationship with the society it would govern. Electoral outcomes are an index of social control, of the capacity of a democratic people to regulate themselves. If elections are chronically indecisive, that reflects disarticulation within the larger social organization and low levels of social control. Political interests are more difficult to aggregate,and a stable consensus about which values and principles should limit the pursuit of individual advantage is more difficult to form. Under such circumstances, the capacity of society to sustain democratic government is strained.

Before moving on, there is an omission in Janowitz's work which ought to be noticed. His analysis of social organization is essentially secular in a way that contrasts sharply with the writings of Émile Durkheim or Edward Shils, both of whom dwell on the idea of the sacred in society. It makes no place for religion or religious institutions and no prominent place for the creative accomplishment of humanist writers and other artists. This omission does not mean Janowitz was ignorant of or indifferent toward "high culture." He was neither. He was solicitous that social science maintain a humanistic stance. Nevertheless, his sociology adopts the attitude of modern naturalism characteristic of Deweyan pragmatism and the psychoanalytic tradition. It is an attitude which in practice understates the relevance of the sacred as a category of sociological analysis.

Primary Groups and Personal Control

Morris Janowitz's abiding concern for examining macrosocial patterns of institutional development never blinded him to the importance of small-group processes and social personality.[119] He stood against sociological reductionism which would ignore mechanisms of socialization and the processes of internalizing norms or the partially autonomous contribution which social personality could make for institutional development. For Janowitz, the critical question about what is now referred to as the "micro-macro link" concerned the formation of an individual's attachment to the larger societal collectivity and his relation to its external authorities. To use an old-fashioned term, it was the question of determining what maintained one's "morale" to participate effectively in large-scale social organizations. His recognition of the problem was influenced by his wartime study with Edward Shils of the cohesion of the Wehrmacht. In substance, his approach to it was shaped by W. I. Thomas's work on social personality, but even more by Sigmund Freud's psychoanalytic theory.

Following Thomas, Janowitz used the term *social personality* to refer to "relatively enduring" predispositions to behave which are exhibited across different interpersonal and social settings. These predispositions are rooted in psychic states, but molded by social processes during childhood and refashioned throughout the life cycle. They are, in other words, one product of socialization, and they have significant consequences for social control. Social control aims to reduce violence and coercion, to rely on persuasion and reason as much as possible in the organization of social life. Achieving the aim depends in no small part on the individual's relation toward external authority. Following Freud, Janowitz distinguished three types of psychological control: *external control,* which entails mere submission to external authority and reflects minimal development of personal autonomy; *superego* or *conscience control,* which acknowledges the need for "higher moral" principles to guide behavior, but requires external agents to reinforce their relevance; and *ego* or *personal control,* which accepts external authority, but includes a critical element of self-generation and self-regulation. Speaking generally, as advanced industrial social organization becomes more complex, complicating the pursuit of a person's self-interest, "higher levels" of personal control are required "to link the person to the nation-state and to contribute to the quality of citizen participation." [120]

Variability in levels of personal control is affected by one's attachments to the larger society as mediated by participation in primary groups. The importance of primary-group attachments for maintaining morale and effective participation in a large-scale organization was demonstrated dramatically by Morris Janowitz and Edward Shils in their study "Cohesion and Disintegration in the Wehrmacht in World War II." [121] It had been commonly thought that "the high degree of organizational integrity and fighting effectiveness" of the German army during the last months of the war was due to the strong national socialist political convictions of the soldiers. More important for the German soldier in fact was "the steady satisfaction of certain *primary* personality demands afforded by the social organization of the army." [122] While ideology may figure prominently in volunteer, revolutionary, or professional armed forces, in a conscript army representative of the total population, the "decisive fact" was membership in a squad or section which had structural integrity, leadership with which the soldiers could identify, and the capacity to satisfy primary needs for physical security (food, weapons, shelter, etc.) and sociability. The German army attempted to maintain the strength of primary-group ties by maintaining unit integrity throughout the war as long as possible and minimizing the probability of divisive political discussions among the soldiers. The army began to break down as these conditions became more difficult to sustain. Isolation from one's unit, aggravating anxieties about one's own physical survival; worries about the well-being of one's family; unit failure to meet the soldier's most basic physiological needs—these all broke the bonds of group solidarity, and increased the incidence of surrender and desertion. As reliance on personal control to support the military mission grew less effective, the officer corps increasingly resorted to threats (either to the soldier himself or to members of his family) to coerce compliance.

The interplay between social personality and attachments to large-scale social structure, however, is frequently direct, and no less important than interactions which are mediated through primary groups. Janowitz's early study with Bruno Bettelheim of ethnic intolerance and hostility speaks to the point. [123] Janowitz rejected the claim that prejudice and outgroup hostility were universal psychological dispositions about which nothing could be done. The forms of ethnic hostility and the motives for its expression varied, he argued, with the particular society in which it appeared. An adequate explanation for anti-Semitism in medieval European society had to draw on a religious ethos and anxiety about salvation. But these factors have little relevance for the contemporary situation. In modern society, anxiety is focused on one's material well-being. Correspondingly, overt expressions of anti-Semitism or other forms of ethnic intolerance are most frequently aroused among those who are downwardly mobile, next most among those who are not mobile at all, and least among the upwardly mobile. This is not to say that the dynamics of one's connection to the societal system for distributing wealth is all-determinative. If the personality is very strong, or strongly committed either to tolerance or intolerance, then the influence of the social field is limited. But it is to suggest that ethnic intolerance is not "purely psychological in origin" or "beyond the reach of social reform." It is at least partly the result of fears generated by one's connection to the larger social order; and so rational reform is possible to the extent that the fears can be addressed or reassured.

Janowitz drew on the findings of these early studies in the third period of his career to consider the relationship between personal control and social organization. In *Social Control of the Welfare State,* he noted that pervasive economic uncertainty accompanied growth of the welfare state. Welfare expenditures increased at a higher rate than real economic growth, budgetary strains were manifest in persistent and growing federal government deficits, and in the 1970s chronic inflation and high unemployment created "stagflation." In this context, levels of personal discontent and discontent with government increased (although overt expressions of prejudice toward minority groups declined).[124]

Moreover, Janowitz argued, levels of personal anxiety about one's material well-being were heightened by two factors highly characteristic of advanced industrial societies. The first was isolation, which increased among key population groups, rendering local socialization less effective. John Dewey and others have long argued, for example, that transition from youth to adulthood was facilitated by comprehensive socialization experiences which combined academic and work experiences. Yet, Janowitz observed, educational institutions under advanced industrialism focused narrowly on academic performance and were largely cut off from the larger social environment, hindering effective socialization. As schools did with youth, so welfare institutions separated and isolated their clients from the larger social structure.[125] While they helped eliminate the misery of poverty, through isolation they "thwart[ed] self-esteem and competence among [welfare] recipients."[126] Second, the affluence of advanced industrial society heightened drives toward impulse gratification, the symptoms of which, Janowitz argued, showed up in "forms of behavior—deviant and otherwise—that must be labeled as self-destructive."[127] Thus, both factors contributed to lowering levels of personal control. Because effective personal control is necessary to strengthen collective self-regulation, the result decreased the prospects for social control.

Social Control, Citizenship, and Democratic Polity

Despite the close connection between personal and social control, Morris Janowitz thought it was misleading to say that social control dealt with relations between "individuals" and "society." He strongly rejected both sociological and psychological reductionism and regarded attempts theoretically to distinguish individual from group processes as largely overdrawn.[128] Macrosocial institutional analyses, he thought, provided evidence about the changing capacity for self-regulation among individuals and groups. This outlook betrayed his desire to know what affected the prospects for maintaining a strong democratic polity, especially under conditions of advanced industrialism. In the last period of his career, Janowitz studied the problem through an intensive, if incomplete, analysis of the institution of citizenship. In general, his conclusions were gloomy. He found many reasons to believe that contemporary citizenship was a weakened institution and that the prospects for social control and democracy suffered thereby.

Typically, sociological study of citizenship in modern Western society follows T. H. Marshall's brilliant analysis of the progressive expansion of citizenship from civil to political to social rights.[129] But Janowitz argued that effective citizenship involved both rights and obligations. Preoccupation with citizens' rights therefore needed to be balanced by concern for citizens' obligations.[130] Nor was it enough simply to list duties; for example, to pay taxes, to be educated, to perform military service, to participate in voluntary (especially community-based) associations, or to participate in various facets of the electoral process. The underlying rationale and purpose of these obligations had to be understood, as did the conditions which promoted or inhibited their enactment. For that reason he took issue with the enumeration of citizen duties offered by T. H. Marshall. Marshall failed to treat obligations in depth, and he understated the importance of performing duties which were compulsory. "A compulsory act," Janowitz wrote, "does not have to be performed mechanically and without critical concern for its justice and relevance."[131] There is substantial variation (and so room for voluntary action) in how obligations are performed. The critical question from this point of view, and one largely unaddressed in the sociological literature, is whether social institutions are organized to help or hinder the enlightened practice of citizen duties. Janowitz was concerned that particular institutions, like public schools or the Internal Revenue Service, discouraged effective expression of citizen obligations because they failed to take seriously their responsibilities for civic education.

Institutional conduct in many spheres defined the meaning of citizenship and influenced its consequences for democratic society. Throughout the nineteenth and early twentieth centuries, parliamentary democracies maintained a strong link between citizenship and the obligation to perform military service.[132] Early democratic revolutions were legitimated partly by arming the "masses" in opposition to feudal regimes. Building on revolutionary traditions, states mobilized mass armed forces of conscripted citizens to fight in defense of their nation. The military effectiveness of these forces depended on a comparatively simple internal division of labor and an industrial economy able to generate huge surpluses to support large armies in the field. But these factors were reinforced by a political culture in which military service became a hallmark of citizenship.

Nevertheless, as Janowitz was first to point out, military organization changed gradually but fundamentally after the Second World War to move away from mass armed forces composed of citizen soldiers toward smaller professional forces composed largely of volunteers. The change was explained partly by the heavy economic and human costs associated with the technology of modern warfare. It was explained also by the material affluence of advanced industrial nations, along with rising levels of education, which increased skepticism about the value of performing military service. Significantly, the change altered the normative and symbolic content of both the citizen's and the soldier's role, posing problems for social control. The military obligation of citizenship was a means for establishing civilian control over the military and integrating the military into larger society. Without the obligation, Janowitz worried, the military could become "a more isolated body" with ideologically "selective linkages" with the larger society. It might become another pressure group and basis for cleavage further to burden the task of parliamentary government.

Effective exercise of citizenship rights and obligations requires an adequate relation to external authorities which is characteristic of high levels of personal control. Besides the military, the mass media are important institutions affecting what level of personal control people achieve, and so contribute markedly to the substance of this relationship.[133] Though Janowitz acknowledged that difficulties attend studies of the effects of mass media, his review of the available evidence led

him to conclude that the mass media, on balance, have not contributed
to the growth of personal control. His assessment rested on the confluence of three themes. First, mass advertising promoted the increased
pursuit of material goods but no corresponding increase in sense of
satisfaction, which requires accepting some limits on consumption.
The resulting consumerism was "a destructive act, one with implicit
and [explicit] aggressive overtones." [134] Second, similarly, the cumulative effects of exposure to violence on television, especially for youngsters, evidently increased aggressive behaviors. While the effects were
difficult to detect and not strong when appropriate controls were in
place, Janowitz observed that if resources "allocated to violence had
been used for civic education, the social personality of the U.S. citizenry would have been discernibly less accepting of illegitimate violence." [135] Finally, the growing dominance of "advocacy" journalism,
coupled with increased reliance on television for news, heightened a
projective and distrustful response toward public affairs. Television
commentators were trusted. But they stressed a personalistic definition
of politics, de-emphasizing concern about underlying issues, and they
helped define public affairs as suspect, directing suspicion away from
themselves to other persons and institutions. As a result, they provided
"a weak basis for rational appeals and for strengthening ego control."
Taken together, while the mass media are essential for integrating any
large-scale democratic polity, they fail to contribute adequately to the
socialization required for effective self-regulation.

Janowitz was convinced that transition from early industrial to advanced industrial society meant the onset of a period of chronic
strain.[136] He believed that strains on social control made Western democratic regimes more vulnerable to coercive and authoritarian appeals.
But he did not expect any revolutionary overthrow. Nor did he allow
the general thrust of his analysis to blind him to countertrends. In
"The Social Ecology of Citizenship," an essay which he wrote with
Gerald D. Suttles, Janowitz described the continuing vitality of urban
communities.[137] Rejecting both romantic complaints that local communities were eclipsed in urban societies and utopian hopes that all
social problems could be resolved through "local control," Janowitz
noted the elaboration of new institutions forging links between local
urban communities and larger metropolitan and national political
structures. Above the local social bloc (the "natural" community),
communities of voluntary associations formed to deal with episodic
crises within a district affecting more than one social bloc. Not infre-
quently, these communities cooperated to create an aggregated metropolitan confederation responsive to supra-district issues of transpor-

tation, housing, sewage disposal, etc. And these confederations have joined forces on the national level in support of federal policies dealing with common problems.

If anything, Janowitz was overly optimistic about what these associations might accomplish for civic education and citizen participation. Typically, involvement in the relevant organizations was highly intermittent and narrowly concerned with a single issue. Their effectiveness moreover assumed levels of government spending which budgets over the last decade have not sustained. Yet he had an abiding faith in community-based voluntary associations as an important vehicle for the exercise of democratic citizenship. They supplied a framework within which communities could internalize and balance contending claims, agree on values superordinate to individual and group interests, and exert real influence on their government. These are essential requirements for maintaining democratic social control.

In sum, Janowitz rejected depictions of democracy as an unremitting struggle for power among competing interest groups and of social control as an exercise of dominance by ruling elites. Personal and social control—the capacity to participate effectively in the regulation of one's own life and in the life of one's community—are prerequisites for the reproduction of liberal democratic society. And they are closely related phenomena. But neither is achieved automatically. Their achievement depends on institutional arrangements, in particular on a normative context for civic action which limits the pursuit of self-interest by concern for a higher good. Janowitz's contribution to the study of citizenship is unique for examining how these limits, in the form of citizen obligations, are eroded or maintained in advanced industrial society.

Institution Building and Social Change

Morris Janowitz knew that political leaders bore ultimate responsibility for dealing with institutional conflicts in advanced industrial societies. Nevertheless, he believed that the social sciences could make an indirect contribution to the success of their work by offering reasoned assessments of the prospects for social change. He used the term *institution building* to refer to this contribution. Institution building, as he defined the term, encompassed "conscious efforts to direct societal change and to search for more effective social control which are grounded in rationality and in turn are supported by social science efforts."[138]

His confidence in the ability of social science to help reconstruct institutions is perhaps out of touch with current fashions in sociological thought. He was not cynical about human motives or radically skeptical about the prospects for changing institutional arrangements to improve human well-being.[139] He recognized "the limitations of rationalistic explanations of human behavior and achievement."[140] It was a task of effective social science to make those limitations clear. Yet this did not detract from the contribution social science made. On the contrary. For Janowitz, who self-consciously continued the tradition of John Dewey in this regard, social science research was part of a larger social process of public discussion supported by modern democratic societies.[141] Institution building was an ongoing product of public discussion within which organized social inquiry was an influential, though not the only, voice.

The effectiveness of social science efforts for institution building depended in part on how social scientists defined their role within this public discussion. Janowitz first dealt with the matter in an essay, published in 1954, "The Ideology of Professional Psychologists."[142] Psychologists at the time were concerned about the influence social values might have on their scientific research and professional practice. Their concern, Janowitz observed, was generated not by introspective worry over some "past positive sins," but by a collective desire to achieve greater influence over human behavior in American society, to engage in institution building, as Janowitz would later call it.[143] Yet they were impeded from realizing their desire because they failed sufficiently to understand the value orientations which guided their practice. Most important, not unlike other social sciences, psychology adopted a naive empiricism and faith in the truth of scientific knowledge which confused scientific knowledge with reality and so devalued other kinds of social knowledge. The resulting failure to recognize limits on psychological knowledge led to a fantastic exaggeration of the potentialities of social science and a caricature of the social scientist as "all-powerful." Not much less important, psychologists adopted a narrow means orientation to their research based upon an overly optimistic belief about achieving rapid change in human relations. Janowitz thought their optimism reflected America's engineering culture. But it led to a wasteful preoccupation with bits of problems, and so limited the social influence of psychological research. Though social scientists ought to be concerned about the usefulness of their research, their concern should not be excessive, as if they alone were responsible for solving public problems. Social scientists must exercise reasonable initiative to become realistic about their roles as scientists and citizens. For Janowitz, these were compatible roles in democratic societies. "The scientific method," he wrote, "remains unspoiled and in fact becomes more effective when the social scientist realizes that the value assumptions that guide his technical research and the value assumptions that guide him as a public citizen ought to be part of the same whole." [144]

Janowitz remained concerned about the contributions social science made to public life throughout his career. A substantial portion of *The Last Half-Century* was devoted to the topic, as was his last book, *The Reconstruction of Patriotism,* and he worked in the mid-1980s to organize a large-scale assessment by qualified scholars of the worth of sociology. (Unfortunately, the progress of his disease limited his participation in this project.)[145] On balance, he concluded that the work of social scientists who were "devoted to the pragmatic—as opposed to the mechanical or ideological—application of the scientific method" had made life in advanced industrial society more tolerable and enhanced the possibility for social control.[146]

For his part, Janowitz contributed to institution building by clarifying alternative possibilities for managing organizations and organizational change, and by indicating how forms of citizen participation in democratic decision making could be made more effective. An example is found in his book *Institution Building in Urban Education.*[147] In that work, Janowitz rejected arguments that attributed declines in educational attainment to the lowering of professional standards. More essential was the failure to organize schools adequately within the urban community. Arguments about low professional standards rested on what he called the specialization model of the school, which had its roots in the assumptions of cognitive psychology. It emphasized the priority of academic over socialization goals and argued for increased use of curriculum specialists whose work would be coordinated through a district-wide administration. In effect, it treated schools as a functionally specific institution within but not fully part of local communities. In contrast, the aggregation model (which Janowitz preferred) assumed that effective learning depended on affective as well as cognitive or rational processes. It sought to balance academic with socialization goals and argued for increased support for "master teachers" with responsibility as "central managers of the classroom" to create appropriate conditions for teaching and learning. Such teachers would have to convince youngsters that they were concerned for their basic needs, which would entail using schools as coordinating mechanisms for formal and informal programs of community intervention. While the specialization model explicitly narrowed the school's role to focus on the task of teaching basic skills, the aggregation model tried to integrate school activities more widely within the life of the community. Janowitz preferred the aggregation model because it would overcome the school's relative isolation, allowing teachers to develop a sense of group affiliation and self-esteem in their students which would stimulate academic learning.

Effective institution building in school systems and elsewhere is made more difficult by tendencies toward "trend thinking." Extrapolation of past trends can replace genuine thought about how institutional processes are affected by changing social contexts. Janowitz was sensitive to this problem, especially as it was found in military organization. The military is a highly bureaucratized organization often preoccupied with the persistence of its distinctive way of life and operational routines. Despite vast changes in structure and mission following the Second World War, military leaders hoped to create a sense of combat readiness and effective group solidarity by strictly enforcing the day-to-day routines of military life and engaging in rigorous training. But these are manifestations of "organizational traditionalism." A military committed to the goals of deterrence and peacekeeping cannot guarantee its combat readiness by relying on organizational routines.[148] Military readiness, Janowitz argued, required innovative and rapid adjustments of routine capacities to emergencies and crises "to restore balance effectively or to create a new balance" in troubled situations.[149] The capacity to respond to the unexpected represented a core military value, and an element of continuity with the past. Yet it was only "dimly perceived and appreciated."[150]

Properly understood, concern about combat readiness represented a genuine problem. Military officers who were uncertain about their ability to carry out their task might feel pressured to adopt postures that distorted the usefulness of military force in international relations. But while traditional reliance on tough training might forge group loyalty, it would not necessarily develop the professional perspectives required for a deterrent force. The essential issue, Janowitz believed, was to modify the military's organizational climate so that combat readiness represented neither personal aggressiveness or ideological rigidity but rather an element of organizational effectiveness. Doing so required novel programs of political education and professional socialization. Education to enhance conceptual clarity about the military's strategic purpose had to be widespread, not confined to the top leadership, but made part of the regular education of the entire leadership cadre. Professional socialization was needed to help form group cohesion and collective motives. "Military men," Janowitz noted, "tend to think of themselves as specialists in violence."[151] But the military's organizational climate cannot be defined by men acting out aggressive impulses. Rather it must express effectively internalized professional norms and values. To be seen as legitimate and reliable, a force which handles nuclear weapons must exhibit high standards of behavior, incorporating different and more constrained personal and social controls than those in civilian society.

As these examples show, the focus of institution building for Janowitz went beyond questions about managing large-scale organizations. The essential concern was over the capacity to participate effectively in the regulation of one's own life and in the life of one's own community, to organize institutions to enhance personal and social control and so to facilitate the reproduction of liberal democratic society. Effective civic consciousness—constructing an adequate micromacro link—requires understanding of the normative content of citizenship obligations and a reduction of barriers that might inhibit their enactment. Yet under the fragmented conditions of advanced industrial society, "the inherent advantages of citizenship are either not obvious or increasingly limited in consequence."[152] To counter these tendencies, and to help supply the minimum cultural unity which democratic rule requires, Janowitz long argued for establishment of a system of voluntary national service.[153] He believed such a program might be modeled after the Civilian Conservation Corps (CCC). In contrast with the Jobs Corps, which assumed the moral worth of people derived solely from their marketplace value, the CCC provided young men with work to meet the needs of the larger collectivity. Public service reinforced their sense of self-worth through the social and moral meaning of their accomplishments. Developing a sense of civic consciousness required active participation in the life of the larger community, not for one's own benefit, but to construct public goods. The experience, he hoped, would help "balance the pursuit of economic self-interest against collective civic obligation."[154]

Janowitz once referred to himself as a "citizen-sociologist."[155] The term captures his belief that sociology was not a scholarly discipline pursued in isolation from the rest of society. For him, it was a calling that required active engagement with the major problems of the day. That did not mean the discipline should be politicized, guided in its conclusions by partisan commitments. He subscribed to Max Weber's ideas of "value free" social science. Nor did it require that sociologists attempt to become "philosopher-kings." He had a realistic sense about the contributions of social science to institution building, which steered between utopian hope and pessimism about the prospects for reform. The task was not to make policy, but to speak with a respon-

sible voice in public discussion. On the basis of rigorous and pragmatic research, social scientists could clarify for policymakers and an
alert public "what the questions are people have to answer and decide,
not [the answers to] specific questions." [156]

Intellectual Impact

Without doubt, Janowitz was judged by his contemporaries to be an
important figure in American sociology during the four decades following the Second World War. Available measures of academic reputations are crude, but support the point. He was appointed to serve on
the faculties of two of the nation's most prestigious universities. He
was elected by his colleagues to serve as vice-president of the American
Sociological Association in 1970–71, this despite the fact that his research on the military was harshly and unfairly judged during the period of bitter division over the war in Vietnam. In 1978, he was elected
a fellow of the American Academy of Arts and Sciences. Five years
later, in 1983, he was elected a fellow of the American Philosophical
Society. The following year, he received the American Sociological Association's Award for a Career of Distinguished Scholarship. Janowitz
was also one of the few sociologists whose reputation was not confined to national borders. He was active in the International Sociological Association, serving on its executive council and founding its research committee on armed forces and society. He was awarded an
honorary doctorate in 1977 by the University of Tolouse in recognition of his contributions to empirical studies of the military. And, in
1986, he was named honorary president of the Israeli Institute for Military Studies.

Janowitz was a man who possessed enormous energy; he was always able to do many things at once. His interests were broad and
diffuse, and in speech he was often loud and flamboyant, given to hy-
perbole as a way to make a point. But his efforts were not scattered or
frenetic. His energy was concentrated on achieving particular goals.
He remained in control over the direction of his work and of its place
in his personal life. He was constant in his friendship, standing by
people even after they disappointed him, helping them if he could. He
exhibited a critical but true loyalty to the institutions with which he
was involved. When added to his prodigious intellectual preparation
and passionate belief in the importance of social science inquiry, these
qualities gave Janowitz a personal magnetism that attracted colleagues, no less than students, and earned their respect. [157]

He was always suggesting what studies should be done and surveying work in progress to discern new directions in the field. In 1951, for instance, he participated in a seminar on political behavior sponsored by the Social Science Research Council. The product of that seminar was a set of project designs to encourage empirical research about political organization and conduct.[158] The political scientist Samuel Eldersveld recalls that Janowitz was a real leader of the group, helping especially to formulate a design for a study of local political party organization which he thought ought to be done.[159] He had an exceptional ability to judge the quality and improve the design of various research projects. This ability was appreciated and relied on not only by his colleagues, but also by editors of major publishing houses in the social sciences, like Jeremiah Kaplan of the Free Press and Ivan Dee with Quadrangle Books. These qualities were essential for his editing of the Heritage of Sociology series.

Janowitz's work on the military exerted direct and palpable influence on the development of sociological research. In part, this was so because of the special place held by his work *The Professional Soldier,* a classic and seminal contribution to the field. But it was also because of his activities as founder and chairman of the Inter-University Seminar on Armed Forces and Society (IUS). From a loose-knit organization of about a dozen scholars in the early 1960s, this association grew to hundreds of members drawn from around the world, all of whom were actively engaged in research about some aspect of armed forces and society. Through this organization, Janowitz encouraged many people to undertake studies of the military and arranged for conferences to be held on a regular basis in places ranging from Chicago to Varna, which provided opportunities for these scholars to present and discuss the results of their work. It was his understanding of the field— as being fundamentally concerned with the issues of (*a*) military professionalism and organization, (*b*) the logic of war and armed conflict, and (*c*) civil-military relations—which lent coherence and significance to the enterprise. It is significant that a recent "Trend Report on Armed Forces and Society" presents a selective bibliography of nearly six hundred entries which are organized in terms of these categories to provide an overview of the field.[160]

Janowitz's direct impact on the discipline cannot be confined to the military, however. He was an energetic teacher who supervised a large number of students in research over the range of his own empirical and theoretical interests. Oscar Grusky, Mayer Zald, and Harvey Molotch, for example, have established distinguished careers of their own in the areas of organizations, collective behavior and social movements, and urban studies. There is no complete listing of all the graduate committees on which Janowitz served over the course of his career. It is certain that he served on at least 130 Ph.D. committees, chairing no less than 45, while teaching at Chicago. Many of the dissertations which he directed—particularly those done when he was at the height of his creative powers in the early 1970s—have subsequently been published, such as James Jacobs's developmental analysis of penitentiary organization in *Stateville,* Albert Hunter's documentation of persistence and change in local community organization in *Symbolic Community,* and William Kornblum's study of the interrelationships between political, neighborhood, and labor organization in *Blue Collar Community.* These works stand as important contributions in sociology, and provide further evidence of the breadth of Janowitz's influence.

A comprehensive assessment of the impact of Janowitz's ideas would have to examine more subtle lines of influence as well. His students found in him a model of how to carry the traditions of their discipline to another generation. He loved lively discussions about the worth of competing hypotheses, and tried to provoke them in the classroom. He encouraged students to argue strongly for their own point of view, but also required that they listen and respond to one another. His was a challenging intellectual style. Although he was sometimes overpowering for passive students, he was tolerant of different methods and points of view, as long as they could be defended on reasonable intellectual grounds. He was often gruff and short in conversation, sometimes to a startling degree. But he was genuinely solicitous about the well-being of his students, and went to extraordinary lengths to help them establish their careers.

He often said that he regretted having just one life to give for sociology. This never meant that sociologists ought to lead monkish lives devoted only to their studies. His belief that social science could contribute to the solution of the larger public issues led him to become active in a wide variety of projects. He had an extensive record of public service at the national level, but never lost sight of the important contributions to be made on the local level. He worked in local politics in Ann Arbor, helping Samuel Eldersveld run a successful campaign for mayor, and ran (unsuccessfully) for a seat in Michigan's state legislature. He organized support to subsidize new- and used-book stores in Hyde Park. He was active in raising money to create a development fund for the Woodlawn Organization. He worked with local schools to improve their level of instruction. He organized the Metcalf Report on police brutality in Chicago and worked with private developers and municipal agencies to encourage the development of economically and racially heterogeneous urban neighborhoods. As one friend recalled:

He went many places every day, and talked to many people, often offering analysis or proposing changes, or concocting projects. Sometimes his tone suggested that the person being spoken to should drop all other matters and move a bookstore, recruit a coffee shop, plan a street fair, find support for a family in distress, tutor an illiterate, or convince the Board of Education to establish a branch school. He tried to make the suggestions doable and practical, and to imply that problems presented were surmountable.[161]

It is unlikely that many people could unite his scholarly abilities with a practical sense of how to improve local communities and how to mobilize others within the university and without to see to it that many projects were carried out. But colleagues and students who worked with him were bound to try.

The unity of theory and action embodied in Janowitz's life evidenced his commitment to pragmatic sociology. It is impossible to forecast how future sociological research and thought will value such an approach. Some hope to establish absolute and grand theories of one kind or another, while others try to establish a paradigm of rational action to the exclusion of affective and other nonrational factors. These are not the grounds on which a pragmatic approach will stand. A pragmatic sociology recognizes the constancy of social change and the need for institutional adaptation which cooperative social action makes possible. Its task and contribution, Janowitz taught, is to identify fundamental trends in societal development, to indicate their substantive implications for social control, and to clarify realistic alternatives for institution building. In the process, the stock of sociological concepts is refined and the prospects for containing the strains of modern society are improved.

Notes

1. Alvin W. Gouldner, *The Coming Crisis of Western Sociology* (New York: Basic Books, 1970); Siegwart Lindenberg, "How Sociological Theory Lost Its Central Issue and What Can Be Done about It," in *Approaches to Social Theory,* ed. Siegwart Lindenberg, James S. Coleman, and Stefan Nowak (New York: Russell Sage Foundation, 1986), pp. 19–24.

2. Dennis Smith's recent work, *The Chicago School: A Liberal Critique of Capitalism* (London: Macmillan, 1988), includes a full chapter on Janowitz's work and its standing in the Chicago tradition.

3. Edward Shils, "Biographical Memoir: Morris Janowitz," *Yearbook, 1989* (Philadelphia: American Philosophical Society, 1990), pp. 201–07.

4. Morris Janowitz, *W. I. Thomas on Social Organization and Social Personality* (Chicago: University of Chicago Press, 1966), p. vii.

5. Robert E. L. Faris, *Chicago Sociology, 1920–1932* (Chicago: University of Chicago Press, 1970).

6. On the history and importance of philosophical pragmatism as a source of ideas for Chicago sociology, see most recently Hans Joas, "Symbolic Interactionism," in *Social Theory Today,* ed. Anthony Giddens and Jonathan Turner (Stanford: Stanford University Press, 1987), pp. 86–93; Donald N. Levine, "On the Heritage of Sociology," in *The Challenge of Social Control,* ed. Gerald D. Suttles and Mayer N. Zald (Norwood, N.J.: Ablex Publishing, 1985), pp. 13–19; and Lester Kurtz, *Evaluating Chicago Sociology* (Chicago: University of Chicago Press, 1984), pp. 8–10.

7. For details in this section, I have relied on Michel L. Martin's "Of Arms and the Man: A Short Intellectual History of Morris Janowitz's Contribution to the Sociology of the Military," in *The Military, Militarism, and the Polity* (New York: Free Press, 1984); personal communications with Morris Janowitz's wife, Gayle, and oldest daughter, Rebecca; and Morris Janowitz, transcript of interview conducted by David Street at the University of Chicago in April 1979. I am grateful to Professor Sally Kilgore for making this unpublished transcript available for my use.

8. Grace Zimel, personal communication.

9. Harold Glazer and Jacob G. Bornstein, personal communications.

10. From "Paterson: Episode 17," in *The Collected Poems of William Carlos Williams: Volume 1, 1909–1939,* ed. A. Walton Litz and Christopher MacGowan (New York: New Directions, 1986), pp. 442–43.

11. Harold Glazer, personal communication.

12. Janowitz chose to study German in high school because he anticipated that another war with Germany was inevitable.

13. Rose Janowitz felt betrayed by the Russian Revolution and hated Lenin. Morris Janowitz attributed his anticommunist outlook to her influence: "I took it in with my mother's milk," he would say. Rebecca Janowitz, personal communication.

14. Janowitz graduated cum laude and was inducted into Phi Beta Kappa. His classmates voted him "the most brilliant boy" of his class.

15. Morris Janowitz, interview (April 1979).

16. Gerald D. Suttles, "A Tribute to Morris Janowitz," in *The Challenge of Social Control,* p. 9. See also Bernard Barber, *Effective Social Science* (New York: Russell Sage Foundation, 1987), p. 66.

17. When Janowitz first read Freud's work is not known with certainty, though it is not unreasonable to suppose he had done so before graduating from college. He did not study psychoanalysis systematically until after the Second World War.

18. Sidney Hook, personal communication. See also his autobiography, *Out of Step* (New York: Harper & Row, 1988).

19. Janowitz, *The Last Half-Century* (Chicago: University of Chicago Press, 1978), p. xii.

20. Janowitz, interview (April 1979); letter from Morris Janowitz to Sid-

ney Hook, 4 June 1968, box 13, folder 6, Morris Janowitz Papers, Regenstein Library, University of Chicago. Hereafter, references to this collection will be designated *MJP.*

21. It was in this role that Edward Shils first remembers seeing Janowitz. He described Janowitz at that time as being a "lively youth, fresh out of university, full of high jinx, never shunning physical exertion, obviously enjoying himself to the hilt, exhilarated by the association with great events." See Shils, "Biographical Memoir."

22. Edward Shils notes that the idea for the unit came originally from Harold D. Lasswell. See his "Biographical Memoir."

23. Members of this unit, who, besides Janowitz, included Edward Shils and W. Phillips Davison, fought unsuccessfully to prevent the internment of Japanese-Americans.

24. W. Phillips Davison, personal communication.

25. Janowitz, interview (April 1979). The qualification about Marcuse is Janowitz's own.

26. While working in this office Janowitz was injured slightly by a piece of glass sent flying by a German bomb; he received the Purple Heart for his injury.

27. See chap. 9, this volume.

28. Janowitz, interview (April 1979). Janowitz rose from the rank of private to that of second lieutenant by war's end.

29. Irving L. Janis, Raymond H. Fadner, and Morris Janowitz, "The Reliability of a Content Analysis Technique," *Public Opinion Quarterly* (summer 1943): 293–96; Morris Janowitz, "The Technique of Propaganda for Reaction: Gerald L. K. Smith's Radio Speeches," *Public Opinion Quarterly* (spring 1944): 84–93; Donald V. McGranahan and Morris Janowitz, "Studies of German Youth," *Journal of Abnormal and Social Psychology* 41 (January 1946): 3–14; M. I. Gurfein and Morris Janowitz, "Trends in Wehrmacht Morale," *Public Opinion Quarterly* (spring 1946): 78–84. While the last two of these articles appeared after Janowitz was discharged, they were both written and submitted for publication while he was in the military.

30. By this time, Harold Lasswell was no longer on the faculty at Chicago, but taught at the Yale law school. (On this, see Edward Shils, "Some Academics, Mainly in Chicago," *American Scholar* [spring 1981]: 192–95.) Janowitz hoped that the atmosphere which inspirited him still lingered at Chicago. Janowitz briefly considered attending Harvard and traveled to Cambridge to visit with Talcott Parsons, but he would later say, "I wasn't moved by that place and its imagery." Quoted in Barber, *Effective Social Science,* p. 67.

31. Bettelheim, a native Austrian, had written an important article in 1943 ("Individual and Mass Behavior in Extreme Situations," *Journal of Abnormal and Social Psychology* 38:417–52) which was based in part on reflections about his experiences while a prisoner in Nazi concentration camps before he was able to flee to the United States in 1940. Though Janowitz had not met Bettelheim beforehand, he and his associates during the war studied this ar-

ticle. Janowitz, interview (April 1979). See also Morris Janowitz, "Bruno Bettelheim," *International Encyclopedia of the Social Sciences,* vol. 18 (New York: Free Press, 1979), pp. 59–63.

32. During the years 1946–48 the faculty included Ernest Burgess, Herbert Blumer, Philip Hauser, Everett Hughes, William Ogburn, Edward Shils, Lloyd Warner, William Foote Whyte, and Louis Wirth. Ellesworth Faris was emeritus until 1953. See Lee Harvey, *Myths of the Chicago School of Sociology* (Brookfield, Vt.: Avebury, 1987), p. 224.

33. Morris Janowitz, foreword to Robert E. L. Faris, *Chicago Sociology, 1929–1932* (Chicago: University of Chicago Press, 1967), p. xi.

34. Attending an informal seminar in Louis Wirth's home, Otis Dudley Duncan, who was reluctant to call attention to himself, noticed another student up front speaking out to challenge what Wirth said. When he asked who this graduate student was, he was told, "That's not a graduate student; that's Morris Janowitz," (Suttles, "A Tribute to Morris Janowitz," p. 9.) The story sounds apocryphal, but it is consistent with other stories that are told. Rebecca Janowitz (personal communication) remembers a British major who had always heard that the American Army was organized differently than the British Army. One day he was sent to meet her father. "When I first saw him," he recalled, "he was seated on his commanding officer's desk pounding it with his fist. I knew then what I had heard about the American Army was true."

35. Letter from Morris Janowitz to Col. Herman Beukema, 28 January 1948, *MJP* box 1, folder 2. Whether Edward Shils had or would have agreed to such a publication outlet is not certain. See letter from Morris Janowitz to Edward Shils, 8 December 1947, *MJP* box 1, folder 2.

36. W. Phillips Davison edited the journal at that time. Janowitz asked him whether the journal would devote a special issue to the study, or else publish it in its entirety over two issues. But the means to do this were not available. Though the paper as it appeared in the summer of 1948 was one of the longest the journal had published, much material was cut from the original. (W. Phillips Davison, personal communication.)

37. Edward Shils, who was also to have worked on the project, but could not, recommended that Janowitz become involved in the study, collecting and analyzing the data from 150 intensive interviews of veterans of enlisted rank from the city of Chicago.

38. Janowitz, interview (April 1979).

39. Harold Wilensky (personal communication).

40. The first time he taught the course, Janowitz relied on his notes from Hook's course when preparing his lectures on Karl Marx. Irwin Goldberg (personal communication).

41. Guy Swanson (personal communication).

42. Janowitz once strongly advised a student to pursue his research in a particular direction. The student faithfully did so, but it led nowhere. A few months later, the student consulted again with Janowitz, who pointed out that the student's path was a dead end. "But you suggested it," the student replied.

"And whose fault is it if you doggedly follow lousy advice?" Janowitz asked in return. William Gamson (personal communication).

43. Janowitz, interview (April 1979).

44. Barber, *Effective Social Science*, p. 69.

45. Kurt Lang (personal communication). The source of the funds for this meeting is unknown. Janowitz reports that he received $5,000 from the Ford Foundation in the 1950s which he used in support of his military studies (Barber, *Effective Social Science*, p. 69). Whether these were the funds he used or some other remains a conjecture.

46. Daniel Bell requested a copy of the paper in a letter he wrote to Morris Janowitz, 29 April 1954 (*MJP* box 2, folder 1). Alexander George received a copy of the paper the same spring, for which he thanked Janowitz in a letter to him, 19 May 1954 (*MJP* box 2, folder 3).

47. Letter to Horace Miner from Morris Janowitz, 18 May 1954, *MJP* box 2, folder 1.

48. Morris Janowitz, "Some Observations on the Ideology of Professional Psychologists," *American Psychologist* (September 1954): 532.

49. Letter from Morris Janowitz to Philip Hauser, 11 July 1960, *MJP* box 5, folder 1.

50. Gayle Janowitz (personal communication).

51. Edward Shils, "Biographical Memoir."

52. Though his appointment to the department was not effective until 1962, Janowitz accepted the offer of an appointment in late February or early March of 1961. Letter from Morris Janowitz to David Riesman, 6 March 1961, *MJP* box 5, folder 7.

53. Foreword to Robert E. L. Faris's *Chicago Sociology, 1920–1932* (Chicago: University of Chicago Press, 1970), p. xii.

54. Edward Shils, "Morris Janowitz." Remarks made at a conference held in honor of Morris Janowitz at the University of Chicago, 14–15 May 1982.

55. Originally this group was named the Inter-University Seminar on Military Organization. Its name was changed in the late 1960s as the focus of research broadened.

56. Harold Wilensky (personal communication).

57. Plans for Center for Social Organization Studies (August 1962), *MJP* box 23, folder 12.

58. Letter from Morris Janowitz to Philip Hauser, 4 December 1961, *MJP* box 23, folder 12. The center continued in operation until the early 1980s, when it was re-formed as the William F. Ogburn/Samuel A. Stouffer Center for the Study of Population and Social Organization. While it always served as an important forum to encourage critical discussion of research being done by graduate students, the center suffered in the mid-1970s and after from lack of financial support.

59. Kurt Lang (personal communication), an original member of the group, dates its formation to the summer seminar held in Ann Arbor in 1953 which Janowitz convened when he was formulating his research design for

The Professional Soldier. It is unclear to me, however, that Janowitz thought to establish an ongoing association at that time.

60. Leonard S. Cottrell, Maury Feld, Oscar Grusky, Kurt Lang, Peter Rossi, and Hana Selvin participated in this meeting, over which Janowitz presided.

61. Report on Inter-University Seminar on Military Organization, *MJP* box 33, folder 12.

62. Terms of a grant to run from 1963 to 1967 are described in a memo from Morris Janowitz to D. Gale Johnson (Dean, Social Sciences Division, University of Chicago), 8 January 1964, *MJP* box 36, folder 6. A four-year extension of the grant was awarded in 1968. See letter from Orville G. Brim, Jr. (President of Russell Sage Foundation), to Morris Janowitz, 12 November 1968, *MJP* box 14, folder 3.

63. Janowitz hoped this book would be the first volume for a series of studies in social organization. See his preface to *The New Military,* ed. Morris Janowitz (New York: Russell Sage Foundation, 1964), p. 7.

64. A bibliography of publications of the IUS from 1964 to 1974 is printed at the end of the current paperback edition of *The Professional Soldier* (New York: Free Press, 1971), pp. 467–68. These publications were facilitated by Sage Publications, which created a book series on armed forces and society for the work of IUS fellows.

65. Gerald D. Suttles and Richard P. Taub (personal communications).

66. He took the place of Nathan Keyfitz, whose sudden illness left him unable to continue his term of office.

67. Edward Shils, "Biographical Memoir."

68. Janowitz, interview (April 1979).

69. Edward Shils, "Biographical Memoir."

70. The tensions vented in the winter quarter at Chicago had been building for some time and were aggravated by societal divisions over the war in Vietnam, urban community development programs, and civil rights issues, not to mention the conflagration at the 1968 Democratic National Convention, which was held in Chicago, and the model of student disruptions at other major universities the year before.

71. *New York Times,* 31 January 1969, p. 18. Their contentions were baseless. There is every reason to believe that Marlene Dixon's work at the time was conventional (not radical) and lacked the promise of originality or distinction which was required for her reappointment. And there is no evidence to the contrary. The decision of the department in her case was carefully reviewed and affirmed in the winter of 1969 by a committee appointed by the Dean of Faculties.

72. For external reflections on the matter, see Wayne C. Booth, *Modern Dogma and the Rhetoric of Assent* (Chicago: University of Chicago Press, 1974).

73. Many details in this paragraph and the next are owed to personal communications with Rebecca Janowitz, William Kornblum, Allan Silver, and Gerald Suttles.

74. Letter from Morris Janowitz to Amos Hawley, 23 May 1969, *MJP* box 14, folder 11.

75. When asked how he was able to continue his work in the midst of the disruptions, Janowitz responded, "By writing and by following the craft of sociological inquiry I gain both motivation and strength to face the very problem [*sic*] of daily life and political involvement." Letter from Morris Janowitz to Jeff M. Elliot, 23 January 1969, *MJP* box 14, folder 6.

76. There are some exceptions to this claim; most notably, two short monographs—*The Military and Political Development of New Nations* (1964), a product of his participation with the Committee for the Comparative Study of New Nations, and *Institution Building in Urban Education* (1969). These broke new ground, the first about the fit between civil-military relations and social structures in nations established through independence movements following World War II, and the second about how the social organization of schools within urban neighborhoods affected efforts to improve public education.

77. Letter from Morris Janowitz to Barbara D. Finberg (Executive Assistant of Carnegie Corporation), 6 February 1966, *MJP* box 23, folder 4.

78. Janowitz was actively involved in soliciting manuscripts for the series in the fall of 1962. Memo from Morris Janowitz to Roger Shugg, 27 November 1962, *MJP* box 52, folder 7.

79. Letter from Morris Janowitz to Vernon K. Dibble, 2 November 1966, *MJP* box 29, folder 6.

80. The quoted phrase comes from an attachment to a letter from Morris Janowitz to Andrew Effrat, 18 December 1969, *MJP* box 15, folder 4.

81. Letter from Morris Janowitz to Milton Rosenberg, 12 October 1970, *MJP* box 16, folder 2.

82. Morris Janowitz, "Review of *Young John Dewey*," *American Journal of Sociology* 83 (March 1978): 1282.

83. In a letter to Dorothy S. Thomas, 28 December 1965 (*MJP* box 29, folder 6), Janowitz confessed that "the work of W. I. Thomas was so important in my intellectual development." And in a letter to Sidney Hook, 4 June 1968 (*MJP* box 13, folder 6), he acknowledged "my profound intellectual debt to the training and outlook I got from your courses."

84. Letter, 14 August 1972, *MJP* box 16, folder 11.

85. Letter from Morris Janowitz to Philip Selznick, 13 November 1968, *MJP* box 29, folder 11. The failure of a hoped-for volume to appear was not unusual. Projected volumes on Buber, Cooley, and Sorokin also failed to be completed.

86. Morris Janowitz, "Review Essay: The Coming of Post-Industrial Society," *American Journal of Sociology* 80 (July 1974): 230–36.

87. Morris Janowitz, *The Last Half-Century* (Chicago: University of Chicago Press, 1978), p. 7.

88. Ibid., p. xi.

89. Ibid.

90. See n. 6 above.

91. See most recently Jeffery C. Alexander's *Twenty Lectures: Sociological Theory since World War II* (New York: Columbia University Press, 1987), pp. 195–214.

92. Morris Janowitz, "Review of *Young John Dewey*," p. 1282.

93. H.S. Thayer, *Meaning and Action: A Critical History of Pragmatism* (Indianapolis: Hackett Publishing, 1981).

94. Hans Joas, "Symbolic Interactionism," p. 83.

95. Ralph Turner, "The Forgotten Paradigm?" *Contemporary Sociology* 9 (1980): 609–12.

96. Hans Joas, "Symbolic Interactionism," pp. 83–84.

97. Cf. Richard J. Bernstein, "John Dewey," *Encyclopedia of Philosophy*, vol. 2 (New York: Macmillan, 1967), p. 383.

98. The pragmatic roots of these postulates are documented in Dmitri Shalin, "Pragmatism and Social Interactionism," *American Sociological Review* 51 (1986): 9–29.

99. See chap. 1, this volume.

100. "Under the influence of philosophical pragmatism and the impact of empirical research, the dichotomous categories of gemeinschaft-gesellschaft were found to be both oversimplified and inadequate." See "The Concept of Social Control," chap. 2, this volume, esp. p. 75.

101. *Psychological Review* 3 (July 1896): 357–70.

102. See "The Concept of Social Control," pp. 73–85, esp. p. 75, chap. 2, this volume.

103. Morris Janowitz, "Sociological Theory and Social Control," *American Journal of Sociology* 81 (July 1975): 100.

104. Bernstein, "John Dewey," pp. 384–85.

105. Fred Davis and Richard Taub, personal communications.

106. See "Theory and Policy: Engineering versus Enlightenment Models," chap. 3, this volume.

107. Ibid., p. 92.

108. This section has not exhaustively described the various lines of influence which justify regarding Janowitz's work as an exemplar of a pragmatic sociological approach. Interesting parallels may be drawn, for example, between the Chicago school's use of a "natural history" model of collective action, which Janowitz often employed, and Dewey's notion of patterns of inquiry as developed in his book *Logic: The Theory of Inquiry* (Carbondale, Ill.: Southern Illinois University Press, 1986 [1938]), chap. 6.

109. *The Last Half-Century*, p. 29.

110. See "Professionalization of Military Elites," chap. 4, this volume. This paper effectively summarizes the main argument of *The Professional Soldier*.

111. Morris Janowitz, *The Professional Soldier*, chap. 20.

112. See below, p. 103.

113. See below, p. 111.

114. See "The Social Dimensions of Local Community," chap. 5, this volume.

115. *The Last Half-Century,* p. 268.

116. See below, pp. 123–125.

117. See "Inequality, Occupations, and Welfare," chap. 6, this volume.

118. See "The Emergence of Weak Political Regimes," chap. 7, this volume.

119. See "Social Personality and Personal Control," chap. 8, this volume.

120. Ibid., p. 159.

121. See excerpt, chap. 9, this volume.

122. Ibid., p. 161 (emphasis in original).

123. See "Ethnic Intolerance and Hostility," chap. 10, this volume.

124. See "The Psychological Context of Welfare," chap. 11, this volume.

125. Ibid., p. 190.

126. Ibid.,

127. Ibid., p. 192.

128. *The Last Half-Century,* pp. 77–78.

129. T. H. Marshall, "Citizenship and Social Class," in *Class, Citizenship, and Social Development* (Chicago: University of Chicago Press, 1977), pp. 71–134. On current literature see Bryan S. Turner, *Citizenship and Capitalism* (London: Allen & Unwin, 1986), and J. M. Barbalet, *Citizenship* (Minneapolis: University of Minnesota Press, 1988).

130. See "Observations on the Sociology of Citizenship: Obligations and Rights," chap. 12, this volume. With this argument, Janowitz anticipated the concerns of communitarian philosophers like Benjamin Barber, Alasdair MacIntyre, and Michael Sandel, who wrote on these themes in the 1980s.

131. Ibid., p. 202.

132. See "Military Institutions and Citizenship in Western Societies," chap. 13, this volume.

133. See "Mass Media and Popular Distrust," chap. 14, this volume.

134. Ibid., p. 240.

135. Ibid., p. 244.

136. See Morris Janowitz, "Review Essay of *Reflections on the Causes of Human Misery and upon Certain Proposals to Eliminate Them,*" *American Journal of Sociology* 79 (March 1974): 1321–26.

137. See chap. 15, this volume.

138. *The Last Half-Century,* p. 400.

139. For an elaboration of this argument, see Alan Sica, "The Rhetoric of Sociology and Its Audience," in *Sociology and Its Publics,* ed. Terence C. Halliday and Morris Janowitz (Chicago: University of Chicago Press, forthcoming).

140. *The Last Half-Century,* p. 400.

141. Janowitz was particularly influenced in his thought on this subject by Dewey's book *The Public and Its Problems* (Chicago: Swallow Press, 1954[1927]), a work which he frequently recommended to students. In that work, Dewey argues that the transformation of large-scale society into a democratic community depends on the formation of a public through communication. Social inquiry is essential to the process: "Communication of the results of social inquiry," Dewey wrote (p. 177), "is the same thing as the

formation of public opinion. This marks one of the first ideas framed in the growth of political democracy as it will be one of the last to be fulfilled."

142. See chap. 16, this volume.

143. Janowitz provided a full evaluation of the contributions of professional psychology to institution building in American society in *The Last Half-Century,* chap. 11.

144. See below, p. 281.

145. One result of these efforts, however, was a conference, "Sociology and Institution Building," held in November 1988, shortly after Janowitz's death. The papers of this conference are to be published in *Sociology and Its Publics,* ed. Terence C. Halliday and Morris Janowitz (Chicago: University of Chicago Press, forthcoming).

146. *The Last Half-Century,* p. 401.

147. See "Models for Urban Education," chap. 17, this volume.

148. See "Institution Building for Military Stabilization," chap. 18, this volume.

149. Ibid., p. 296.

150. Ibid.

151. Ibid., p. 298.

152. See below, p. 305.

153. See "Toward the Reconstruction of Patriotism," chap. 19, this volume.

154. Ibid., pp. 305–306.

155. Barber, *Effective Social Science,* p. 75.

156. Ibid., pp. 75–76.

157. Guy E. Swanson (personal communication).

158. See "Research in Political Behavior," *American Political Science Review* 46 (December 1952): 1003–1045.

159. Samuel Eldersveld (personal communication). Eldersveld eventually used the design to guide his study of Detroit party structures, which he did with Daniel Katz.

160. Gwyn Harries-Jenkins and Charles C. Moskos, Jr., "Trend Report on Armed Forces and Society," *Contemporary Sociology* 29 (1981): 1–164.

161. Margaret Fallers (personal communication). Her description of Janowitz's behavior is confirmed by the vivid recollections of many others, ranging from Richard Stern, the novelist, to Leon Despres, former Chicago alderman.

I

THE LOGIC OF
SOCIOLOGICAL INQUIRY

1

Styles of Theory Construction

Sociologists entertain differing notions about the nature of sociological explanations. As sociology became an academic discipline, it became philosophically concerned with the applicability and limits of positivism, and in time, the potentials of logical positivism as a basis of sociological inquiry. This involvement with positivism has not resulted in the partition of sociology. While there are extreme phenomenologists in sociology who reject the relevance of positivism, most "working" sociologists are concerned with the appropriate balance of emphasis in the discipline. It is as if the participants required the close proximity of their opponents for stimulation.

The basic issues become clear if one considers the inquiries that sociologists actually undertake rather than the formulae they claim to adhere to. However, because sociology is incremental, each sociologist does not start afresh. The investigator must make a number of decisions about the logic of his approach which are influenced by past accomplishments. He has a set of alternative ways of constructing his categories and defining the properties of social organization which can be thought of as his style of theory construction. (The possibility of a revolutionary breakthrough is never denied, but there is no basis for anticipating its immediate or even remote eventuality.) Systemic analysis as one style of theory construction supplies a set of decisions about five categories of analysis: general versus middle-range theory; equilibrium versus developmental analysis; interdependent versus autonomous structures; generalized versus differentiated units of analysis; and social versus socioenvironmental boundaries.

General Theory versus Middle-Range Theory

Immediately after 1945, sociologists debated the alternative merits of general theory versus theory of the middle range. Like many such sociological issues, it has subsided without clear-cut resolution. How-

From *The Last Half-Century*, pp. 60–75. © 1978 by The University of Chicago. All rights reserved.

ever, on this issue, systemic analysis is explicit: it rejects the relevance of these alternative formulations because they are both part of a common approach. The terms of reference in the distinction were offered with specific intellectual objectives in mind by Robert K. Merton. He was concerned that sociological theory not be limited to the history of ideas, but that theory construction have an influence on empirical research and that empirical research, in turn, on the reformulation of sociological theory.[1] He was writing in the context of his own work as a member of a university-affiliated center during a period of expansion of survey research methodology. He wanted to relate the findings of this methodology to the broader, more enduring interests of academic sociologists. It may well be that the language of his argument created a debate which he did not intend. His formulations gave rise to an antithesis between his approach and that of the comprehensive-system builders, particularly Talcott Parsons and his colleagues. The difference between these approaches is one in preferred degree of abstraction and generality of concepts and propositions.

Merton argues, "from all of this it would seem reasonable to suppose that sociology will advance in the degree that its major concern is with developing theories of the middle range and will be frustrated if attention centers on theory in the large. I believe that our major task today is to develop special theories applicable to limited ranges of data, theories, for example, of class dynamics, of conflicting group pressures, of the flow of power and the exercise of interpersonal influence, rather than to seek at once the 'integrated' conceptual structure adequate to derive all of these and others."[2] There is a close affinity between this style of theory construction and that of systemic analysis. The emphasis is on a range of testable hypotheses for which no single postulated schema will suffice. . . .

But any set of hypotheses requires a group of givens on which they can rest. Systemic analysis refers to testable and delimited hypotheses to be found in theories of the middle range. But there can be no testable hypotheses without some elements—explicit, at that—of a general theory.[3] The argument appears overdrawn at best, except to the extent that particular general theories do not generate testable hypotheses. Naturally, there is considerable latitude in the logical structure, specificity, and their substantive content of the givens. The result of the

1. Robert K. Merton, *Social Theory and Social Structure* (Glencoe, Ill.: Free Press, 1957), pp. 85–117.

2. Ibid., p. 9.

3. See Ralf Dahrendorf, "Out of Utopia: Toward a Reorientation of Sociological Analysis," *American Journal of Sociology* 64 (September 1958): 115–27.

enormous discussion of this so-called controversy is to point out that some theories, because of their global character or their internal definitions and categories, do not produce testable hypotheses.[4] In the language of systemic analysis, such testable hypotheses do not have a life of their own but are derived in part from, or at least dependent on, elements which are to be found in what Robert K. Merton calls grand theory.

An essential aspect in the debate between the advocates of grand theory and advocates of middle-range analysis centers on the appropriate theoretical terms of reference in a sociological analysis. Again, at this point, the observer might be struck by the lack of agreement in the theoretical terms of reference which sociologists employ in their empirical research efforts. Every abstraction is not a theory, nor can the term "concept" be applied to every abstraction. Much of the discussion in sociology about appropriate theoretical terms of reference is both commonplace and arbitrary. But to dismiss these problems as being a form of oversophistication and to engage in excessive elaboration is self-defeating. It is more important to note the degree of operative convergence in sociological analysis, since systemic analysis does require terms which will expedite the translation of findings from one investigation to another and from one subject to another.

The implicit and explicit issues in the debate between grand theory and middle-range theory resolve themselves when there is a degree of logical clarity which makes it possible to separate the hypotheses that are being tested in a given research from the assertions (assumptions) on which they rest and which are therefore taken for granted in the course of the investigation.[5] This distinction is essential if any real progress is to be made in codification of research findings.

It is important to distinguish between types of givens. There are those givens which are no more than assumptions. They are taken for granted during the course of a particular investigation, and can be weakened by specific empirical findings. Such assumptions are different from the "overarching" givens, those *postulates* found in grand theory, which represent basic outlooks and are not likely to be rejected by particular empirical research but can be abandoned or modified only by the longterm superiority of alternative sets of hypotheses drawn from an alternative theoretical perspective. In the absence of revolutionary science, this is indeed slow, difficult, and painful. . . .

4. For an explanation of this, see Maurice Mandelbaum, "Societal Laws," *British Journal for the Philosophy of Science* 8 (1957): 211–23.

5. I am indebted to my colleague Amos Hawley for the assistance he has given me on these issues of analytic terminology.

Equilibrium versus Development Analysis

Sociology reacts strongly to developments in other research disciplines. In particular, it continues to reflect the imprint of biological and physiological constructs. . . . The intellectual record spans attempts to incorporate Charles Darwin's evolution and natural selection to the contemporary development of cybernetics and the biology of the brain.[6] The most persistent influence has been by the use of the analogy of equilibrium. Distinct from such analogous reasoning has been the effort to explore the linkages of biological factors and social organization or social behavior as a research task.

Equilibrium, as a property of social organization heavily emphasized by L. J. Henderson and his disciples, has to be juxtaposed to the alternative which might best be called developmental analysis.[7] Systemic analysis acknowledges the priority of the developmental posture, at least as a point of entry; at this decisive point it finds equilibrium analysis too confining.

In the extensive literature on equilibrium analysis, the underlying postulate is the inherent tendency of the component subsystems and the overall system of social organization to remain in a steady state. Modifications and deviations tend to be eliminated, reduced, or narrowly restricted. The equilibrium approach, in effect, perpetuates the older distinction between static and dynamic analysis. It asserts the necessity of stipulating in advance all the variables required. In this view, understanding social structure is a prerequisite for explicating social change.[8]

6. Of the extensive literature on cybernetics, the following references are illustrative of those which have been widely read and cited by sociologists: Norbert Wiener, *Cybernetics* (New York: Wiley, 1948); William R. Ashby, *Design for a Brain* (New York: Wiley, 1952); and W. Sluckin, *Minds and Machines* (Baltimore: Penguin, 1960).

7. Bernard Barber, ed., *L.J. Henderson: On the Social System* (Chicago: University of Chicago Press, 1970). For a discussion of the alternative developmental approach see Harold D. Lasswell, *World Politics and Personal Insecurity* (New York: McGraw-Hill, 1935), pp. 3–26; see also G. Poggi, "A Main Theme of Contemporary Sociological Analysis: Its Achievements and Limitations," *British Journal of Sociology* 16 (1965): 283–94. For a penetrating analysis of history and the analysis of social change which converges with "systemic analysis" in its concern with the appropriate level of analysis and abstraction see Ernest Gellner, *Thought and Change* (London: Weidenfeld and Nicholson, 1964).

8. See particularly Talcott Parsons, *The Social System* (Glencoe, Ill.: Free Press, 1951), chap. 11, "The Process of Change in Social Systems," pp. 480–535. Parsons argues that "a general theory of the processes of change in social systems is not possible in the present state of knowledge" (p. 486).

Theoretical orientations which make use of the property of equilibrium handle the question of change by the "principle of emergence," a philosophical construct of long tradition. However, as pointed out by various philosophers, including Abraham Edel, this "principle" is not without problems and limitations for empirical investigators.[9] As applied to social organization analysis, the "principle of emergence" has been described: ". . . at various levels of organizational complexity systems emerge which have properties which cannot be inferred from or explained in terms of the operation of their component parts or elements and that these emergent properties must be treated as causally relevant variables in the theory. By implication, at each emergent level, certain new degrees of freedom are created."[10] This formulation asserts that the new properties cannot be inferred from the prior state, but it is still causally relevant. The property of emergence violates the development toward theoretical closure which the equilibrium format is designed to facilitate. Thus equilibrium analysis is as much an aspiration as a reality.

Developmental analysis is both more time-bound and more interested in making explicit so-called emergent properties. It does not make the sharp distinction between static and dynamic analysis or between structural analysis and the analysis of social change. There are many unsolved and unsolvable problems of such a format, but it supplies a more realistic and comprehensive orientation, beginning with the aspiration that the postulates of change be explicit and substantive, rather than implicit and purely formal—as is often the case in the equilibrium format. To use such an orientation may well "mess up" the analysis. For example, secondary, intervening variables are stated in advance; but the possibility that additional elements will be introduced to the analysis cannot be ruled out in advance.

If equilibrium analysts, or some of them, postulate that social change occurs gradually, developmental analysis postulates that the rates of social change vary and are a subject for empirical investigation.[11] Likewise, if equilibrium analysis implies that change has its locus outside the system under analysis, in developmental analysis change can originate within and outside the social organization under investigation.

9. Abraham Edel, "The Concept of Levels in Social Theory," in F. Gross, ed., *Symposium of Sociological Theory* (Evanston, Ill.: Row Peterson, 1959), pp. 167–95.

10. Ibid., p. 171.

11. President's Research Committee, *Recent Social Trends* (New York: McGraw-Hill, 1933).

It is a primary responsibility of the sociologist to collect and chart empirical indicators of social change. At this point, sociology and "history" converge. All empirical sociology is history, but history is not all empirical sociology. The collection of social indicator data cannot be limited to particular hypotheses but must reflect the collective judgment of social scientists about the range of descriptive data required to write contemporary social history. In the 1920s such a research notion was presented in the writings of William F. Ogburn. Almost a half-century later, the institutionalized collection of such indicators in sociology has begun to occur." [12]

Developmental analysis at times postulates some hypothetical end state, for example, Harold D. Lasswell's "garrison state." [13] The goal is to examine social change in terms of movement toward or away from this construct. This emphasis in developmental analysis includes the charting of "master trends," to use C. W. Mills's term, which supply the societal context for the investigation of particular institutions.[14] Within such a historical and analytic framework, it becomes feasible to explore the limits of equilibrium analysis.

To argue that developmental models are more appropriate for the study of society hardly implies that systemic analysis of social control has no aspirations for general formulations. It does mean that sociologists must pay attention to "historical" issues in research. To aspire to narrow the distinction between history and sociology is commendable only if the sociologists remain aware of the looseness of notions such as the "principle of emergence" and other escape hatches that historians have allowed themselves.[15]

12. Eleanor B. Sheldon and Wilbert E. Moore, *Indicators of Social Change* (New York: Russell Sage Foundation, 1968).

13. Harold D. Lasswell, "The Garrison State," *American Journal of Sociology* 46 (January 1941): 455–68. See also Guenther Roth, "Socio-historical Model and Developmental Theory," *American Sociological Review* 40 (April 1975): 148–57.

14. Hans Gerth and C. Wright Mills, *Character and Social Structure: The Social Psychology of Social Institutions* (New York: Harcourt, Brace and World, 1953).

15. There is no reason to suppose that modern research efforts, with their better resources and elaborate methodology, are always superior to earlier efforts. Studies of racial tension and violence make interesting comparisons possible of the period immediately after World War I and the 1960s. One of the most comprehpensive analyses deals with Chicago during 1919, Chicago Commission on Race Relations, *The Negro in Chicago* (Chicago: University of Chicago Press, 1922). The detailed documentation for this volume was collected by the sociologist Charles S. Johnson under the guidance of Robert E. Park, and the published report is based on an integrated effort. For 1965–1970, immense amounts of data were collected by the Congress, federal commissions, and univer-

Likewise, there is a question of the appropriate time span involved in developmental analysis, a subject on which sociologists have not displayed great expertise. There is no general answer; but sociologists have erred in limiting the periods in their developmental analysis, whether the object of study is a particular institutional innovation or a pattern of societal change. Explanations of the limits vary; the dramatic character of particular contemporary events, inherent limitations of sociological inquiry and available data, or even the desire to participate in policy making. However, intellectual criticism of sociological research has had an increasing influence on broadening and extending sociological time perspectives.[16] In summary, systemic analysis encompasses a concern with the equilibrium model and an emphasis on developmental analysis; the actual admixture is related to both the specific research issue and the style of the investigator.

Interdependent versus Autonomous Structures

One aspect of sociological theory which has fairly general acceptance is that embodied in the holistic approach. The elements of social organization have meaning in terms of all other elements. Most of the founding figures of sociology made some equivalent reference to the idea of holistic analysis. The incremental development in sociology has reaffirmed this notion; the influence of social anthropology has reinforced it.[17] However, sociologists require frequent reminders of this aspect of sociological theory, because it is very difficult to implement in research.

The emphasis of holistic analysis makes the meaning and relevance of any factor or dimension of analysis rest on an understanding of all the other factors and dimensions; this is an essential part of the pursuit of macrosociology. For better or worse, sociology is the discipline concerned with "the context." However, sociological theories based on a

sity and social research groups. Some of these materials permitted refined measures of statistical analysis, including the use of Guttman-type scaling procedures. But not for a single community did these efforts produce the penetrating analysis presented in *The Negro in Chicago*.

16. For a brilliant example of comprehensive historical treatment of the persistence and change of a complex social entity which encompasses the full and necessary temporal sequences, see Donald Levine, *Greater Ethopia. The Evoution of a Multi-ethnic Society* (Chicago: University of Chicago Press, 1974).

17. Lloyd A. Fallers, *Social Anthropology of the Nation State* (Chicago: Aldine, 1974).

holistic framework, as Pierre L. van den Berghe points out, can use fundamentally different conceptions of explanation and causality.[18]

In fact, to speak of a holistic orientation is to refer to no more than the view that, in social organization, causation is to some degree reciprocal among the component elements.[19] It does not answer the question of the degree of interdependence of the components in any particular social organization. On this essential issue—the degree of postulated interdependence among component structural elements—sociological writers differ consistently and to a considerable degree; the direction of systemic analysis is to take for granted at least a considerable degree of actual and potential autonomy between elements, or to assert that there are conditions under which such autonomy is operative.

The distinction of equilibrium versus developmental analysis is relevant at this point. Equilibrium versus developmental analysis postulates different degrees of interdependence. Equilibrium orientations assert a great degree of effective interdependence of component elements of any given social organization. In this type of theory construction, the structure of a society is characterized by a continuous network of persons and groups, so that a change in one component has a direct and discernible effect throughout the entire social organization.

However, if one proceeds by means of systemic analysis, the degree of interdependence is problematic; more specifically, developmental analysis asserts that some autonomous groups are required to achieve effective integration in a given social organization. Thereby systemic analysis, which uses developmental constructs, rejects the idea of complete and comprehensive interdependence.

In particular, the very notion of social control in an advanced industrial society underlines the crucial role of autonomous or relatively autonomous groups. This asserts no less than that some groups in an advanced industrial society will be autonomous or relatively so if the process of social control is to be effective. There is no reason to deny the possibility that in a primary group, a community, a large bureaucracy, or [a] nation, effective social control is compatible with and requires some autonomy in particular constituent groups. In fact, examination of social control in an advanced industrial society indicates that, because of the increased complexity of the division of labor, the

18. Pierre L. van den Berghe, "Dialectic and Functionalism: Toward a Theoretical Synthesis," *American Sociological Review* 28 (October 1963): 695–705.

19. See Alvin Gouldner for a related analysis of reciprocal and autonomous relations in social organizations, "The Means of Reciprocity: A Preliminary Statement," *American Sociological Review* 25 (April 1960): 161–78.

importance of such autonomous structures is enhanced if social rather than coercive control is to be achieved.

Generalized versus Differentiated Units of Analysis

Directly related to the degree of interdependence is the decision which sociologists must make about the units of analysis (and the objects of analysis). In this decision, systemic analysis differs from the dominant motif, since there is a strong tendency in sociological theory to develop and utilize a single basic, highly generalized unit for sociological analysis. For example, sociologists use various notions of a basic "social atom" from which the component elements of social organization are derived and in terms of which social structure can be analyzed. Social role is one formulation of the basic social molecule and the social act is in effect the atomic element.[20]

Talcott Parsons advanced this type of analysis. He spoke of the institutionalization of the social role, the mechanism by which more complex systems are created.[21] The intellectual goal is to produce an orientation of the widest generality, applicable to all institutional arrangements. It is interesting to note that theories of social organization which stress the close interconnection of the component elements are the ones which tend to postulate a single basic unit of analysis. These theories also tend to proceed by means of an equilibrium approach.

Likewise, an orientation which rests on a single, generalized unit of analysis tends to use a single object of analysis. The analogy with the biological notion of organism is again at work. Talcott Parsons offers the social system as his object of analysis, and he holds that society—the nation-state in the modern context—is the most complete social system.[22] While the notion of social system can be applied to other objects of analysis, they are all derivative from the nation-state as a social system. In this regard, George Homans's theoretical orientation has many common features with Talcott Parsons's conception of social systems. He presents the human group as the appropriate object of analysis. The human group is best characterized as the obverse of total society, namely, the primary group defined in classic terms of the small, face-to-face collectivity.[23] Homans builds his case on the argument that "perhaps we cannot manage a sociological synthesis that will ap-

20. For an early contribution, see Florian Znaniecki, *The Social Role of the Man of Knowledge* (New York: Columbia University Press, 1940).
21. Talcott Parsons, *The Social System* (Glencoe, Ill.: Free Press, 1951), passim.
22. Ibid., p. 19.
23. George Homans, *The Human Group* (New York: Harcourt, Brace, 1950).

ply to whole communities and nations, but it is just possible we can manage one that will apply to the small group.[24] In other words, the small group, the human group, for George Homans, like the social system (the total society) for Talcott Parsons, is not only the appropriate object of analysis; it is also a conception of sociological inquiry and a strategy of analysis.[25]

Systemic analysis, drawing on empirical practices as much as on theoretical forms, takes a very different stance with respect to the units and objects of analysis. The notion of a single molecular unit of analysis does not generate a guide to the variables to be employed in research. Likewise, to postulate a single unit or object of analysis—particularly if it is couched in a highly abstract format, such as the social system or the human group—is incomplete. It remains necessary to construct additional taxonomies of group structure to generate testable hypotheses.

There is, of course, a strong element of taste or preference in this theory construction. The unitary approach excessively detaches theory construction from social reality. On the other hand, an elongated collection of units and objects, reflecting the wide research interests of sociologists and having no internal logic, is self-defeating.[26] In short, an appropriate set of units and objects of analysis seeks a balance between concreteness to guide empirical research and a degree of analytical generality.

In the elaboration of sociological theory, the simple distinction between "community" and "society" served to identify units and objects of analysis. These terms are not simply empirical entities; they are also analytical categories. The independent variables are linked to the "community" (the unit of analysis) and were designed to explain its

24. Ibid., p. 31.
25. Both approaches have intellectual attractions. Talcott Parsons's focus on the total society not only supplies continuity with long-standing concerns about the social order but also carries a face validity, namely, that total society is obviously most complex and therefore the core of sociological inquiry. George Homans's posture appears to carry with it an important seed of intellectual restraint and modesty. In his view, how can sociologists attack the total society when they do not understand the small group? Actually, sociologists have not been constrained to accept either formulation of a single object of analysis, nor need they do so.
26. At this point, systemic analysis converges with the idea of grounded theory. Grounded theory, however, does not sufficiently emphasize the positive assistance that the intellectual heritage of sociology affords the empirical investigator, nor does it specify the formal issues that must be resolved by the investigator. See Barney Glaser and Anselm Strauss, *The Discovery of Grounded Theory: Strategies for Qualitative Research* (Chicago: Aldine, 1967).

transformation into "society" (the object of analysis); these distinctions also imply the reverse flow of influence from "society" to "community." The schema presents a balance between abstract categories and concrete realities which continues to have a strong appeal to empirical sociologists.

But the distinction between "community" and "society" was hardly sufficient to incorporate the empirical observations of the founding figures in sociology. Sociologists like Charles Horton Cooley identified the primary group as an essential component in accounting for the social order. Likewise, since the earliest writings of Herbert Spencer, sociologists have sought analytically to distinguish "institutions" from "society."

By the turn of the century, a relatively standardized set of units and objects of analysis had come into the terminology of primary groups, communities, institutions, and societies.[27] For students of social control, these early distinctions have remained crucial, although the definitions have been refined and modified. These structures were offered as elements of "holistic" analysis and not the result of ad hoc observation. Each rested on analytic definition and delimitation. For systemic analysis these analytic categories continue to serve as rubrics for research and for codification of existing empirical research.

Systemic analysis seeks to avoid the investigation of primary groups, communities, and institutions that are detached from their social context and their interrelations.[28] A great deal of empirical research into social organization has emerged as the study of samples of such structures, as if they were detached and self-contained objects of analysis. In essence, systemic analysis focuses on a set of differentiated analytic entities. This focus is designed to supply a framework sufficiently comprehensive to pursue the investigation of macrosociology. Macrosociology is the study of the most complex and most comprehensive social group, namely, the nation-state. The nation-state must be seen in its relations to the world-wide system of nation-states. For other historical periods, macrosociology encompasses other sociopo-

27. In *The Polish Peasant in Europe and America*, 5 volumes (Boston: Richard G. Badger, 1918–20) by W. I. Thomas and Florian Znaniecki, published in 1918, one of the earliest systemic studies of comparative social organization and social structure, these categories were defined as the irreducible minimum and more were thought of as merely residual.

28. Charles P. Loomis and Zona K. Loomis's observations on systemic linkages are relevant here. "This is the process whereby the elements of at least two social systems come to be articulated so that in some ways and on some occasions they may be viewed as a single system." Charles P. Loomis and Zona K. Loomis, *Modern Social Theories* (Princeton, N.J.: Van Nostrand, 1961).

litical objects, for example, the city-state. But in the modern period, the nation-state has emerged as the "universal" format, although there are some nation-states which are no more than urban centers without hinterlands. . . .

Social versus Socioenvironmental Boundaries

Systemic analysis must address itself to the boundaries of social organization. This is a crucial decision in social theory, since it involves imputing causal processes. The interplay of the "material" conditions of society and the "normative" elements of social control has been at the center of sociological inquiry. One solution—implicit or explicit in many normative perspectives—has been to narrow the boundaries of social organization, to exclude the material environment, and to focus on social interaction. Normative theories take cognizance of the external environment in terms of the manner in which it is defined by social institutions and by the "strains" that develop over the allocation of resources. Theoretical orientations of this variety often emphasize the equilibrium mode of analysis. The advantage of such an approach is that the sociologist can claim that he is operating at one level of analysis—and the appropriate one, at that. From Émile Durkheim onward, such a direction has been explored in the interest of logical rigor, analytic simplicity, and theoretical closure. Such theories are very attractive, precisely because they challenge sociological thinking and popular thinking which emphasize the importance of the material environment.

But systemic analysis seeks to incorporate the environment into the boundaries of social organization more directly and explicitly, whether the environment is considered in ecological, technological, or economic terms, or a combination of these. Systemic analysis of this kind presents a "socioenvironmental" framework. Sociological writers have tried in different ways to deal with these environmental boundaries. First, the ecological orientation postulates the external environment as an essential (even *the* essential) dimension of social organization which operates directly and without mediating mechanisms, by means of competitive and associational processes.[29] Second, and more often, technological and economic dimensions are incorporated as the prime variables in generating the forms of social structure and social organization. This is, of course, the logic of classic "economic deter-

29. Amos Hawley, *Human Ecology; a Theory of Community Structure* (New York: Ronald, 1950).

minist" theories of social class conflict. Alternatively, technological and economic sectors of society have been explicitly juxtaposed to the normative and cultural sectors by sociologists like William F. Ogburn. The resulting "imbalance" between these spheres determines patterns of social change and social control.[30] Third, there are those sociologists who proceed on a much delimited basis and identify particular aspects of the external environment, for example, geographic distance, for exploring specific "vulnerabilities" of social organization.[31] All these strategies are relevant for systemic analysis, although they do not postulate invariant causal priority for any particular environmental or economic-technological element. (If one had to select a single "prime cause," technology might be the most effective and satisfactory—or rather, a technological-economic determinism—but at least sociology has kept itself from that self-defeating requirement.) Instead, some reciprocal influence is thought to be operative. To define the boundaries of social organization as being socioenvironmental in this sense implies that one's orientation has a degree of openness to reflect historical specifics. It weakens the effort to create a highly deductive system. But such is the problem of a systemic-analysis approach to social control in an advanced industrial society.

Thus, to summarize partially, systemic analysis rejects the distinction between grand theory and theory of the middle range. It rests on a series of givens in order to put forward a body of testable hypotheses. Systemic analysis attributes the greater relevance to developmental over equilibrium analysis and, correspondingly, takes into account those component elements of social control which are not completely interdependent. The degree of interdependence is problematic, but effective social control in an advanced industrial society requires at least some relatively autonomous social groupings. In turn, rather than to postulate a basic and universal social unit of analysis, such as social role, and a highly abstract object of analysis, for example the social act, it requires a set of analytically differentiated units and objects of analysis. These should be linked to the imputed causal processes. Finally, systemic analysis is not limited to a set of social interactional boundaries but makes use of a socioenvironmental conception of boundaries.

From the beginnings of sociology as an organized discipline, total

30. William F. Ogburn, *Social Change: With Respect to Culture and Original Nature* (New York: Huebsch, 1922).

31. Arthur L. Stinchcombe, *Constructing Social Theories* (New York: Harcourt, Brace and World, 1968), pp. 216–30, "Geopolitical Concepts and Military Vulnerability."

societies have been taken as the central objects of analysis, with analytic entities, such as the primary groups, communities, and institutions, as the irreducible components.[32] It is interesting that the term "macrosociology" has become prominent to describe the comparative analysis of total societies in terms of complex linkages of these constituent elements. The goal of systemic analysis is not to arrive at a single body of propositions which conform to a unified theoretical perspective. The objective is to establish overlapping hypotheses which are given a degree of coherence by related assumptions and by master societal trends which describe the historical context. This is the essential character of systemic analysis. Likewise, sociological knowledge is thought of not only as more generalized formulations but also as substantive findings—the contents of its monographs and its charting of social trends.

Such a stance does not mean the slightest retreat from the "principles" of scientific inquiry. It does not mean that theory construction in sociology seeks to make a virtue out of imputed weaknesses. On the contrary, it means that the investigator seeks to make a series of appropriate decisions about both the formal and empirical aspects of his undertaking, which reflect the heritage of the discipline as well as his own immediate experiences.

32. Regional and worldwide patterns of "international" relations among total societies are hardly excluded thereby. On the contrary, social control in advanced industrial societies is directly influenced by the supranational systems which modern technology and organization have helped to fashion.

2

The Concept of Social Control

In the emergence of sociology as an intellectual discipline, the idea of social control was a central concept for analyzing social organization and the development of industrial society. Originally, the term dealt with a generic aspect of society and served as a comprehensive basis for a sociological examination of the social order. In fact, it was one intellectual device for linking sociological analysis to the human values and philosophical orientations employed by some pioneer sociologists interested in "social progress" and the reduction of irrationality in social behavior. In the most fundamental terms, "social control" referred to the capacity of a society to regulate itself according to desired principles and values. Sociological analysis has the task of exploring the conditions and variables likely to make this goal attainable. . . .

The intellectual investment in the idea of social control derives from a rejection of economic self-interest theories. Social control has been an expression of the outlook that held that the individualistic pursuit of economic self-interest can account for neither collective social behavior nor the existence of a social order and does not supply an adequate basis for the achievement of ethical goals. Much of the writing about social control must be understood as sociologists' efforts to accept the relevance but at the same time to identify the limitations of marginal-utility analysis.

In formal terms, one can think of social organization, the subject matter of sociology, as the patterns of influence in a population of social groups. Social control, therefore, is not to be conceived as being the same as social organization; it is instead a perspective which focuses on the capacity of a social organization to regulate itself; and this capacity generally implies a set of goals rather than a single goal.

From "Sociological Theory and Social Control," *American Journal of Sociology* 81:1 (July 1975): 82–87, 101–8. © 1975 by The University of Chicago. All rights reserved.

This paper is a section of a larger study, "Macrosociology and Social Control." I am indebted to the Russell Sage Foundation, New York City, for a generous grant in support of this work.

Social control is a perspective which, while committed to rigorous hypothesis testing, requires the explication of a value position.

Social control was not originally and subsequently has not been necessarily the expression of a conservative political outlook. Many early American sociologists who used the term were religious socialists; others were adherents of a "progressive" view. It is more to the point to emphasize that these early formulations parallel sociologists' contemporary interests in "value maximization." While social control involves the capacity of constituent groups in a society to behave in terms of their acknowledged moral and collective goals, it does not imply cultural relativism. The term has continuity because social control can be conceived as resting on a value commitment to at least two elements: the reduction of coercion, although it recognizes the irreducible elements of coercion in a legitimate system of authority, and the elimination of human misery, although it recognizes the persistence of some degree of inequality. One should also mention a third element: a commitment to procedures of redefining societal goals in order to enhance the role of rationality, although this may be considered inherent in the first two.

The opposite of social control can be thought of as coercive control, that is, the social organization of a society which rests predominantly and essentially on force—the threat and the use of force. Of course, even in the most repressive totalitarian nation-state the agents of repression are limited in scope by some primitive, if unstable, set of norms. However, and more pertinent to the issue at hand, any social order, including a society with a relatively effective system of social control, will require an element of coercion, but presumably a limited one circumscribed by a system of legitimate norms.[1]

There is no doubt that early sociologists in the United States were vague about their social goals and their notions of the "ideal." Frequently, the ideal they offered was no better defined than as the spontaneously emergent and spontaneously accepted consensus. At times, they were no more specific than to assert that the ideal referred to norms that were rationally accepted and [internalized] in contrast with the conditions of coercive controls. Sociologists have become much more specific about the goals they wish to see maximized and therefore

1. Personal control is the psychological and personality counterpart of social control. The former focuses on a person's capacity to channel his energies and to satisfy his needs while minimizing disruption and damage to himself or others. It implies mastery over one's psychological environment and encompasses those psychological conditions that enhance rationality (Bettelheim and Janowitz, 1964).

far more precise about the analysis of different patterns and mechanisms of social control.

Obviously, there are a variety of types and mechanisms of social control. Each is the result of particular antecedent variables and, in turn, each form has a different impact on social behavior. The task of empirical social research is to investigate the forms and consequences of social control. In essence, this means answering the hypothetical question, Which forms of social control are most effective, that is, which enable a social group to regulate itself in terms of a set of legitimate moral principles and result in the reduction of coercive control?[2]

This perspective explicitly negates the assertion that social organization per se represses personality, social creativity, and collective problem solving. In the simplest terms, social control is not the achievement of collective stability. The vital residue of the classical standpoint is that social control organizes the cleavages, strains, and tensions of any society—peasant, industrial, or advanced industrial. The problem is whether the processes of social control are able to maintain the social order while transformation and social change take place. There is no question that, from this point of view, there is a parallel between social control and stability or repression. The argument that is relevant here is just the opposite: social control, to the extent that it is effective, "motivates" social groups. All this seems painfully obvious; but one purpose of a theoretical orientation is to make the obvious inescapable.

Exploration of the idea of social control requires one to recognize that its emergence was part of a continuing critique of and response to the gemeinschaft-gesellschaft model. Under the influence of philosophical pragmatism and the impact of empirical research, the dichotomous categories of gemeinschaft-gesellschaft were found to be both oversimplified and inadequate (Tönnies, 1887). I speak not only of Ferdinand Tönnies's exposition but also of the stream of parallel or related writers. These include Henry Maine (status and contract), Émile Durkheim (mechanical and organic solidarity), Charles Horton Cooley (primary and secondary groups), Robert Redfield (folk culture and urban culture), Louis Wirth (urbanism as a way of life), Ralph Linton (ascription and achievement), and Talcott Parsons (pattern var-

2. In the contemporary period, Amitai Etzioni defines control in a fashion similar to the classic orientation found in social control. "Control—the process of specifying preferred states of affairs and revising ongoing processes to reduce the distance from these preferred states." His theoretical model is derived from cybernetics (1968, p. 668).

iables) (Maine, 1861; Durkheim, 1893; Cooley, 1909; Redfield, 1947; Wirth, 1938; Linton, 1936; Parsons, 1951).

The converging elements of these formulations have had a powerful impact on sociological theory and analysis. At the same time, there is a tradition of criticism of the writings of Tönnies and those who have followed his formulations that is almost as long-standing and enduring as the gemeinschaft-gesellschaft model itself. Among the European sociologists who have dissented from Tönnies's orientation are Georg Simmel (1922), Herman Schmalenbach (1961), Theodor Geiger (1926, 1963), and René Koenig (1955). The accumulated empirical evidence from anthropological and sociological sources with a historical perspective indicates that peasant societies are not wholly Gemeinschaft entities, as Tönnies used the term. The inability of the model to account for the variety of solidary collectivities that emerge in advanced industrial societies is equally noteworthy.

Much of the criticism of the gemeinschaft-gesellschaft approach is not an effort to reject its central concern with societal transformation.[3] Instead, it is an attempt to recast the approach to make it effectively applicable to the analysis of the alternative historical paths by which societies have become urbanized and industrialized. It is difficult, if not impossible, to think of the emergence of modern society in terms of an "evolutionary" transformation from "community" into "society" that is the result of a limited number of basic variables and a linear model of social change and societal transformation. Thus, the criticism has had the consequence of freeing the model from its historical mythography and refashioning its conceptual dimensions and variables into testable hypotheses.

As a result, the notion of social control has been formulated and elaborated to provide a more adequate approach to problems of social change and social order. Sociological theories of the social order thereby have come to reject the assertion that the gemeinschaft aspects of societal structure are only residues of some previous stage of social organization while the gesellschaft dimensions constitute the reality of industrial and urban society. Instead, social organization encompasses, at any given historical moment, essential and elaborated elements of both gemeinschaft and gesellschaft in varying scope, inten-

3. Robert A. Nisbet is representative of those sociological theorists who are aware of the centrality of the concepts of gemeinschaft-gesellschaft in contemporary research and emphasize the necessity of departing from the original mechanistic and linear model of change. He writes, "A relationship that begins as a gesellschaft type may in time become increasingly characterized by gemeinschaft relationships among members" (1970, p. 107).

sity, and consequence. The analysis of social control is an analysis of the interplay of those variables which can be related to both gemeinschaft and gesellschaft attributes. Moreover, the concept of social control is directly linked to the notion of voluntaristic action, to articulated human purpose and actions—that is, to various schemes of means and ends. Therefore it is designed to avoid the overdeterministic sociology which has come to be inherent in the gemeinschaft-gesellschaft model. Social control presents a format of influence based on the notion of interaction and mutual (two-way) relations among social groups. To speak of mutual influence is hardly to deny the elements of inequality and imbalance in social relations.

Sociologists who have used the concept of social control have in effect been following the intellectual lead of Auguste Comte, for whom the central problem of sociological analysis was the impact of industrialization on the social order and the consequences of the resulting individualism on the moral order. Obviously, the classic writers, including Karl Marx, Émile Durkheim, and Max Weber, addressed themselves to the issues Comte raised. One can translate much of the corpus of sociological writing on macrosociology into the language of the social control framework, but to do so would obscure rather than clarify the issues involved. It is preferable to focus directly on that distinct sociological stream which in varying degree makes explicit use of the idea of social control. Though mainly an American stream, it is influenced by and in turn has influenced European thought and research. It presents both a unity and a continuing elaboration.

First, the original writers and, in time, the subsequent ones as well have manifested a philosophical outlook concerned with the limits of rationality in pursuing social and moral aims. Their outlook has reflected pragmatism in the majority of the writers, but for some it also has included aspects of phenomenology. An essential element of this orientation has been the rejection or, rather, the avoidance of either idealism or materialism.

Second, the adherents of social control have been concerned with informal, face-to-face relations as aspects of social structure. In contemporary language, they have been preoccupied with the interface between micro- and macroanalysis.

Third, the style of these sociologists has been one of persistent concern with empirical exploration of their ideas. They have been self-critical about appropriate empirical techniques, continually in search of various types of documentation and data, and fully aware of the complexities and elusive character of proof in sociology.

Therefore there is a direct line of intellectual continuity from the earliest efforts to formulate the component elements of social control to its usage by contemporary research sociologists aware of its intellectual background and theoretical purpose. The concept hardly implies that the subject matter of sociology is the "adjustment" of men to existing social reality; on the contrary, since its early use, the thrust of this stream of sociological discourse has been to focus on efforts of men to realize their collective goals. The continuity between the early writers on social control and particular efforts in contemporary research is manifested in such works as the penetrating research on juvenile delinquency by Albert J. Reiss, Jr. (1951). . . .

The reemergence of a focus on social control in its traditional sense (or relabeled variously, for example, as "social regulation," in contemporary language) has the advantage of being able to draw on increased intellectual self-consciousness among sociologists. The following points are essential . . .

First, the social control perspective, as it has developed, supplies an appropriate level of abstraction for the study of social organization and social change. In fact, the social control perspective stands in contrast to the post–World War II trend, in which much theorizing used a high level of generality. Originally, social control theory was formulated at a more concrete level of abstraction. It required a set of taxonomic and analytically differentiated categories as the basic elements of analysis. Specifically, social control scholars postulated that social stratification and social class categories were insufficient for the analysis of social organization and social change. There was an explicit concern with institutions and institutional analysis. Under the rubric "institutions," sociologists investigated an endless range of subjects that reflected their personal tastes more than a set of analytic units and objects of analysis. But from the very beginning of their empirical research, sociologists concerned with social control have been aware of the necessity of grouping their subject matters in a broader analytical category system—but one which would not lose sight of the substantive reality.

Thus, slowly, the variety of research on delinquent gangs, work teams, play groups, and the like became more and more explicitly fused into the study of primary groups, reflecting the writings of Charles H. Cooley and W. I. Thomas. Under Robert E. Park's stimulus, the host of analyses of territorial units and residential patterns merged into a common interest in community structures. Another core of these subject-matter concerns was the transformation of the study of specific corporate institutions into the analysis of bureaucratic organizations, under the influence of Max Weber and Chester Barnard. From study of a myriad of interesting institutions, there emerged the perspective that such categories as primary groups, community structures, and bureaucratic organizations were essential elements for converting the description of social stratification and socioeconomic class patterns into effective analysis of the "social system" or the nation-state. The random investigation of particular institutions that had fascinated the earlier sociologists has given way to a more pointed focus on the interrelations between basic structural "entities." In the effort to avoid excessive reification or a flight into empiricism, the style of theorizing about social control developed in the 1920s—and explicated thereafter—appears to be markedly viable and appropriate for the continuing tasks of sociologists.

Second, the analysis of social control can be pressed with more pointed concern for causal sequences in social change in particular, with a more explicit and adequate overview of the articulation of "social structure" and political institutions. Sociological analysis is only slowly coming to grips with the crisis of political legitimacy that constitutes the key problematic issue in advanced industrial society, particularly in those nations with multiparty parliamentary institutions.

The noteworthy defect of the early formulations of social control was a viewpoint that saw political institutions as derivative from the social stratification system, almost as if political institutions were thought to be epiphenomenal. The contribution of political sociology since the 1920s has only partially overcome this defect. As sociologists have progressively sought to articulate the relations between social structure and political institutions, they have emphasized the causal priority of the elements of social stratification. They have perceived politics and "political conflict" as manifestations of the underlying social stratification rather than augmenting their approach to politics with an institutional framework associated with the idea of social control (Janowitz, 1970). Sociologists have been interested in describing community stratification, in the mode of Robert and Helen Lynd's *Middletown* (1929), or national stratification patterns, by means of the national survey sample, in order to trace the consequences of these hierarchies for political control. In their view, politics is mass political participation, especially electoral behavior. The causal pattern has been from underlying ecological, economic, and occupational structures to social strata to a set of group interests which fashion mass political participation.

Sociologists have yet to explore adequately the implications of an institutional approach to the political process. No doubt the sociological tradition contains examples of an institutional perspective on politics, that is, the viewpoint that political institutions constitute an independent source of societal change and an element for fashioning social structure. But sociologists, including those attached to the social control perspective, have been slow to implement the comprehensive implications of such an assertion. However, the rise and sociopolitical consequences of the welfare state have moved this intellectual agenda into prominence.

The modern political party and modern political institutions penetrate all sectors of society. It is necessary to speak of their decisive consequences for social structure and to recognize that the supremacy of modern political institutions does not insure either their effectiveness or their legitimacy. As a result, trends in political behavior, especially measures of electoral behavior, become key indicators of the effectiveness of social control in advanced industrial societies with multiparty systems. The crisis in political legitimacy emerges thereby not as a sudden manifestation but rather as the outcome of continuing social change. The cumulative impact of the technological and organizational developments associated with World War II can be taken as the threshold to the new historical era. World War II not only created the institutional base for the welfare state but also contributed to the demand for more extensive political participation.[4]

After a short period of limited adaptation following World War II, Western parliamentary institutions have demonstrated their increased inability to produce effective majorities and to create the conditions for authoritative decision making. Therefore, the task of students of social control is not only to explain patterns of personal deviant behavior, such as suicide, criminality, and personal unhappiness, important though these may be. The core issue is to help account for the decline of parliamentary opposition and the rise of unstable executive leadership.

The grave difficulties of parliamentary control can be seen in the patterns of mass political participation common to Western nations. In the briefest terms, there have been a long-term increase in the proportion of the population who declare themselves unaffiliated with the major parties, an increase in shifting of the electoral choice from one national election to the next, and a decline in belief in the effectiveness of the legislative process.

4. For an analysis of the transformation of Great Britain into a welfare state under the impact of World War I and World War II, see especially Arthur Marvick (1968).

The changes in social stratification resulting from technology, occupational structure, patterns of urbanization, and economic resource allocation do not appear to have increased or produced a highly alienated or anomic electorate. On the contrary, the social stratification patterns result in a highly fragmented electorate with a powerful degree of solidarity within the component social elements. These groupings increase their demands for economic benefits, especially governmental benefits. Thereby persons find themselves, under an advanced industrial society, with their own built-in competing self-interests that are not easily resolved or aggregated into integrated and stable political preferences.

In the three decades since the end of World War II, the structure of political parties in the advanced nations, including the United States, has remained relatively unchanged. The descriptive literature on party organization has not been effectively integrated into macrosociology and the analysis of social control. No doubt the parties require vastly greater resources to perform their political tasks, and the mobilization of these resources paradoxically appears to make them less responsive. Nor has the influx of a new cadre of personnel acting for underrepresented groups altered the internal functioning of the major parties. The issue that the social control perspective must face is deep. The opportunity to express political demands and to balance them by periodic national elections becomes less and less effective as a crucial element in social control.

During the second half of the 1960s, the strain of social change and political constriction produced a marked escalation of parapolitical movements, outside the institutionalized parties, that frequently used violent symbolism and elements of violence. There has also been a striking increase in efforts to extend civic participation into the management of administrative agencies of government and of voluntary associations. These later efforts, in part a response to the impact of the parapolitical movements, have reflected an implicit recognition of the limitations of periodic national elections as mechanisms of social and political control.

There can be no doubt that sociological literature failed to anticipate the scope and intensity of these social movements, although one can find penetrating analyses of the high levels of societal strain and the constriction of the processes of social control that an advanced industrial society was producing. The sociological writings about these agitations often followed the classic model of the natural history of social movements. Such writings were perceptive in focusing on the impending transformation of these social movements into "interest groups" and highlighted their built-in limitations for influencing patterns of social control.

It was no profound sociological discovery that the protest movements of this period would lead to increased diffuse political violence but hardly to a revolution or a "revolution situation." Nevertheless, their explosive character requires students of social control to reexamine the issue of violence and coercion in social change. In the sharpest terms, what is the relationship between reliance on violence and coercion and the search for effective social control in an advanced industrial society? The question manifests itself at every point in sociological analysis where existing patterns of social control are ineffective.

Historians have made it clear that, regardless of the vast and immeasurable amount of human misery which coercion and violence have produced, the threat and use of force in the past have been essential for achieving, on specific and important occasions, more effective social control. But to explicate the "principles of force" is another matter—that is to formulate propositions of the conditions under which force produces positive contributions to social control. Sociologists have speculated repeatedly on this issue; but how much further has the analysis been pressed beyond the hopeful aspirations of Georges Sorel in *Reflections on Violence* (1914)?

The perspective of social control is grounded in assumptions about interaction and mutual influences. Therefore it raises the persistent and vexatious issue of the consequences of force and coercion for those who initiate or manage their use—whether the goal be the maintenance of a social structure or its change. Perhaps the central proposition that can be explored is that the use of force and coercion in the search for social control operates within progressively narrower limits in relations both within and between industrial societies.[5] This assertion obviously does not deny the extensive and diffuse patterns of violence under advanced industrialism; nor does it deny violence's decisive importance in particular circumstances. But it does emphasize the emergence of a calculus which points to the expanded self-defeating implications for those who must rely extensively on force and coercion in their efforts to achieve social control in its traditional meaning. Such a calculus of force and coercion reflects at least two trends. There has been an increase in the professed moral sensibilities of the citizenry (which is compatible with political indifference under conditions of

5. For this process in international relations, see Morris Janowitz (1974).

ineffective political institutions). Furthermore, the sheer complexity of societal organization has made anticipating the consequences of force—especially given the expanded power of force—much more difficult.

In a period of weakened and ineffective social control in advanced industrial societies, continued conflict and disintegration are alternative or even simultaneous outcomes. Social disintegration implies a reduction in the ability of a group to control the behavior of its members and a decline in interaction and influence; social conflict implies an increase in interaction between social groups on the basis of antagonistic means and goals. In evaluating the consequences of persuasion and coercion with respect to direct social change, we must confront the problem of whether the existing categories of political ideology— the language of political discourse which dominates sociological analysis—are adequate for analyzing social control.

The alternative outcomes of the search for effective social control cannot be analyzed adequately in terms of conventional ideological categories—radicalism, conservatism, or incremental liberalism. There exists a mass of empirical data which highlight the conclusion that these categories are limited in describing mass opinion as well as the realities of institutional practice. Moreover, these categories of political analysis imply a final result, a resolution, and an end state, when in effect we are dealing with a continuous and continuing social process. But the macrosociology and, as a result, the analysis of social control are too often dominated by a narrow format fashioned by political discourse. Thereby the "resolution" or "outcome" of ineffective social control does not necessarily conform to the categories of political ideology. It is necessary at least to assume that, for an advanced industrial society, the alternatives could include such results as chronic and persistent tension and a variety of patterns of stagnation.

In conclusion, it is necessary to return to the point of departure. The core element in social control is the idea of self-regulation of the group—whether the group be a face-to-face primary group or the nation-state. In essence, social control is a perspective toward social organization—one which focuses on the outcome of regulative mechanisms. To use the language of empirical social research, it thereby identifies a set of dependent variables applicable to the fullest range of institutional settings. The empirical content of social control depends on the sociologist's ability to clarify and explicate the content and criteria of self-regulation.

Although some sociologists have transformed the content of the term "social control" into that of social conformity and even social repression, the classical usage has persisted. The major advance in the intellectual history of social control has been its linkages to the political process and to the crisis of "political legitimacy." These linkages can be accomplished, not by means of a sociological reductionism, but by a recognition of the boundaries of political institutions and the "supremacy" of politics in an advanced industrial society.

References

Bettelheim, Bruno, and Morris Janowitz. 1964. *Social Change and Prejudice.* New York: Free Press.

Cooley, Charles Horton. 1909. *Social Organization: A Study of the Larger Mind.* New York: Scribner.

Durkheim, Émile. 1893. *De la division du travail social.* Paris: Alcan.

Etzioni, Amitai. 1968. *The Active Society.* New York: Free Press.

Geiger, Theodor. 1926. *Die Masse und ihre Aktion: Ein Beitrag zur Soziologie der Revolutionen.* Stuttgart: Enke.

———. 1963. *Demokratie ohne Dogma; die Gesellschaft Zwischen Pathos und Nuchternheit.* Vol. 5. Munich: Szczesny Verlag.

Janowitz, Morris. 1970. *Political Conflict: Essays in Political Sociology.* Beverly Hills, Calif.: Sage.

———. 1974. "Toward a Redefinition of Military Strategy in International Relations." *World Politics* 26 (4): 473–508.

Koenig, Rene. 1955. "Die Begriffe Gemeinschaft und Gesellschaft bei Ferdinand Tönnies." *Kolner Zeitschrift fur Soziologie und Sozialpsychologie* 7:348–420.

Linton, Ralph. 1936. *The Study of Man.* New York: Appleton-Century.

Lynd, Helen, and Robert Lynd. 1929. *Middletown.* New York: Harcourt, Brace.

Maine, Henry. 1861. *Ancient Law.* London: Murray.

Marvick, Arthur. 1968. *Britain in the Century of Total War: War, Peace and Social Change, 1900–1967.* Boston: Little, Brown.

Nisbet, Robert A. 1970. *An Introduction to the Study of Society.* New York: Knopf.

Parsons, Talcott. 1951. *The Social System.* Glencoe, Ill.: Free Press.

Redfield, Robert. 1947. "The Folk Society." *American Journal of Sociology* 52, no. 4 (January): 293–308.

Reiss, Albert, Jr. 1951. "Delinquency as the Failure of Personal and Social Control." *American Sociological Review* 16, no. 2 (April): 196–206.

Schmalenbach, Herman. 1961. "The Sociological Category of Communion." Pp. 331–47 in *Theories of Society,* edited by Talcott Parsons and Edward Shils. Glencoe, Ill.: Free Press.

Simmel, Georg. 1922. "Die Kreuzung sozialer Kreise." Pp. 305–44 in *Soziologie*. Munich: Duncker & Humboldt.

Sorel, Georges. 1914. *Reflections on Violence*. New York: Huebsch.

Tönnies, Ferdinand. 1887. *Gemeinschaft und Gesellschaft*. Leipzig: Reisland.

Wirth, Louis. 1938. "Urbanism as a Way of Life." *American Journal of Sociology* 44 (July): 3–24.

3

Theory and Policy: Engineering versus Enlightenment Models

Since 1945, as the interests and activities of sociologists have rapidly enlarged, there has been an increase in efforts to establish new bridges to the practice professions and to policymakers. As a result, a number of studies have appeared which contain participant observations and detailed case studies of the concrete experiences of sociologists in using their knowledge for social policy.[1] Generally these materials focus on institutional resistance to the utilization of sociological knowledge. They probe the dilemmas the sociologist faces when he seeks to maintain the objectivity and social distance required for research and at the same time seeks to influence directly practice and policy. From the point of view of the sociology of knowledge, however, it is equally or perhaps even more important to examine the notion that different conceptions of sociological knowledge influence the social role of the social scientist, including the sociologist.

Sociologists in general, or at least those who fall within the scope of this analysis, are committed to the scientific method and to the need to be empirical. Yet adherence to these basic commitments does not result in a generalized sociological approach. Important differences in sociological "schools" persist rather than disappear, even though sociologists are prepared to tolerate these differences with less and less recourse to polemics. These differences are not merely methodological but concern the nature of sociological knowledge and the relationship between social science knowledge and policy. As a result, it is possible

From "Sociological Models and Social Policy," *Archives for Philosophy of Law and Social Philosophy*, vol. 1969 LV/3, pp. 307–19. Reprinted by permission of Franz Steiner Verlag. © 1969 by Morris Janowitz.

1. Alvin W. Gouldner and S. M. Miller, eds., *Applied Sociology: Opportunities and Problems* (New York, 1965); Donald W. Valdes and Dwight G. Bean, eds., *Sociology in Use: Selected Readings for an Introductory Course* (New York, 1965); Arthur B. Shostak, ed., *Sociology in Action* (Homewood, Ill., 1966); Paul F. Lazarsfeld, William H. Sewell, and Harold L. Wilensky, eds., *The Uses of Sociology* (New York, 1967).

to speak about differing professional perspectives among sociologists which encompass epistemological, substantive, and policy dimensions.

There are, of course, alternative ways of categorizing such professional perspectives, especially as the institutionalization of sociologists still is relatively diffuse. The distinction between quantitative and non-quantitative sociologists does not supply a comprehensive point of entrance into these issues. Nor does the notion of empirical versus theoretical sociology have great relevance. Although there are wide differences in styles of scholarship, most empirical sociologists are committed to the strategy that sociological knowledge is generated by an interplay between both elements. Likewise, even the most "abstract" sociologist assumes that the collection of basic descriptive data—especially of a trend variety—is essential. As a way of characterizing basic perspectives in sociology, I note the existence of two different models of sociological knowledge: the "engineering model" and the "enlightenment model." My own preference is for the enlightenment approach, but this is no judgment of the intellectual adequacy of work done under either model. Brilliant and highly systematic work comes from men of the engineering orientation; in turn, a great deal of mediocre scholarship is offered in the name of enlightenment assumptions.

In analyzing the essential elements of these two different approaches, the underlying hypothesis is that the social backgrounds of sociologists or social stratification affiliations are less important than the institutionalized process of academic recruitment, discipleship, and university organization in determining adherence to one of these perspectives.

Engineering Model

The engineering model makes a sharp distinction between basic research and applied research. The sociological enterprise is defined as a group of highly trained, theoretically oriented specialists supported by methodologists and, as required, by fieldworkers. The task of the basic researcher is to develop and test a logico-deductive system of hypotheses. Theoretical knowledge is highly general. There is great concern with either abstract or quantitative formulations. Theoretical contributions are designed to systematize knowledge and to stimulate empirical research.

In this conception, the division of sociological labor requires a larger group of applied research experts who are concerned with the research application of existing theoretical knowledge. Their work does, of course, contribute to new theoretical formulations. But fundamentally the applied researchers collect empirical data, on request, to solve specific problems. They are skilled in on-the-spot data collection and have the interpersonal orientations and skills to communicate their findings in direct terms to policymakers and professional practitioners. They are, so to speak, social engineers.

The engineering model is most highly developed and elaborate in psychology, where special branches of engineering or applied psychology are institutionalized. Its intellectual origins rest in the strong emphasis on operationalism in the social sciences that developed in the 1920s and 1930s in the United States. One of the most powerful intellectual advocates of this view was George Lundberg.[2] But the institutionalization of the engineering model in sociology is to be found in the work of Paul F. Lazarsfeld, who organized the Bureau of Applied Social Research. While Lazarsfeld has written very little explicitly on the theory of the engineering model, the Bureau of Applied Social Research in the 1950s was a testament to the vigor of this approach in the research services it rendered for public and private clients. Even in *The Uses of Sociology,* of which Lazarsfeld was an editor, there is no statement of his orientation.[3] In fact, the introduction to the book was written jointly with William H. Sewell and Harold L. Wilensky; the latter held an outlook which is part of the enlightenment model. But Lazarsfeld and his disciples have strongly emphasized that they seek to make use of the findings of applied social research for more basic theoretical analysis.

Robert K. Merton, a close associate of Lazarsfeld, has presented one of the most carefully reasoned expositions for the engineering approach.[4] For Merton, basic theory embraces key concepts, postulates, theorems, and laws. "Applied science consists simply in ascertaining (a) the variables relevant to the problem at hand, (b) the values of the variables and (c) in accordance with previous knowledge, setting forth the uniform relationships between these variables." The description of applied science as "simply ascertaining," that is, as essentially an empirical operation, warrants emphasis. Merton is fully aware that in real life this simple distinction is difficult to observe. For him, therefore, the problem of the sociology of knowledge is to account "for the discrepancies and coincidences between the 'ideal pattern'

2. George Lundberg, *Can Science Save Us?* (New York, 1947).

3. Lazarsfeld, Sewell, and Wilensky, *Uses of Sociology.*

4. Robert K. Merton, "The Role of Applied Social Science in the Format of Policy: A Research Memorandum," *Philosophy of Science* (July 1949), pp. 161–181.

and the 'actual pattern' of relations between basic and applied social science."[5]

Inevitably this type of orientation implies an explicit set of assumptions about the career development and institutional affiliations of the "basic sociologist" versus the applied researcher. They are seen as different persons who have different career lines. The basic researcher is a member of an academic department of sociology, while the applied researcher has an affiliation with a university-based research institute or is employed by a business or governmental institution. Merton has explicitly argued this issue in terms of organizational access and bureaucratic power rather than intellectual and scientific elements.

> Here we come upon a central problem confronting the policy-oriented social scientist today, as he faces the choice of affiliations with the academic, business, or government communities. If he is to play an effective role in putting his knowledge to work, it is increasingly necessary that he affiliate with a bureaucratic power structure in business or government. This, however, often requires him to abdicate the academic privilege of exploring policy possibilities which he regards as significant. If, on the other hand, he remains unaffiliated to a power structure in order to preserve fuller freedom of choice, he usually loses the resources to carry through his investigations on an appropriate scale and the opportunities of getting his findings accepted by policy-makers as a basis for action.[6]

The engineering model emphasizes the prescriptive recommendations that the applied sociologist offers. An explicit statement of the engineering model is presented by Hans L. Zetterberg in *Social Theory and Social Practice*.[7] Zetterberg, who was also for a time a member of the Columbia University sociology faculty, explicitly criticizes contemporary sociology because of its failure to recognize a sharp distinction between theoretical and applied studies. He uses physiology and medicine as the basic example for his analogy, because the doctor is able to offer precise prescriptive recommendations. The doctor, or better still the engineer, is the model of applied sociological research.

Enlightenment Model

By contrast, the enlightenment model does not stress the distinction between basic and applied sociology. The sociologist recognizes that

5. Ibid., p. 178.

6. Robert K. Merton and Daniel Lerner, "Social Scientists and Research Policy," in Daniel Lerner and Harold D. Lasswell, eds., *The Policy Sciences* (Stanford, 1951), pp. 212–93.

7. Hans L. Zetterberg, *Social Theory and Social Practice* (New York, 1964).

he is part of the social process and not outside of it. Sociologists who adhere to this point of view strive for a high degree of generality. Yet they recognize that sociological knowledge is not to be found in formal propositions alone but in the concrete facts and empirical data which give meaning to the search for generalizations. Of course, some sociologists are more skilled in logical or formal analysis, and others have stronger skills in quantitative or field work. But excessive differentiation of the organization of the discipline could only serve to thwart the growth of sociological knowledge.

Applied research that is not grounded in effective theory has little likelihood of supplying a basis for policy. Basic theory that is not continuously checked against trend data or specific social contexts or experimental situations is soon likely to lose its relevance.

Applied research, if the term has any meaning, refers to the circumstances under which a client hires a social scientist to do a particular piece of research which he hopes to use as soon as it is completed. It refers to sponsorship and time perspectives.[8] At times applied research may be narrowly circumscribed and concerned with limited aspects of a problem, but this is not inherent in such research. The advocates of the enlightenment model reject the view that sociological knowledge produces definitive answers on which policy and professional practice can be based. Sociology is but one aspect of the social sciences, and the social sciences themselves are but one type of knowledge required for policy.

Sociologists perform a number of interrelated research functions, each of which potentially contributes in a different way to social policy. First, sociologists collect descriptive data and chart social trends. These materials are a form of social intelligence which gives professionals and public leaders a better "picture" of the societal and institutional context in which they must operate. These data are concentrated forms of experience, which men can use according to their intelligence and capacities. Second, sociologists seek to test hypotheses about specific institutions and conflict problems. In their efforts to develop generalizations, sociologists use concepts which may stimulate new ideas and new approaches to problem-solving. Third, the testing of hypotheses is primarily designed to evaluate the relative effectiveness and the social costs of different strategies and policies for dealing with social change and political conflict. The enlightenment model encompasses both the explication of "causes" of social behavior and the

8. Philip M. Hauser, "Social Science and Social Engineering," *Philosophy of Science* 16:3 (1949): 209–18.

systematic analysis of planned or managed efforts at social change. These relationships, both quantitative and nonquantitative, are relevant "inputs" to the decision-making process. Fourth, the sociologist may be engaged in developing models or broadscale studies of the most complex social systems. The end results of such undertakings are new bodies of data and new models which may help society to clarify or even alter its social and political goals and objectives.

Under the enlightenment model it is assumed that the sociologist recognizes that he is interacting with his subject and a variety of publics to which he must be responsible. His work has an impact on himself, and his findings influence his subjects and his public in an ongoing fashion. Sociologists who adhere to this concept are also concerned with issues of privacy and the rights of the subjects under investigation. Some of their findings remain highly specialized and have limited circulation. But their work should not remain the property of a single client. Much research becomes widely disseminated. For example, the notion of social change and culture lag is not merely a technical sociological concept but part of the broader discourse of our society. To use a more extreme case, the delinquent gang leader has incorporated the language of sociologists into his defensive ideology. In the enlightenment model, the sociologist as a professional has the model of the teacher with all the complexities, ambiguities, and unanticipated consequences that this involves.[9]

The intellectual background of the enlightenment model can be found in a variety of sociological perspectives. Writers as diverse in theoretical perspective and methodology as Florian Znaniecki and William F. Ogburn give expression to this outlook. In *The Social Role of the Man of Knowledge,* which appeared at the same time as Robert Lynd's *Knowledge for What,* Znaniecki speaks of the fusing of the roles of the sage and the technological leader.[10] He is concerned with sociology as a "cultural science," and he opposes the view that the technical specialist alone can effectively apply social science knowledge.

William F. Ogburn devoted a lifetime to scholarly and detached research on social change and sought to collect and organize statistical data in a scholarly framework. At the same time, he pioneered in developing the descriptive social intelligence function of sociology as, for example, in his work for President Hoover's Commission on Recent

9. Alvin Gouldner, "Theoretical Requirements of the Applied Social Sciences," *American Sociological Review* (February 1957), pp. 92–102.
10. Florian Znaniecki, *The Social Role of the Man of Knowledge* (New York, 1940).

Social Trends. In setting forth his "Observations on Sociological Research," his commitment to the enlightenment model is stated with his usual clarity and judicious temperament. "The distinction between fundamental and applied research is not, I think, as sharp in sociology as it is in a natural science, such as physics or chemistry.[11]

In terms of the enlightenment model, what makes a piece of "applied" research undertaken for presumed practical ends relevant for sociological scholarship is the ability to place the particular and specific findings in a broader context. This means the data must be integrated in terms of some general (or theoretical) notions. This same ability makes the piece of research relevant for social policy and practical ends. Lasswell used the phrase "policy science" or "policy approach" to emphasize this point. "The basic emphasis of the policy approach, therefore, is upon the fundamental problems of man in society rather than upon the topical issues of the moment." [12]

As a partial summary, the engineering model focuses on the need to identify specific cause-and-effect relations. It is concerned with definitive answers to specific questions and particular hypotheses in order to make concrete recommendations. The enlightenment model assumes the overriding importance of the social context, and focuses on developing different types of knowledge which can be utilized by policymakers and professions. While it seeks specific answers, its emphasis is on creating the intellectual conditions for problem-solving. Its goal is a contribution to institution-building.[13]

Both the engineering and the enlightenment models encompass what is called evaluation research, that is, the assessment of alternative strategies and techniques of influencing social change and social control. For the engineering approach, evaluation research is pursued by applied specialists who are seeking specific answers to the effectiveness of a particular social innovation or social experiment. Emphasis is on the analysis of manifest data and indicators that will supply specific criteria of performance. It tends to neglect the underlying reasons for the experiment. In the enlightenment model, evaluation research cannot neglect the social context of the experiment and the social definition of the participants. The analysis of planned change must include a concern for the conditions under which the experimental program

11. William F. Ogburn, "Some Observations on Sociological Research," in Otis Dudley Duncan, ed., *William F. Ogburn on Culture and Social Change* (Chicago, 1964).

12. Harold D. Lasswell, "The Policy Orientation," in Lerner and Lasswell, *The Policy Sciences,* p. 8.

13. See Barbara Wootton, *Social Science and Social Pathology* (London, 1959). See Morris Janowitz, *Institution Building in Urban Education* (New York, 1969).

developed, the professional and ideological factors that helped develop the program, and an institutional analysis of the social experiment itself and of cooperating or competing institutions. Without these dimensions there can be no understanding of the potentials and limitations of the emerging institution to survive and to develop.[14]

Both the engineering and the enlightenment concepts of sociological knowledge are explicit in accepting the scientific method. Sociological language has become so diffused in the United States and in other Western industrialized nations that social criticism incorporates significant amounts of sociological terminology. Social criticism is not to be confused with either of these conceptions of sociological knowledge, though both imply a commitment to intervening in social change. Neither point of view requires sociologists to abandon their personal opinions or civic responsibility. Sociologists are kinds of people who feel very strongly about social problems and are therefore likely to address themselves to public issues in dramatic terms which attract widespread attention. The sociologist has therefore emerged as a kind of folk hero whose opinions are constantly being quoted in the mass media.

It is not likely that sociologists will give up their activities as popular social critics, nor is it desirable. But these activities are different from their professional responsibilities that derive from either one of the two conceptions of sociological knowledge. The role of the sociologist as social critic clearly complicates the institutionalization of the sociologist's professional responsibilities. It is difficult for the various publics of the sociologist to separate these activities, for there is clearly a different basis in logic and evidence when he operates as a sociologist or a popular critic.

Institutionalization of Sociology

It is possible to point to broad social and cultural influences which have helped to shape these two different models of sociological knowledge. One can argue that the enlightenment approach was built into sociology from its origins as part of the intellectual aspiration of the discipline, and because at least a few of the early American sociologists strove to become professors and to be accepted as professors in the university system. For the United States, in particular, the engineering model reflects the impact on sociology of a set of societal values which

14. See David Street, Robert Vinter, and Charles Perrow, *Organization for Treatment: The Comparative Analysis of Correctional Institutions* (New York, 1966), as an example of this type of evaluation research which rests on basic organizational analysis.

give high prestige and ample rewards to scientific-based engineering. The university system has been oriented to the contributions to practical engineering which the natural and biological sciences have made. In seeking to develop and expand the social sciences, it was natural that this formula should be used as a model.

The growth of funds both for higher education and for social research [has] increased the number of sociologists and contributed to the institutionalization of the different conceptions of sociological knowledge. Social background does not seem to have been a powerful factor in accounting for affiliation with one or another professional perspective, but there is clearly an absence of adequate data on this vital point. It is also doubtful whether economic rewards are crucial factors in accounting for recruitment into posts which are designated as applied research. There is probably some differential in pay for employment in such settings, and economic incentives are at work in recruiting sociologists for short-time [sic] assignment in such organizations. Personal preferences for different styles of life are as important as actual salary differences. The prestige and stable career routes built around teaching assignments are at the core of professional preferences in sociology. In other words, because the impact of graduate training is very powerful, it is here that professional attitudes are fashioned or made explicit.

I would argue that the development of the engineering model is to a considerable degree the result of the personal entrepreneurship of outstanding sociologists and the system of discipleship that operates in the social sciences. Advocates of the engineering model are to be found not only in those institutions that are committed to an engineering philosophy but also among members of academic departments that subscribe to this point of view as a result of intellectual convictions which are strengthened in graduate school. (These observations do not encompass the experience of "radical" sociologists who generally enter graduate school with fixed and explicit conceptions of "theory and practice.")

There exists little data on the distribution of professional perspectives among sociologists; these must be inferred from the work they perform. Even information on the jobs that sociologists hold is most limited. Nevertheless, it is abundantly clear that despite the rise of the scale [of] research grants and independent research institutes, sociology is basically a teaching profession with implicit commitments to the enlightenment model. This is the case despite extensive publicity and public discussion about applied research and the public image of sociologists as social engineers. Most sociologists are teachers, with a minority, difficult to estimate, who combine academic-based research work with their teaching. To be a teacher does not insure a well-developed conception about the relationship between sociological knowledge and practice. Many sociologists perform their duties as craftsmen without explicit professional perspectives. But the requirements and pressures of the teacher move the sociologist in the direction of the enlightenment approach.

II

SOCIAL ORGANIZATION: INSTITUTIONAL DEVELOPMENT IN ADVANCED INDUSTRIAL SOCIETY

4

Professionalization of Military Elites

. . . Despite aspirations for generalized explanations of social conflicts, social scientists cannot overlook the highly distinctive aspects of war as a process of social change.

First, as of the second half of the twentieth century, wars are "unique" forms of social conflicts because they are waged only by nation-states. War implies social conflict between nation-states with their ideologies for legitimizing the use of violence in the national interest. The nation-state is a territorially based social system which monopolizes the use of the instruments of violence for both internal and external objectives. This is not to exclude from consideration armed conflict between established "imperial" nation-states and revolutionary political groups seeking to establish new and independent nation-states. In the last two decades important political movements of national independence have been able to arm themselves. In the process of expelling imperial powers, these revolutionary political movements only create new nation-states which become potential and actual warmakers.

Second, war is differentiated from other forms of social conflict because war-making relies on a highly professionalized and specialized occupation, the professional soldier. By contrast, for example, conflict in the family, in community affairs, and even in wide aspects of economic relations involves no or little specialization of personnel. In these arenas the personnel are the same in conflict and in nonconflict situations. Nevertheless, in most nation-states—totalitarian and democratic—the decision to threaten war or to make war involves "politicians" and "civilian" leaders with broad manipulative skills and not primarily the military professionals. Regardless of the political power of the military elite, the classical forms of absolute military dictatorship are not applicable to a modern mass-industrialized social structure.

From "Military Elites and the Study of War," *Journal of Conflict Resolution* 1:1 (March 1957): 9–18. Reprinted by permission of Sage Publications, Inc. © 1957 by Morris Janowitz.

Third, the transition from peace to war and from war to peace is determined by a calculus which cannot be found in other types of social conflict. The essential calculus of war-making does not rest on the postulate that any prolongation of peace will increase the probabilities for the further prolongation of peace. On the contrary, given the dynamics of the traditional arms race, the prolongation of peace brings with it increased uncertainty about the enemy's war-making potential and therefore may increase the probability of war in order to maintain existing advantages (Lasswell, 1950). In other forms of social conflict, social inertia and the postponement of decisions may contribute to the nonviolent resolution of conflict and differences.

In the language of social science, simple equilibrium models are difficult to apply to the process of war-making.[1] Instead, a process or developmental analysis which highlights the voluntaristic efforts and calculations of the elites within each nation-state is more appropriate. These considerations lead to the analysis of the organization of political and military elites as a crucial mechanism in the analysis of war and war-making.

Is it possible to identify different models of political-military elite organization—models which are reflective of different social structures? Can the consequences of the vast technological developments in war-making on the organization of elites be traced out, in order to infer emerging trends? Can important uniformities in the motivational and ideological components of differing political and military elites be established?

Models of Political-Military Elites

Four models of political-military elites can be identified—aristocratic, democratic, totalitarian, and garrison state. For a base line, it seems appropriate to speak of the aristocratic model of political-military elite structure. The *aristocratic model* is a composite estimate of western European powers before industrialism began to have its full impact (Vagts, 1937). In the aristocratic model, civilian and military elites are socially and functionally integrated. The narrow base of recruitment for both elites and a relatively monolithic power structure provide the civilian elite with a method of "subjective control" of the military (Huntington, 1956).

There is a rigorous hierarchy in the aristocratic model which delineates both the source of authority and the prestige of any member of

1. For a discussion of equilibrium models and social change see Moore, 1955.

the military elite. The low specialization of the military profession makes it possible for the political elite to supply the bulk of the necessary leadership for the military establishment. The classical pattern is the aristocratic family which supplies one son to politics and one to the military. Birth, family connections, and common ideology insure that the military will embody the ideology of the dominant groups in society. Political control is civilian control only because there is an identity of interest between aristocratic and military groups. The military is responsible because it is a part of the government. The officer fights because he feels that he is issuing the orders.

In contrast to the aristocratic model stands the democratic one. Under the democratic model the civilian and military elites are sharply differentiated. The civilian political elites exercise control over the military through a formal set of rules. These rules specify the functions of the military and the conditions under which the military may exercise its power. The military are professionals in the employ of the state. They are a small group, and their careers are distinct from the civilian careers. In fact, being a professional soldier is incompatible with any other significant social or political role. The military leaders obey the government not because they believe in the goals of the war but because it is their duty and their profession to fight. Professional ethics as well as democratic parliamentary institutions guarantee civilian political supremacy. The officer fights because of his career commitment.

The *democratic model* is not a historical reality but rather an objective of political policy. Elements of the democratic model have been achieved only in certain Western industrialized countries, since it requires extremely viable parliamentary institutions and broad social consensus about the ends of government. The democratic model assumes that military leaders can be effectively motivated by professional ethics alone, and this is most difficult. Paradoxically enough, certain types of officers with aristocratic background have made important contributions to the development of the democratic model.

In the absence of a development toward the democratic model, the *totalitarian model* tends to replace the aristocratic one (Speier, 1952). The totalitarian model, as it developed in Germany, in Russia, and to a lesser degree in Italy, rests on a form of subjective control, as did the older aristocratic model. But the subjective control of the totalitarian model arises not from any natural or social unity of the political and military elites. On the contrary, a revolutionary political elite of relatively low social status and based on a mass authoritarian political party fashions a new type of control of the military elite. The revolutionary elite, bedecked with paramilitary symbols and yet forced into temporary alliance with older military professionals, is dedicated to reconstituting the military elites. Subjective control of the totalitarian variety is enforced by the secret police, by infiltrating party members into the military hierarchy, by arming its own military units, and by controlling the system of officer selection. Under subjective control of the totalitarian variety the organizational independence of the professional military is destroyed. The officer fights because he has no alternative.[2]

The *garrison-state model,* as offered by Professor Harold D. Lasswell, is the weakening of civil supremacy which can arise even out of an effective democratic structure (Lasswell, 1941). While the end result of the garrison state approximates aspects of the totalitarian model, the garrison state has a different natural history. It is, however, not the direct domination of politics by the military. Since modern industrial nations cannot be ruled merely by the political domination of a single small leadership bloc, the garrison state is not a throwback to a military dictatorship. It is the end result of the ascent to power of the military elite under conditions of prolonged international tension. Internal freedom is hampered, and the preparation for war becomes overriding. The garrison state is a new pattern of coalition in which military groups directly and indirectly wield unprecedented amounts of political and administrative power. The military retain their organizational independence, provided that they make appropriate alliances with civil political factions. The officer fights for national survival and glory.

It cannot be assumed that all forms of militarism involve "designed militarism." "Designed militarism"—the type identified with Prussian militarism—involves the modification and destruction of civilian institutions by military leaders acting directly and premeditatedly through the state and other institutions. Equally significant and more likely to account for crucial aspects of the garrison state, as well as for contemporary American problems, is "unanticipated militarism." "Unanticipated militarism" develops from a lack of effective traditions and practices for controlling the military establishment, as well as from a failure of civilian political leaders to act relevantly and consistently. Under such circumstances a vacuum is created which not only encour-

2. The totalitarian model which developed in western Europe is not the same as the survival of feudal-like military dictatorship still found in parts of South America, in which a military junta directly dominates civilian military life. The Perón model was a strange combination of the old-style military dictatorship plus the newer devices of the totalitarian model.

ages an extension of the tasks and power of military leaderships but actually forces such trends.

The threats to the democratic model cannot be meaningfully analyzed merely from the point of view of "designed militarism." "Designed militarism" emphasizes the impact of military leadership on the civil social structure. "Unanticipated militarism" requires an analysis of the manner in which the military profession responds and reacts to the developments in civilian society. The technology of war, which is the advanced technology of civilian society, lies at the root and sets the preconditions in the trends toward "unanticipated militarism."

Consequences of Technological Trends

The long-term technological development of war and war-making required the professionalization of the military elite. Such technological developments were compatible with the democratic model of political-military elites, since this model rests on the differentiation of the functions of politicians and soldiers. However, the current continuous advance in the technology of war begins to weaken the possibility of the democratic elite model.

The vast proliferation of the military establishments of the major industrialized nations is a direct consequence of the continuous development of the technology of warfare. The "permanent" character of these vast military establishments is linked to the "permanent" threat of war. It is well recognized that under these conditions the tasks which military leaders perform tend to widen. Their technological knowledge, their direct and indirect power, and their heightened prestige result in their entrance, of necessity, into arenas which have in the recent past been preserved for civilian and professional politicians. The result is the tremendous stress on the traditional assumptions about the effectiveness of the democratic model for regulating political-military relations. The need that political leaders have for active advice from professional soldiers about the strategic implications of technological change serves only to complicate the task of redefining spheres of competence and responsibility. Totalitarian, as well as democratic, nations are faced with these problems.

The impact of the technological development of warfare over the last half-century leads to a series of propositions about social change:

A larger percentage of the national income of modern states is spent for the preparation, executing, and repair of the consequences of war.

There is more nearly total popular involvement in the consequences of war and war policy, since the military establishment is responsible for the distribution of a larger share of civilian values and since the destructiveness of war has increased asymptotically.

The monopolization of legal armed violence held by the military has increased so greatly that the task of suppressing internal violence has declined, as compared with the external tasks of the national security (Chorley, 1943).

The rate of technological change has become accelerated, and a wider diversity of skill is required to maintain the military establishment.

The previous periodic character of the military establishment (rapid expansion, rapid dismantlement) has given way to a more permanent maintenance or expansion.

The permanent character of the military establishment has removed one important source of political-military conflict, i.e., the civilian tendency to abandon the military establishment after a war. Instead, because of the high rate of technological change, internal conflicts between segments of the military elite have been multiplied.

The diversification and specialization of military technology have lengthened the time of formal training required to acquire mastery of military technology, with the result that the temporary citizen army will become less important and a completely professional army more vital.

The complexity of the machinery of warfare and the requirements for research, development, and technical maintenance tend to weaken the organization line between the military and the nonmilitary.

Because of these technological and large-scale administrative developments, civilian society as well as the military establishment is undergoing basic transformation. The contemporary tension in political-military organization within the major industrialized powers has a common basis to the degree that the technological requirements of war are highly universal. Yet the differences in the amount or character of political power exercised by military leaders and the methods for resolving conflicts between political and military leaders as between the major nation-states cannot be explained primarily, or even to any great extent, by differences in the technological organization of their armed forces. This is not to deny that each weapon system—land, sea, or [air]—tends to develop among its military managers characteristic orientations toward politics based on the technical potentialities of their weapons. The political outlook of any military establishment will be influenced by whether it is an organization dominated by army, navy, or air force. Nevertheless, technological developments merely set the limits within which the civilian and military elites will share power. National differences in the influence patterns of military elites must be linked to national differences in social structure and elite organization.

These technological trends in war-making have necessitated extensive common modification in the military profession in both democratic and totalitarian systems and regardless of national and cultural differences. The changes in the military reflect organizational requirements which force the permanent military establishment to parallel other civilian large-scale organizations. As a result, the military takes on more and more the common characteristics of a government or business organization. Thereby, the differentiation between the military and the civilian—an assumed prerequisite for the democratic elite model—is seriously weakened. In all these trends the model of the professional soldier is being changed by "civilianizing" the military elite to a greater extent than the "militarizing" of the civilian elite.

What are some of these modifications in the military profession? They include (*a*) "democratization" of the officer recruitment base, (*b*) a shift in the basis of organization authority, and (*c*) a narrowing of the skill differential between military and civilian elites. Propositions concerning these trends for the United States military during the last fifty years are applicable in varying form to the military establishment of the other major industrialized nations. (Janowitz, 1953)

(a) "Democratization" of the Officer Recruitment Base

Since the turn of the century the top military elites of the major industrialized nations have been undergoing a basic social transformation. The military elites have been shifting their recruitment from a narrow, relatively high-status social base to a broader, lower-status, and more representative social base.

The broadening of the recruitment base reflects the demand for large numbers of trained specialists. As skill becomes the basis of recruitment and advancement, "democratization" of selection and mobility increases. This is a specific case of the general trend in modern social structure of the shift from criteria of ascription to those of achievement. In western Europe the "democratization" of the military elites displaced the aristocratic monopoly of the officer corps; in the United States an equivalent process can be observed, although social lines are generally less stratified and more fluid. The sheer increase in size of the military establishment contributes to this "democratization." The United States Air Force, with its large demand for technical skill, offered the greatest opportunity for rapid advancement.

From the point of view of the democratic model, "democratization" of social recruitment of military leaders is not necessarily accompanied by "democratization" of outlook and behavior. By "democratization of outlook and behavior" is meant an increase in accountability or an increase in the willingness to be accountable. In fact, the democratization of the military profession carries with it certain opposite tendencies. The newer strata are less aware of the traditions of the democratic model. Their opportunities for mobility make them impatient and demanding of even greater mobility. Their loyalty to the military establishment begins to depend more and more on the conditions of employment rather than on the commitment to the organization and its traditions.

The increased representativeness of social background of the military profession also results in an increased heterogeneity of the top leaders within the various military services. Under these conditions it is more difficult to maintain organization effectiveness and at the same time enforce the norms of civilian political control. (In a totalitarian society, it likewise becomes more difficult to maintain organization effectiveness and enforce party loyalty.) Of course, any large-scale organization develops devices for overcoming these forms of disruption. The military profession emphasized honor as a unifying ideology, and intra-service marriage patterns have been a power device for assimilating newcomers into the military establishment. But requirements of bureaucratic efficiency corrode honor, and the military marriage, like civilian marriage, is currently more limited in its ability to transmit traditions.

Even more fundamental, the new "democratization" changes the prestige position of the military profession. The older traditional soldier has his social prestige regulated by his family of origin and by the civilian stratum from which he came. What society thought was of little importance as long as his immediate circle recognized his calling. This was true even in the democratic model. The British officer corps, with its aristocratic and landed-gentry background and its respectable middle-class service families, is the classic case in point. In varying degrees before World War II it was true for the United States Navy, with its socialite affiliations, and even the United States Army, with its southern military family traditions. But with democratization of the profession, the pressure develops for prestige recognitions by the public at large. A public relations approach must supplant a set of personal relations. Public relations becomes not merely a task for those specialists assigned to developing public support for military establishment policies. Every professional soldier, like every businessman or government official, must represent his establishment and work to enhance the prestige of the professional military. In turn, a military figure becomes a device of enhancing a civilian enterprise. Under these circumstances, objective control gives way to subjective identity.

(b) Shift in the Basis of Organization Authority

It is common to point out that military organization is rigidly stratified and authoritarian in character because of the necessities of command. Moreover, since military routines are highly standardized, it is generally asserted that promotion is in good measure linked to compliance with existing procedures and existing goals of the organization. (These characteristics are found in "civilian" bureaucracies but supposedly not with the same high concentration and rigidity.) Once an individual has entered into the military establishment, he has embarked on a career within a single pervasive institution. Short of withdrawal, he thereby loses the "freedom of action" that is associated with occupational change in civilian life.

From such a point of view, the professional soldier is thought to be authoritarian in outlook. Status and the achievement of status are thought to be fundamental motivations. The organizing principle of authority is domination—the issuing of direct commands. The professional soldier is seen as limited in his ability and skill to participate in "civilian" political affairs which require flexibility, negotiation, and the "art of persuasion."

However, it is not generally recognized that a great deal of the military establishment resembles a civilian bureaucracy as it deals with problems of research, development, supply, and logistics. Even in those areas of the military establishment which are dedicated primarily to combat or to the maintenance of combat readiness, a central concern of top commanders is not the enforcement of rigid discipline but rather the maintenance of high levels of initiative and morale. This is a crucial respect in which the military establishment has undergone a slow and continuing change since the origin of mass armies and rigid military discipline (Marshall, 1947).

Initiative rather than the enforcement of discipline is a consequence of the technical character of modern warfare, which requires highly skilled and highly motivated groups of individuals. Often these formations must operate as scattered and detached units, as opposed to the solid line of older formations. It is also a consequence of the recruitment policies of modern armies, which depend on representative cross-sections of the civilian population rather than on volunteers. Modern armies increasingly draw their recruits from urbanized and industrialized populations and less from illiterate agricultural groups, for whom response to discipline is a crucial and effective form of control. Tolerance for the discomforts of military life decreases. The "rationality" and skepticism of urban life carry over into military institutions to a greater degree than in previous generations. The rationalization of military life makes necessary the supplying of more explicit motives. Social relations, personal leadership, material benefits, ideological indoctrination, and the justice and meaningfulness of war aims are now all component parts of morale.

Short of complete automation, specialized units manning the crucial technical instruments of war must display fanatically high morale in order to achieve successful military offensive action. Although military formations are still organized on the basis of discipline, military command involves an extensive shift from domination to manipulation as a basis of authority. Manipulation implies persuasion, negotiation, and explanation of the ends of the organization. Direct orders give way to the command conference. Since manipulation involves high social interaction, differences in status are tempered by morale objectives. Shifts from domination to manipulation, from status to morale, are present in many aspects of civilian society. However, the peculiar conditions of combat have obscured the extent to which morale leadership is especially required for military formations. This is not to imply that the military establishment has found a formula for approximately balancing domination and manipulation.

(c) Narrowing the Skill Differential between Military and Civilian Elites

The consequences of the new tasks of military management imply that the professional soldier is required more and more to acquire skills and orientations common to civilian administrators and even political leaders. He is more interested in the interpersonal techniques of organization, morale, negotiation, and symbolic interaction. He is forced to develop political orientations in order to explain the goals of military activities to his staff and subordinates. Not only must the professional soldier develop new skills necessary for internal management; he must develop a "public relations" aptitude, in order to relate his formation to other military formations and to civilian organizations. This is not to imply that these skills are found among all the top military professionals, but the concentration is indeed great and seems to be growing. The transferability of skills from the military establishment to civilian organizations is thereby increased. Within the military establishment, conflicts occur and deepen with greater acceleration between the old, traditionally oriented officers and the new, who are more sensitized to the emerging problems of morale and initiative.

Trends in Indoctrination

In the past, institutional indoctrination of the military professional in the United States avoided discussion of human factors in the military establishment and the political consequences of military operations. (It is, of course, difficult, if not impossible, to intellectualize at any length about the enforcement of discipline.) Before World War II, the United States professional military had a schooling which supplied little realistic orientation except to emphasize a simple mechanical version of ultimate civilian supremacy. However, even before the outbreak of World War II, slowly and painfully, important sectors of the military elite had to reorient themselves on these matters. Reorientation came about as a result of the realities of the war. Of course, much of the crucial work merely devolved upon lower-rank staff officers and technical specialists, with the "top military cadre" not fully in sympathy.

In the absence of institutional indoctrination for these tasks, impressive indeed is the extent to which self-indoctrination succeeded in producing the number of officers capable of functioning in these areas. Nevertheless, the military establishment continues to be characterized by deep inner tensions because of its new responsibilities and because of the absence of a sufficiently large cadre of top officers sensitized to deal effectively with its broad administrative and political tasks.

Before World War II, whatever training and indoctrination existed for handling the complexities of civil-military relations and political tasks was primarily a self-generated mission. Some deviant career officers were not only sensitive to the emerging problems within the military establishment, but many of these officers sought to indoctrinate themselves about emerging problems of civil-military relations and of the political aspects of military operations. They often accepted specialized assignments of a quasi-political nature or those involving communications skills which supplied relevant opportunities for indoctrination and training. (These assignments included military attaché, foreign-language officer, intelligence officer, and public relations.) Voluntary acceptance or pursuit of these assignments represented genuine efforts at self-indoctrination and thereby selected out for training those who felt inclined and had potentials for growth. In the United States especially, before 1939, these assignments had relatively low prestige. In fact, they were seen as interfering with one's career, and therefore they were avoided by all except those who had sufficient foresight to see their high relevance. For many, these assignments did involve risk and short-term disadvantages. However, the results of such assignments in crucial cases were just the contrary. They assisted officers in entering the very top of the military elite, since they did, in fact, represent realistic indoctrination for emerging tasks.

Since the end of World War II, at all levels of the military establishment institutional indoctrination encompasses much wider perspectives—social and political. Although much of the new indoctrination appears to be oriented to the broader problems of the military establishment—internal and external—it is very much an open question as to what the consequences are likely to be for civil-military relations in a democratic society.

Ideological indoctrination is now designed to eliminate the civilian contempt for the "military mind." The "military mind" has been charged with a lack of inventiveness and traditionalism. The new indoctrination stresses initiative and continuous innovation. This is appropriate for the career motives of the new recruits and is important in creating conditions for overcoming bureaucratic inertia. The "military mind" has been charged with an inclination toward ultra-nationalism and ethnocentrism. Professional soldiers are being taught to de-emphasize ethnocentric thinking, since ethnocentrism is detrimental to national and military policy. The "military mind" has been charged as being disciplinarian. The new indoctrination seeks to deal with human factors in combat and in large-scale organization in a manner similar to contemporary thought on human relations in industry. In short, the new indoctrination is designed to supply the professional soldier with an opinion on all political, social, and economic subjects which he feels obliged to have as a result of his new role.

The new "intellectualism" is a critical capacity and a critical orientation. The military officer must be realistic, and he must review the shortcomings of the past and contemporary record of political-military relations. Will the growth of critical capacities be destructive, or will it be productive of new solutions? The consequence could be a growth in hostility toward past arrangements, in particular toward past political leadership of the military establishment and toward the dogmas of civilian supremacy. The military profession runs the risk of confusing its technical competency with intellectual background. As a result, it could become critical and negative toward the military bureaucracy and toward civilian political leadership in the same way that Joseph Schumpeter speaks of the university-trained specialist becoming critical of the economic system. In the United States at least, such hostility is hardly likely to lead to open disaffectation but more to passive resentment and bitterness.

In the long run, under either the democratic or the totalitarian model, the military establishment cannot be controlled and still remain effective by civilianizing it. Despite the growth of the logistical dimensions of warfare, the professional soldier is, in the last analysis, a military commander and not a business or organizational administrator. The democratic elite model of civilian supremacy must proceed on the assumption that the functions of the professional military are to command soldiers into battle. There is no reason to believe that the characteristics of the ideal professional soldier as a military commander are compatible with the ideal professional soldier as an object of civilian control, although the differences seem to be growing less and less as the automation of war continues. The quality of political control of the professional soldier is not to be judged by examining those aspects of the military establishment which are most civilian but rather those which are least civilian. Here the willingness to submit to civilian control, rather than the actuality of civilian control, is most crucial.

There is no reason to believe, in a democratic society, that the military can be controlled by offering them the conditions of employment found in civilian society. In the long run, civilian establishments would draw off all the best talent, especially in a business-dominated society. To achieve the objectives of the democratic elite model, it is necessary to maintain and build on the differentiation between civilian and military roles. A democratic society must accord the professional soldier a position based on his skill and on his special code of honor. He must be integrated because his fundamental differentiation is recognized. Under these circumstances, standards of behavior can be established and political directives enforced. The current drift toward the destruction of the differentiation of the military from the civilian cannot produce genuine similarity but runs the risk of creating new forms of hostility and unanticipated militarism.

References

Chorley, Katherine. 1943. *Armies and the Art of Revolution*. London: Faber & Faber.

Huntington, Samuel P. 1956. "Civilian Control of the Military: A Theoretical Statement." In Eulau, Heinz, Eldersveld, Samuel, and Janowitz, Morris (eds.), *Political Behavior: A Reader in Theory and Research*, pp. 380–85. Glencoe, Ill.: Free Press.

Janowitz, Morris. 1953. *The Professional Soldier and Political Power: A Theoretical Orientation and Selected Hypotheses.* University of Michigan: Bureau of Government, Institute of Public Administration.

Lasswell, Harold D. 1950. *World Politics and Personal Insecurity.* Glencoe, Ill.: Free Press.

————. 1941. "The Garrison State," *American Journal of Sociology* (January).

Marshall, S. L. A. 1947. *Men against Fire: The Problem of Battle Command in Future War.* Washington: Infantry Journal.

Moore, Barrington, Jr. 1955. "Sociological Theory and Contemporary Politics," *American Journal of Sociology* (September), pp. 107–15.

Speier, Hans. 1952. *War and the Social Order: Papers in Political Sociology.* New York: G. W. Stewart.

Vagts, Alfred. 1937. *The History of Militarism.* New York: W. W. Norton & Co.

5

The Social Dimensions of the
Local Community

... The contents of the community press, the social attributes of its readers, and the social role of its publishers when viewed as elements of a communications system make possible inferences about social cohesion in the urban metropolis. In such a process of synthesis, the interpretative conclusions are likely to outrun the data at hand and become rather speculative because of the complexity of the task of understanding the urban community.

The analysis of the community press if it reveals nothing else indicates that significant proportions of the residents of the urban metropolis are not "rootless" individuals. Countertrends to large-scale organization continually develop which modify the impact of technological impersonalization and make possible the gratification of individual needs in the local community. This is a crude statement. Ultimately, the task at hand is to emerge with a theoretical "model" of the local community. Such a "model" will present a meaningful analysis of the complexities of the local community and point the way toward constructive support of those mechanisms and institutions which maintain social cohesion.

In moving toward such a "model" or generalized description of the local urban community, three basic social dimensions of analysis are required, similar to those relevant for analyzing most social systems;[1] (*a*) the motivational involvements and gratifications (or nongratifications) connected with community residence, (*b*) the social organization of the local community, and (*c*) the resultant patterns and mechanisms of social control on the local community level.[2]

From *The Community Press in an Urban Setting*, 2d ed. (Chicago: University of Chicago Press, 1967), pp. 195–213. © 1952, 1967 by Morris Janowitz. All rights reserved.
    1. See Talcott Parsons, *The Social System* (Glencoe, Ill.: The Free Press, 1951), for an elaborated frame of reference for analyzing social systems.
    2. Moreover, it is necessary to delimit the "spatial" boundaries of the local community in order to differentiate community research from certain other types of social system analysis. Social scientists have charted the historical boundaries of the local com-

Motivational Involvement in the Local Community

On the one extreme, . . . there is a minority of residents (nonreaders; 16 percent) for whom the community press had no meaning and who can be presumed to have practically no commitment or involvement in the community regardless of the amount of their use of local facilities. These individuals are most likely to constitute the "rootless" individuals on whom community social controls have little or no effect. On the other hand, there is another minority (fans; 11 percent) who find themselves heavily involved with the local community and who are most likely therefore to respond to the pressure of the local community. For the remainder, varying levels of involvement emerge.

Interpersonal contacts around the use of local facilities, and not mere use of local facilities, mold these commitments and involvements. The most direct way in which the social organization of the local community seems to serve these individual needs and motives hinges on its ability to serve the primary-group requirements of child-rearing. The local community functions as a community particularly around the needs of its most conspicuous consumers—the children . . .

Thus, family cohesion becomes central for understanding the inner dynamics of local community involvement since it seems more explanatory than the age, education, income, and other such characteristics of the residents. Involvement, within a given community, seems hardly to be associated with attributes such as renters vs. home owners, or single-family dwellers vs. multiple-dwelling-unit residents. Length of residence increases community involvement, but here again children act as catalysts in the process.

Community involvement is also linked, but to a lesser degree, to primary-group attachments outside of the family, but rooted in the local community. There can be no doubt that given the same community facilities there is a level of involvement which reflects an underlying personality orientation . . . A clue to the influence of these personality variables can be seen in the fact that community orientation was con-

---

munity and plotted "natural" areas on the basis of location of industry, commerce, transportation, and residence. The community areas employed in this research were derived in large measure through such a procedure. The residents' subjective definition of the "spatial" boundaries of the community are also required.

In addition, the residents' estimates of the prestige or status position of their community as compared with adjoining and nonadjoining communities are relevant. These rankings are crucial since the mechanisms of social stratification in the metropolis involve not only sensitivity about economic class but also consciousness about the status of one's community.

centrated in those individuals who perceived their local community in terms of its human "resources" as compared with those who were preoccupied with its physical "resources."

In any case, it is difficult to designate the frequency of these personalized contacts as being considerable or inconsiderable. . . . How easily could these contacts be broken? Perhaps more relevant are some of the consequences of these contacts and involvements. The data at hand indicated that where stable primary groups existed in the local community, the community press tended to operate as an extension of real social contacts. Where these contacts were absent, the contents of the community press operated merely as a substitute for contact, and thereby negated the impact of the community press in developing local social cohesion. The role of these primary-group contacts and involvements which conditioned the impact of the community press certainly seems relevant to other sources of symbolism as well as participation in local voluntary associations.

Social scientific efforts to analyze community involvement have been dominated by a typology involving a sharp distinction between those individuals who display local-community orientation and those who are reputed to have a broader or metropolitan outlook.[3] At numerous points, the data at hand question the advisability of considering urban personality in these sharply opposing terms.

The study of community involvement and orientations by means of the community press seems to highlight a developmental view of the distinction between "community" orientation and "metropolitan" orientation. Local orientations for some broaden out to include wider needs and perspectives, but which do not necessarily eliminate local orientations, although a predominant balance between the two can be discerned. It is as if the individual had the opportunity to make use of community facilities but he augments the satisfaction of his needs by making use of noncommunity facilities and thereby creating metropolitan orientations. The balance between the two varies from community to community . . . Yet . . . the use of local facilities is impressive and has a significance that wider and broader orientations and identifications do not destroy automatically. It is hardly a case of either one or the other. For the bulk of the population, it is a matter of relative commitment. How else could one explain that, by and large, community-newspaper readership is compatible with high levels of ex-

3. Such a dichotomy often implies either a hidden value judgment of the social desirability of the metropolitan outlook, or, on the other hand, a judgment of nostalgia for a return to some sort of rural-type community orientation.

posure to broader mass media? This does not deny that a small group may, because of occupation or specialized life experiences, develop metropolitan orientations without local identifications. It would be a grave error to view this group as typifying the balance between community and metropolitan involvement.

The Social Organization of the Local Community

The analysis of the community press as a communications system reveals immediately some of the complexities of the process by which the individual and his primary-group affiliations are integrated into the large-scale organization of the urban metropolis. It reveals that despite the growth of mass communications and large-scale organization most individuals are not living in a "mass society" in which they are directly linked to the major agencies of concentrated social and political power. Rather, the growth of large-scale organization has been accompanied by a proliferation of intermediate haphazard-like social arrangements and communication patterns. The local urban community appears to be a complex of social interactions which tends to identify a local elite and local institutionalized patterns for controlling social change. The community press is but one institution that stands intermediate between the individual and the major institutions of the metropolis; and the publisher is but one of the members of this intermediate elite.

In power terms, the scope of this elite and the significance of its actions are obviously limited by the character of the decision-making process that finds a context on the local level. This local elite is composed of business, political, religious, voluntary association, and professional community leaders. At first glance it might appear that they constitute a network of individuals whose significance arises out of their hierarchical position midway between top metropolitan leadership and the bulk of the population whose consensus is required for collective action. In this view, interpersonal connections among community elite within a given community or group of communities do not loom significantly and the local elites are considered merely as agents rather than effective leaders.

This view of local leadership is conditioned by the lack of clear-cut correspondence between the geographical limits of the community and the geographical limits of the leaders' social influence. But this is an erroneous view of community leadership. The pattern of group leadership that emerges around the community press and its operations highlights a clear-cut pattern of interpersonal contact among local leaders within the community. The various institutions and associations which penetrate into the local community have no manifest geographical homogeneity or unity. Nevertheless, the lateral interactions of the local leadership within the geographical limits of the local community have a definite pattern which contributes to the self-consciousness and power of these local leaders. This process can be understood better only through prolonged participant observation, which social scientists seldom undertake.

Moreover, community leadership does seem strikingly associated with residential stability. It is worthwhile noting the degree to which community leaders display residential stability (twenty years or over at the same address), again in contradistinction to the view of the urban community as a "rootless" mass. Beyond this simple fact, the social personality and the social techniques of local leaders remain to be investigated. The level of community management that this study probed uncovered again and again the effort at adjudication of conflict by emphasis on areas of common agreement and the postponement of disagreement. The role of the community newspaper in the political life of the community with its curious nonpartisanship reflects this approach and makes it more difficult to uncover the realities of political conflict.

Today, local community organization is perhaps most threatened in precisely those areas where the socially articulate leaders of the community are in the process of departure or are unable to replace themselves. The development of social absenteeism, as the process can be called, need not be viewed as inevitable, for it does get altered, slowed, or temporarily stopped.

The removal of leadership with strong community identifications through the process of social absenteeism can develop to the point where ultimately profound changes in local politics take place with most unfortunate implications. In a city such as Chicago, social absenteeism in certain traditional Democratic wards, located near the center of the city, with lower-class constituencies has fundamentally weakened the Democratic party organization. The ward organizations have been weakened to the point where the wards have suddenly turned Republican. This shift hardly represents the normal and desirable workings of the two-party system. These wards have not turned to traditional Republicanism, for the working-class elements of these depressed local communities are not expressing a political allegiance to the platform of the national Republican party. They have been forced and intimidated into support of a Republican machine so completely weakened through absenteeism that it fell easy prey to the underworld and a new kind of hoodlumism in politics.

Social absenteeism expresses itself in a variegated set of problems in the local community less dramatic than the collapse of traditional political institutions of the most depressed areas. Social absenteeism affects the public educational and social welfare system and even the religious institutions, although religious hierarchies are more aware of the need to act to offset these effects.

Because of the wide variety of functions which gravitate to a community publisher, he operates as a limited counterforce to social absenteeism. In those areas where social absenteeism is less of a problem, the publisher's role seems to be one of galvanizing the local leaders to collective action. Community publishers are self-conscious men because of the kinds of life experiences which have led them into their enterprises and which they have had in operating their enterprises. The peculiar skills of the publisher and the role he plays in seeking to adjust conflicting interests sensitize him to the evolving trends in the local community. Economic interests, of course, condition his outlook. Nevertheless, he is less reluctant to accept the inevitability of adverse changes and more prone to press for desired change than the members of the business community. His promotional background and in part his quasi-intellectual outlook are here at work.[4]

In particular, no group is more sensitive to the political and economic inequalities inherent in the present trends toward suburbanization than the urban community-newspaper publishers. The divergence between the long-established political boundaries and the changing patterns of population in a metropolitan area such as Chicago seems to increase continuously. Throughout the research, specific problems of social action took meaning in this overriding political context. The metropolis is an outgrowth of a machine technology which made possible large concentrations of population. While the distribution of

4. One cannot help contrasting the publisher and the editor of the community newspaper with those types of mass media specialists who for some reason or other seem to be beset by ever-increasing amounts of self-hatred and cynicism. Even the highest priced movie scenario writer develops these attitudes which involve not only a contempt for the self but a contempt for the audience. The factors involved are complex, but a comparison with the community-newspaper publisher and editor reveals at least one striking difference. There can be no doubt that the community publisher has some sense of inferiority about his position and his limited economic achievement. But this hardly constitutes the basis for self-hate and cynicism. He has too many specific and concrete gratifications from his activities; he has too much direct evidence of the response to his medium to feel isolated and self-deprecatory.

commerce and transportation conditioned the form and location of the residential community, political boundaries seemed to coordinate, or discoordinate, social adaptations to these movements. The outmoded character of the legal limits of the urban metropolis is a striking case of a basically discoordinating element of local social organization.

It is not within the power of the community press to have a central role in altering these administrative and political trends. Yet if politicians in the near future seek to deal with this fundamental issue, either through boundary changes, new forms of political representation, or new taxation basis, the community press—both in Chicago and throughout the entire country—constitutes an important resource for clarification and action.

Social Control at the Local Community Level

Social control at all levels involves the clash between individual motives and effective social organization. The code of ethics for operating a community newspaper is a skeleton of the social attitudes and group pressures that are operative in most collective actions at the local community level.

Much research which has been concerned with community social control implies that, as one moves from the center of the metropolis outward, the rates of "disorganization" decreased. The rates usually refer to crime, insanity, and similar indices. Regardless of the validity of these particular findings, it is doubtful whether these differential rates measure variation in effective and overall social control. For example, if, in the case of crime, the definition was broadened to include white-collar crime, would these straight-line relationships still hold true? Probably not. Extremely "disorganized" areas exist in the shadow of the central business districts and adjoining the inner belt of industry. But there hardly seems to exist a clear body of data to link well-defined measures of "disorganization" to types of community areas for the metropolitan district as a whole.[5]

There is no reason to believe that the community press increases in readership or significance with removal from the center of the city. By inference, moreover, analysis of the community press indicates that . . . location from the center of the city is not a distinguishing indicator of the level of community social control. Family cohesion and

---

5. The more relevant problem seems to be to account for the different types and modes of deviant behavior as between community areas.

primary-group contacts seemed more relevant for predisposing an individual toward the acceptance of the community's controlling institutions and associations. There can, however, be no doubt that income and class mold the forms and technique of these institutions and associations as well as condition the outlook of community leadership. This does not carry the implication that lower income and lower status mean less social control from these sources but rather different norms of control.

The range of collective action which involves the community newspaper—from blood-bank campaigns to support for police action—grows out of the leadership position and contacts of the publisher. But, in addition to collective action, social control involves the quest for respectability and morality. The ideology of the community newspaper, and of many other community institutions, seeks to present appropriate symbols of respectability and morality to those who have such motives. Yet for that substantial minority who seek anonymity, avoidance of community involvement and its consequent controls requires little effort.

Local social controls assume particular meaning when a link between these controls and the norms of the larger society can be established. The decisions made in the local community are of limited consequence for the "big" political issues of the moment; yet the motivational commitment toward the local community is certain to bear some relationship to the individual's orientation to the "politics" of the larger community.

In this context, a final hypothesis is presented. Individuals who display high local identifications are people who are likely to display higher political competence than those who have low or no local identification. This hypothesis is presented in its most general form; a minority who are "overidentified" in the local community might display low political competence, while on the other end of the continuum a minority with low community identification might display high political competence derived from ideological considerations. But leaving aside these subgroups, should political competence correlate with community-newspaper readership some light might be thrown on compatibility of local autonomy and local identification and the requirements of the larger political process.

Those portions of the readership survey which dealt with local community affairs included indirect questions on the individual's contacts and estimates of his local precinct captain, alderman, and ward organization. Specific questions involved the problems of the local community and the capabilities of the political offices and officers to deal with these concrete issues. These questions were not designed to determine whether the respondent was a "Democrat," a "Republican," or an "Independent," but rather to probe his trust in and reliance on politics. They produced a flow of material revealing underlying attitudes toward the political process and made possible inferences about self-conceptions of competence in this area. For example, the following respondent leaves no doubt about his own low competence in politics:

> "I think it's all the bunk. I'm a Democrat. I been a Democrat for years. If Truman runs again I don't think I'll vote for him. I don't think the little persons can do anything. The politicians may start out all right but they end up the same—corrupt. They can't help it. You need someone to rule. Everyone can't be for himself."

Regardless of the respondents' political affiliation, relative confidence in the effectiveness and honesty of local politics—projective measures of personal political competence—tended to be associated with high community-newspaper readership. However, in the case of the political parties the association was larger and more statistically significant than for precinct captains.

These conclusions point to the ambiguities of the social roots of political agreement in the urban local community. Social scientists and reformers are frequently preoccupied with the political type whose competence is operative without a sense of specific local community identification. Indispensable as such individuals are for politics, it is likely that in the near future such individuals alone cannot maintain or strengthen the basis of democratic organization in a metropolis such as Chicago. To the contrary, further weakening of local community identifications is inextricably bound up with the growth of even greater antidemocratic potential among the rank-and-file residents than now besets the urban community.

An issue of social and political control which had mobilized a great deal of local community interest is that of federally supported public housing. This study was initiated before the outbreak of the hostilities in Korea, in a period in which a great deal of attention was being expended on the problems of developing new communities and the redeveloping of old ones. Since this was a period of full employment, it was understandable that urban development and redevelopment would be a fundamental concern. Conceptions of local autonomy and local community, which have so long been the basis of democratic organization, were subjected to a searching criticism on a very pragmatic basis.

Each community newspaper has implicit rules as to the role it in-

tends to play in fashioning the real estate composition of its local community. This, of course, depends on whether the newspaper is confronted realistically with the urban development and redevelopment
problems in its own area, or whether it deals with the problem in terms
of principle. In general, the community press in the Chicago area has
been in opposition to federally supported public housing, including
some in a most outspoken fashion. Moreover, because of parochialism
the local community and its community newspaper, it was felt by certain critics, were likely, in fact certain, to have created undemocratic
standards for residence, particularly with respect to ethnic composition.

This issue can be considered a key to understanding the "manipulative" aspects of community journalism, for underneath the issue is
the fear of altering the ethnic and racial composition of the community. Systematic attitude data is not available on public housing, but
there is enough data on ethnic and racial attitudes in metropolitan
areas to indicate that often the community press reflects rather than
molds attitudes in its opposition to unsegregated public housing.

Therefore, for these same critics of the community press, democratic objectives frequently implied the elimination of local community autonomy if urban redevelopment and residential mobility were
to be guaranteed. To justify such an attack on a traditional preconception of the democratic process, they frequently argued that, in effect,
the local community no longer exists or could never possibly exist in
an urban community. In this view, much is made of the "artificial"
attempts to stimulate local autonomy in a world in which local autonomy has been rendered meaningless.[6]

But a solution to the dilemma between local autonomy and freedom
of residential mobility is not possible by denying the power of the local
orientations that persist in the metropolitan community—the mass of
evidence to which this study contributes is too great to be denied. Although the elimination of segregation is a basic and fundamental democratic value, its achievement through the destruction of local auton-

6. The rhetoric with which these matters concerning the ethnic composition of the
local community are discussed in the columns of the community press at times makes
use of "factual" reportage of events which are designed to remind the resident of the
local community of the "collective danger." . . . Perhaps the criticism leveled at the community press in this area arises from the fact that the majority tend to avoid the issue,
and thereby they fail to discharge their social responsibility. It is a matter of individual
discretion to judge the community press by this standard. Such a point of view also fails
to recognize that at times it is constructive to engage in deliberate avoidance of a problem if that makes possible a desired solution whereas recognition would prevent the
solution.

omy would be undesirable. The destruction of all local community autonomy and all sense of local identification would seem to lead the individual as indicated previously to a sense of personal incompetence which can only result in an even greater antidemocratic potential than is present today.

The Community of "Limited Liability"

The findings of this study call into question theoretical formulations which see the local community merely in the time perspective of a historical shift from "gemeinschaft" (simple—intimate) social forms to "gesellschaft" (complex—indirect) social forms.

The analysis of the collapse or survival of postulated earlier and simpler social arrangements in the urban community eliminates much significant data on how community social controls operate. This observation has become increasingly evident to social scientists who are interested in the workings of power and voluntary association in the local community. The large-scale organization of the urban community hardly eliminates the necessity of theoretical analysis of the networks of intimate and cohesive social relations which supply the basis of collective action on the local community level. In a fundamental sense, the contemporary balance and interrelations between "gemeinschaft" and "gesellschaft" social forms in the local community are as relevant as estimates of long-term trends. (All too frequently, these estimates of the long-term trends in gemeinschaft merely focus on the formal aspects of social organization.)

Recent theoretical reorientations have sought to free the concepts and definitions of the sociology of the urban community from the limitations linked to the bias of implied value premises. The disrepute in which the concept "disorganization" has fallen in certain types of sociological writings is reflective of this issue.[7]

It seems appropriate to point out that the generalized description of the urban residential community implied by this research is a community of "limited liability." Our community is clearly not one of completely bureaucratized and impersonalized attachments. In varying degrees, the local community resident has a current psychological and social investment in his local community. In varying degrees, use of

7. Robert Merton in his theoretical work *Social Theory and Social Structure* (Glencoe, Ill.: Free Press, 1949) seeks to deal explicitly with this problem. A careful reading of Thomas and Znaniecki's *Polish Peasant* will indicate that even earlier, when these authors used the term "disorganization," they were not oblivious to the value implications of the term.

local facilities is accompanied by community orientations. The extent and character of these attachments are in good measure linked to the individual resident's predispositions and acts. Raising a family and, to a lesser extent, length of residence and local social contacts predispose him to an acceptance of local community institutions and social controls. In the process, purely "rational" and "instrumental" relations are modified. In this regard, individuals vary in the extreme; some are more capable (or have more need) than others of developing these orientations.

But, in all cases, these attachments are limited in the amount of social and psychological investment they represent. Thus, the notion of a community of "limited liability" emerges. (The term is viewed as similar in many aspects to the individual's commitment of "limited liability" in economic affairs.) The individual, responding to the general cultural norms, is likely to demand more from his community than he will invest. But more significant, his relation to the community is such—his investment is such—that when the community fails to serve his needs, he will withdraw. Withdrawal implies either departure from the local community or merely lack of involvement. Withdrawal to some extent takes place with individual aging. More often it accompanies changes in the ethnic or social composition of the community. For some the withdrawal is slight since the original investment was slight or nonexistent. Finally the point of withdrawal may vary from community to community, from class to class, from ethnic group to ethnic group; but for each individual there is a point at which he cuts off his losses. Seldom is the investment so great that the individual is permanently committed to a community that cannot cater to his needs.[8]

Thus, in summary, the dimensions of the local community point

8. Such a view of the community eliminates the necessity of employing the orientations of small and isolated community research where frequency of personal acquaintance is viewed as the basis of social stratification. The common indices of frequency of contact are mostly misleading for analyzing these local interlocking directorates. In the urban community, influential contacts do not necessarily require high frequency of contact. Models of influence based on the observation by social anthropologists of small isolated communities hardly reflect the social realities of the urban metropolis, where "rational" and "instrumental" considerations mold elites into power blocs.

Into the "limited liability" conceptualization can also be built dimensions of indirect social control involving the mass media, as well as the leadership and power relations of the local community. From this general orientation, the sharp distinction between mass communications and interpersonal communications research begins to fade. Instead analysis of the interrelated patterns of mass communications and personal communications in the context of a particular social structure becomes more relevant.

toward emerging social change in the largest metropolitan districts. Motives for community orientation center around the family with its gravitational pull toward the community and to a lesser extent around other primary-group contacts. Within a specific local community, significant aspects of social organization operate without respect to socioeconomic status, although deviations (both higher or lower) from the status norms of the community tend to some degree to interfere with community cohesion. Local leadership functions in a social milieu of apparent rationalistic interpersonal contacts, but these contacts are surrounded by a network of purely personalistic relations. Local leadership also involves a heavy emphasis on nonpartisanship, which is in effect an emphasis on the perpetuation of the status quo. Compromise is the general theme except when fundamental values in the community are impinged [upon] by external threats.

The resulting balance of social control at the local community level is one which leaves relatively untouched only a minority of residents, heavily involves another perhaps smaller group in the community, and creates varying degrees of involvement for the bulk of the residents. Many of these elements are indicative of socially adaptive mechanisms seeking and struggling to modify the impact of industrialism and large-scale organization on the local community. This perspective eliminates the necessity of overemphasizing the impersonalized aspects of urban personality, and thereby the character of social manipulation in the local community can be seen in its proper limits.

6

Inequality, Occupations, and Welfare

In the dominant sociological perspective, the social stratification of an advanced industrial society, as well as its transformation, is best understood in terms of the division of labor; that is, by occupational categories. The intellectual heritage of sociological theory dictates such a research strategy. Social stratification obviously encompasses the economic, bureaucratic, and cultural forms which regulate relations within and between occupational and professional groups, as well as ownership of and access to property.

From this point of view, the first step in the macrosociology of industrial society is to construct indicators of social strata and social classes based on occupational analysis. These indicators are supplemented by measures of human settlement and urbanization. The obvious, persistent realities of inequality—economic, social, and political—reinforce the vast energy expended in the measurement of occupational structure. The complexity of the subject and its potential for statistical and mathematical analysis also make it one of continued academic fascination.

Disputes among advocates of different "theories of society" and social change often proceed on a level concerned with the appropriate definition of social stratum and social class. In these debates, the concept of occupational groups is the key issue. From these efforts has come the conviction that a central task of contemporary sociology is to construct societal-wide morphologies of social structure—that is, of social classes and strata. To use the critical terminology of Lloyd Fallers, the dominant sociological perspective is that of a "stratigraphic" image of society.[1] The result is the view of social stratification as an analog to geological strata—massive layers in hierarchical

From *The Last Half-Century*, pp. 123–26, 128, 131–38, 143, 145–48. © 1978 by The University of Chicago. All rights reserved.

1. Lloyd A. Fallers, *Inequality: Social Stratification Reconsidered* (Chicago: University of Chicago Press, 1973), pp. 3–29; see also Talcott Parsons, "An Analytical Approach to the Theory of Social Stratification," *American Journal of Sociology* 45 (May 1940): 841–62.

array which pervade uniformly throughout the entire society or nation-state.

The limits of this perspective are marked, especially from the point of view of the systemic analysis of social control. Therefore this chapter probes alternative formulations of social stratification—which, of course, must be rooted in the sociological tradition of the division of labor and occupational indicators.[2] To assert that a person's social position is a function of his relations to the mode of production makes sense, but requires a realistic notion of the complexity of this relation. The goal is to "break with" the "stratigraphic" image of social stratification for the more differentiated, multifaceted conception epitomized in the notion of the "ordered social segmentation" of an advanced industrial society.[3] To move in this direction, it is necessary to remember that the division of labor and the resulting occupational structure are more than a manifestation of the productive processes of industrialism. They continue to be grounded in the effect of the collective enterprise of the state, in particular, the effect of military institutions and war-making, and, in the twentieth century, the consequences of the rise of the welfare state. . . .

The sociological perspective which stressed the interplay and juxtaposition of industrial and military society was first elaborated by Saint-Simon.[4] He was influenced by Condorcet, who had sought to fuse the aspiration of Francis Bacon for a science of society with his own interest in the social and political values of Rousseau and Locke.[5] Saint-Simon emphasized the antithetical character of military society to industrial society and his premature conclusion that, with the growth of industrialism, "military society" would decline and become useless. Subsequently, both Comte and Spencer maintained the distinction between industrial and military society and anticipated a decline in militarism with the growth of industrial organization.[6] This juxtaposition of military institutions and industrialism led Marx also to observe that in the long run industrial forms would make military insti-

2. Emile Durkheim, *De la division du travail social* (Paris: Alcan, 1893).

3. The notion of ordered segmentation focuses on the spatial or social ecological dimensions of social stratification. It is in part derived from the writings of British and American social anthropologists, although equivalent formulations are to be found in the sociological traditions of urban community research.

4. C. Saint-Simon, *L'Industrie, Oeuvres de Saint-Simon,* ed. Barthélemy d'Enfantin (Paris: E. Dentu, 1868), vol. 18.

5. Keith Baker, *Condorcet: From Natural Philosophy to Social Mathematics* (Chicago: University of Chicago Press, 1975).

6. Spencer, *Principles,* vol. 1, part 2, pp. 576–96.

tutions obsolete. However, for this stage of development, war and proletarian revolution were essential preconditions.[7] While these exercises in "futurology" appear naive in retrospect, they remain pertinent in their focus on the tensions between industrial and military institutions.

However, our task is to examine the results of the preoccupation of sociologists with the long-term development and changes in the division of labor produced by advanced industrialism. The continuing analysis of the influence of industrialism on internal social structure has produced descriptive and analytic materials which in effect have undermined the "stratigraphic" image of social stratification. Sociologists have so extensively elaborated and modified their view of the occupational structure that they have begun to undermine the "classic" formulations of societal-wide social strata based on occupational categories.

Social scientists, mainly by means of the data assembled by the U.S. Bureau of the Census for the Bureau of Labor Statistics, have classified occupational categories into social strata and charted the shifts from 1900 to 1970. The results give empirical meaning to the notion of an advanced industrial society.[8] . . . We are dealing with a dramatic decline of the agricultural sector (41.7 percent of the male working force in 1900 to 8.4 percent in 1960) and the emergence of a "middle" white-collar stratum (from 17.6 percent of the male working force in 1900 to 41.2 percent in 1975). While the "lower" blue-collar stratum expanded (from 40.8 percent of the male working force in 1900 to 53.9 percent in 1975), the rate was slower than those of the white-collar stratum and more specifically the "lowest" grouping, laborers, except farm and mine, actually declined (14.7 percent to 7.4 percent). These trends contribute to the image and reality of the proliferation of the "middle majority."

This type of occupational categorization gives the impression of the persistence of sharp boundaries between the social strata and the continuing relevance of a "stratigraphic" format. The categories remain the same; the changes which have taken place are in the relative concentration in specific groupings. In reality, the occupational structure

7. Karl Marx, *The Communist Manifesto*.

8. Otis Dudley Duncan, "Occupation Trends and Patterns of Net Mobility in the United States," *Demography* 3:1 (1966): 1–18; Alba M. Edwards, "Comparative Occupation Statistics for the United States, 1870 to 1940" (Washington, D.C.: Bureau of the Census, Government Printing Office, 1943) presents an early analysis of trends in occupational distribution.

during 1900 to 1970 has undergone a process of increased differentiation. The number of readily discernible skill groupings within each of the two major strata (white-collar–blue-collar) has greatly increased and the boundaries between the strata are less clear-cut.[9]

Of course, the ordering from the top to the bottom is systematically related to income and education, but two changes can be noted. The disparity between income and education is considerable and has probably increased; the number of occupations which do not fit directly into a continuous hierarchy is noteworthy and has probably increased.[10] The consequence is that the boundaries between the white-collar and blue-collar strata are not sharply discernible and represent a high degree of arbitrary designation. The same holds true for the more specific occupation groupings within the two strata. The notion of ordered social segmentation becomes more applicable and relevant to describe the realities of social stratification.

In addition, a "stratigraphic" format has been associated with a pyramidal structure, but the movement from industrialism to advanced industrialism transforms this pattern to more of a "flask"-shaped labor force. This transformation implies a greater degree of complexity than that encompassed by the "stratigraphic" model. . . .

Closely related is another major limitation in the stratigraphic model, namely, its inability to capture the multiple bases of social differentiation. An industrial society separates work from family and community; this observation may well be the enduring relevance of Karl Marx's sociological analysis. The social hierarchies of work and of family and community are intertwined, but with important elements of disarticulation. In effect, to separate work from residential community attenuates but does not extinguish the network of localistic social relations and the primordial attachments which are nour-

9. Gerhard Lenski, "American Social Classes: Statistical Strata or Social Groups?" *American Journal of Sociology* 58 (September 1952): 139–44; Edward O. Laumann, *Prestige and Association in an Urban Community* (Indianapolis: Bobbs-Merrill, 1966); Richard Hamilton, *Class and Politics in the United States* (New York: Wiley, 1972); William Form, *Blue Collar Stratification: Autoworkers in Four Countries* (Princeton: Princeton University Press, 1976); Reeve Vanneman, "The Occupational Composition of American Classes: Results from Cluster Analysis," *American Journal of Sociology* 82 (January 1977): 783–807.

10. The notion of status crystallization has been coined to handle such inconsistencies; see especially Gerhard Lenski, "Status Crystallization: A Non-Vertical Dimension of Social Status," *American Sociological Review* 19 (August 1954): 405–13; Gerhard Lenski, "Social Participation and Status Crystallization," *American Sociological Review* 21 (August 1956): 458–64.

ished, fashioned, and developed in urban settlements, and reinforced by voluntary associations and the mass media.[11] While the functions of local residential communities become more specialized, the consequences of these territorial attachments are not merely derivations of "social class." . . .

While inequality remains a dominant characteristic of an advanced industrial society, broad socioeconomic strata are less adequate as correlates of sociopolitical behavior than a combination of social origin, education, and career, plus elements of social differentiation such as sex, age, and community attachments (including ethnic-religious identification). There is every reason to substitute for the stratigraphic image or to supplement it with a perspective of the ordered social segments if one seeks to explore political perspective and the resulting patterns of social control. When the idea of ordered social segments is applied, the distinction needs to be made between the bureaucratic occupation setting and the primordial communal affiliations of the individual and his household.

However, the most critical assessment of the conventional analysis of stratigraphic perspective does not derive from empirical critiques, but from an assessment of the intellectual history and political usage of the inherent terms of reference. As is often the case in social-science analysis, the vitality of a frame of reference has its own momentum—or inertia, if you will—which resists scrutiny because it imposes a sense of order on the human environment. Only a direct attack on the origins—both intellectual and political—can overcome such rigidities. Thus the "stratigraphic" approach to social structure in language and political consequences is a modern invention. Its limitations result in part from the fact that it has served both as a device for sociological analysis and as a rhetorical basis for political activity. And it is very difficult to separate the two.

This argument, which reflects the analysis presented by Lloyd Fallers, focuses on the historical relevance and political utility of appeals in the name of social class as a strategy in the struggle and pursuit of political democracy and subsequently in its subversion. We are speaking of the experiences of Western parliamentary systems and their emergence before advanced industrialism. For this historical context, the claim is made that the "stratigraphic" mode was the appropriate language of political appeals during the "age of democratic revolutions."

11. Talcott Parsons, "Age and Sex in the Social Structure of the United States," *American Sociological Review* 7 (October 1942): 604–16.

No doubt the experiences of the Greek city-states and of the early Roman Republic are relevant to this intellectual and political heritage. The particular accomplishments of city-states of Italy, the Hanseatic League, and the record of the Netherlands are germane for such analysis.[12] But the focus at this point is on the emergence of the nation-state, as epitomized by the English, American, and French revolutions, during the period in which national revolutions emerged as the precondition for the development of parliamentary political regimes—a historical sequence of most limited frequency. My reading of the range of comparative historical and macrosociological treatises (in particular R. R. Palmer, *The Age of Democratic Revolution,* and Barrington Moore, Jr., *Social Origins of Dictatorship and Democracy*) leads to the necessity of confronting this basic issue.[13] The emergence of these parliamentary regimes, while they are linked to the expansion of the middle class, cannot be accounted for in the conventional terms of social-stratification patterns, either by comparisons with those industrializing nation-states which did not develop parliamentary institutions or by comparisons of the timing and format of those which did develop such political agencies. To speak of the emergence of Western representative institutions in the eighteenth and nineteenth centuries involves reference to the content and form of ideological movements and political leadership. Of the elements involved, two are crucial. First is the political definition offered by the "revolutionaries" to justify the use of force and the political meaning they imposed on citizen participation in military institutions. . . . Second, the use of social-class appeals creates a political system for containing communal and primordial differences, for expanding political participation, and for creating political formulas for handling competing economic interests by balancing them or at least modulating them by means of limited parliamentary intervention.[14]

Terms such as "class" and "stratum" are modern constructs even in the West. It is extremely important that the *Shorter Oxford English Dictionary* (third edition) gives 1772 as the date of first occurrence for

12. Henry Kamen, *The Iron Century: Social Change in Europe, 1550–1660* (London: Weidenfeld and Nicolson, 1971).

13. R. R. Palmer, *The Age of Democratic Revolution: A Political History of Europe and America,* 1760–1800, 2 vols. (Princeton: Princeton University Press, 1970); Barrington Moore, Jr., *Social Origins of Dictatorship and Democracy* (Boston: Beacon, 1966).

14. For a description of the expansion of mass political participation, see Reinhard Bendix, *Nation-Building and Citizenship: Studies of Our Changing Social Order* (New York: Wiley, 1964); Stein Rokkan, *Citizens, Elections, Parties* (Oslo: Universitets forlaget, 1970), especially chap. 1.

"class" as in the social layer sense. The more technocratic term "social stratum" apparently did not appear until as late as 1902. How were the various forms of inequality described before these terms were used?

Available scholarship underlines that forms of inequality were referred to and debated in a medieval context. This meant that the debate about the nature of the church in relation to the evolving secular state and associated institutions was overriding; equality had to do with the religious and the secular. At the same time, the language of feudalism created an organic conception of society—a collection of orders and estates; and the system of subinfeudation and localism before the emergence of a centralized monarchy and the nation-state rejected the notion of societal-wide strata.[15]

The emergence of parliamentary political regimes rested on the exclusion of particular groups, and on the partial inclusion and participation of others. The exclusion and containment of specific groups assisted in maintaining the political and economic advantages of traditional feudal elements. These exclusionary practices in retrospect highlight the gradualism in the process of political institution building; but the gradualism cannot obscure the transformation in political authority and power which the "age of democratic revolution" produced. Legitimate sovereignty came to be lodged in a set of secular institutions which permitted competitive national elections; elections were the basic instrument both for generating consent and for exercising political power.

From the point of view of strengthening social control, both nationalism and parliamentary regimes required extensive and expanding reliance on universalist principles. The political achievement of nation building in Western industrializing societies was the formula that was used to extend and to "universalize" political participation. It was to draw and develop a political construct—the citizen; symbolized and sloganized by the notion of "one man, one vote." The notion of the citizen avoided formalizing political power in terms of primordial and communal groups, an approach which would have been and has been fatal. Nor was political participation formalized in terms of corporate economic groups, but in terms of individual persons. Of course, the citizen's effective power was a function of his position in the social structure; and explicit property requirements set the standard for the extension of the franchise. But the idea of citizen serves to contain,

15. Marc Bloch, *Feudal Society* (Chicago: University of Chicago Press, 1961).

limit, and make manageable the political issues generated by economic differences.

The citizen was essentially a person who had an occupation; this tended to exclude the economically marginal and women. But it meant that citizens came to think of themselves and to be appealed to in terms of the occupational social strata with which they were affiliated. Political activists who sought to aggregate power came more and more to emphasize the universality of social status.

The language of the students of society both reflected and influenced this political process. The designation of the citizenry as members of occupationally based social classes served ideological and political functions which were initially compatible and conducive to parliamentary regimes. It was an effective basis for enlarging the citizenry and the electorate. It was, in fact, the most universal criterion and one that could be effectively used. But it could also be manipulated so that "paupers" and persons with very small incomes could be excluded. Also, it created a balance of political elements which expanded and diffused political power. In the main, it initially assisted those who came to think of themselves as members of the middle stratum in their conflicts with the older upper status groups. Subsequently, it supplied the basis for alliances between the middle-income skill groups and the lower-income labor groupings. In addition, the political appeals that were generated and the self-conceptions of social class that were implanted in the citizenry could, in varying degrees, operate without producing political divisions that were irreconcilable by parliamentary procedures. Throughout the nineteenth century, Great Britain escaped such divisions by expanding the franchise; in the United States the issue of slavery presented such a cleavage. In France, social class–based demands interrupted the stability and legitimacy of parliamentary institutions, but never undermined them. Prussia and modern Germany as nation-states represent one of the variants of paths toward industrialism, in which parliamentary institutions failed to take hold until the onset of advanced industrialism and then in good measure because they were externally imposed.

In part, this argument rests on the observation that the "stratigraphic" model has greater plausibility in the nineteenth century than in the twentieth century, although even for the earlier period it failed to capture the realities of the interplay of the division of labor and the other bases of social differentiation. The language of social class was most effective as a political strategy in developing industrialism in the Western mode. While the apparatus of the central region and local government operated to the advantage of particular elite groups, the legislative organs of government adapted to the changing demands of emerging groups. The rise in the standard of living was a result of developments in the "private sector." Thus the economic tasks assigned to parliamentary institutions were manageable by the available political mechanisms of debate and bargaining. These economic tasks were more regulative than distributive of the results of economic enterprise. But with the extension of the welfare state, especially after World War I and the Great Depression, the tasks of the legislative arena changed. The very notion of a person and his household's position in the social structure and their relation to the means of production altered fundamentally and, as shall be argued, the relevance of [the] stratigraphic notion of social structure became attenuated.

"Welfare state" here refers to governmental practices of allocating at least 8 percent to 10 percent of the gross national product to welfare, i.e., public expenditures for health, education, income maintenance (including deferred income), and community development (including housing). These allocations can take the form of monetary transfers, expenditures for services, and in-kind benefits (for example, food stamps, public housing). By 1935, the United States had almost reached this level; by 1975, the percentage was approximately 20 percent.

The "welfare state" and welfare expenditures are not synonymous. The welfare state rests on the political assumption that the well-being of its citizens is enhanced not only by allocations generated from their occupations and the marketplace but also from grants regulated by the central government. The welfare state involves at least two additional elements. Under the welfare state, the extent and nature of welfare expenditures are conditioned decisively by parliamentary regimes; that is, they reflect political demands and consent, and not authoritarian decisions. Second, it is accepted as legitimate for the political system to intervene through governmental institutions in order to assist its citizens in the pursuit of their personal and "household" goals. . . .

The effects of increased welfare expenditures and the associated economic trends are pervasive on the pattern of social stratification, although the precise details and consequences are very difficult to identify. The social incidence of the welfare system varies widely. The welfare state is based on the assumption that the lowest social stratum requires additional resources. The emergence of the welfare state has produced a system whose official goal is "assisting" those at the bottom of the social structure. But the long-term trend has been one in which there has been a diffusion of social welfare upward and throughout the social structure. The upward direction of welfare expenditures has been increased by the regressive character of social security taxes. A person who earned $16,500 in 1976 paid 5.85 percent of his income in social security taxes, while a person who earned $100,000 contributed less than 1 percent. For millions of workers, social security taxes exceeded income taxes.

The classic question, "What are the consequences of the mode of production on the social structure?" is valid to the extent that it encompasses the consequences of the social welfare system. The normative rationale of social welfare is based on aspirations for universal treatment and standards. Thus, as such, welfare operates in direct opposition to the particular rewards of occupation and work systems of exchange. As a result, efforts are constantly being made to link welfare payments for income maintenance to work and work incentives; but this linkage is most difficult to achieve. Welfare payments are designed not only for the lowest social stratum but also to deal with the life problems of the population of an advanced industrial society in which inequality is linked to race, sex, age, family composition, and medical and mental health. . . .

But the influence of the welfare state on social structure requires a broader approach than the assessment of the degree of equality of disposable income for households. In addition to money transfers, the welfare state renders direct services or extends benefits at reduced costs. We are particularly interested in those which extend beyond the lower income groups, particularly in the areas of housing, higher education, and medical services.

One of the most important mechanisms for creating new economic equities has been the widespread diffusion of home ownership under extensive mortgage assistance that started after World War I and expanded after World War II.[16] Home ownership penetrates deeply into modest- and low-income families (except for the very lowest, it is not strongly related to family income). Home ownership by modest and middle income families has been facilitated by government-subsidized insurance of mortgages, and low-interest federal- and state-insured veterans' mortgages, which are a form of social welfare that has extended upwardly throughout the social structure.

The dispersion of welfare allocations received impetus from the ex-

16. Glen H. Beyer, *Housing and Society* (New York: Macmillan, 1965), pp. 117–249; Raymond J. Struyk and Sue A. Marshall, *Income and Urban Home Ownership* (Washington, D.C.: Urban Institute, 1974); Congressional Budget Office, *Homeownership: The Changing Relationship of Costs and Income, and Possible Federal Roles* (Washington, D.C.: Government Printing Office, 1977).

tension of higher education. Expenditures for education have produced high rates of economic return and have influenced the pattern of social mobility. Since 1945, there has been massive extension of public support for education. The federal contribution went disproportionately to support higher education until the middle of the 1960s. Access to higher education is directly related to occupational position; as a result, these educational benefits serve to link the middle class—old and new—to the structure of the welfare state.[17]

At the core of the welfare state benefits are the income-maintenance programs, from old age payments to rent supplements to food stamps. These programs extend well beyond the lowest social stratum. Thus, for example, over 100,000 members of the armed forces in the early 1970s were eligible to receive food stamps; for a period students were eligible for food stamps. Old age insurance has become important for members of the middle strata to relieve themselves of or shift the burden of caring for aging parents. Veterans' benefits are social welfare, since they are as much designed to overcome liabilities as they are to be rewards. The emerging medical insurance programs are more and more broadly based. It is significant that aspects of these programs are closely linked to the cost of living index rather than to levels of productivity.

Efforts to diffuse stock ownership as an approach to altering wage earner–employer relations have been studied. Ownership of stock, like that of insurance policies, serves as a vehicle for underwriting welfare payments. However, the ownership of stock has not been a major device for weakening the distinction between wage earner and owner of equity capital. The direct ownership of stock has not diffused deeply and extensively into middle income groups in the United States. Nor have the schemes by which industrial establishments distribute stock been noteworthy in their impact.[18] The 1974 legislation on employee stock ownership was designed to facilitate such schemes by adding a tax deferment advantage.

But it is the vast growth of health and pension plans in industrial and commercial firms, often in conjunction with trade union groups,

17. Joseph A. Rechman, "The Distributional Effects of Public Higher Education in California," *Journal of Human Resources* 5 (summer 1971): 361–70; Richard Freeman, *The Overeducated American* (New York: Academic Press, 1976).

18. According to the New York Stock Exchange data, the 1975 profile of stockowners indicated that there were 25.2 million Americans who held stock, a drop of 18.3 percent from the 30.8 billion in 1970. The average owner was 53 years of age and had an annual household income of $19,000, compared with an $11,000 average for the total population.

which creates new linkages between wage earners and the "mode of production." These schemes depend on the economic returns of investments. As of 1975, by means of pension funds, employees of U.S. firms owned at least 25 percent of the existing equity capital and the figure was projected to rise to 50 percent by 1985. There are inadequate data on the social incidence of this type of welfare equity claim, but it can be estimated that between one-third and one-half of the blue-collar families by 1970 had such "stakes," of real importance to their standard of living. Such private welfare schemes are closely linked with and supported by the welfare state. The federal government seeks to facilitate them by research and information. In 1974 legislation was passed establishing governmental standards and regulations; these programs are in effect subsidized, as they are closely monitored by the government.

Interest-group politics is at the heart of the expansion of welfare expenditures. The claims and demands of occupational groups are expressed by voluntary association networks. Ideological and humanitarian goals—and the realities of inequality and disability of an advanced industrial society—supply the political and rhetorical context. Each occupational group has a short-term, relatively clear-cut interest that competes and conflicts with those of other groups. The political process is unable to impose a national scheme or an integrated economic policy and instead reacts by a series of compromises without "grand design" and without effective contribution to social control and self-regulation of the welfare state. (Some innovations have been inconsistent.) Each claim for social welfare has its inherent relevance, legitimacy, and high priority; the ranking of one claim against another is theoretically very difficult and in the political arena even more difficult to adjudicate. How do elected officials balance the demand for increased old age benefits against youth employment training programs without resort to the strength of pressure groups?

But this analysis needs to be extended in order to explain the emergence of weak and "stalemated" political regimes; it is necessary to assess the effect of the welfare benefits on popular political perspectives and participation. The influence of the welfare state on the social structure modifies and transcends conventional interest-group politics. Political conflict becomes more than the struggle between competing occupational and interest groups. Each person and each member of the household must confront an elaborate set of contradictory or competing and often ambiguous issues in the pursuit of self-interest—immediate or long term. The new social and economic structure produces a fusion of claims and expectations about wages, property, income, and welfare. A person's relation to the means of production is by no means characterized by a simple set of alternatives. One's linkage to the mode of production under these conditions is based both on one's occupation and on the institutions of social welfare.

The claims and expectations of one's occupation remain central. Yet the spread and increased weight of welfare equity claims mean that the admixture of property rights, private welfare returns, and benefits of social welfare are also important components of one's socioeconomic self-conception and realities. The task of assessing one's self-interest becomes continuous and more complex, and the pursuit of one's personal or group goals almost defies direct political and programmatic articulation. . . .

7

The Emergence of Weak Political Regimes

The difficulties of the welfare state contribute to the emergence of weak political regimes at the national level. The problem is not the personalities of the presidents or prime ministers in the Western political democracies but rather the inability of the electoral system to generate a decisive majority for one political organization or for an effective coalition. The narrow and unstable balance of power between legislative groupings, the opposition of chief executive to legislature members, the fragmentation of political factions—these difficulties are widespread in the Western industrialized nations and have been developing at least since the middle of the 1960s and in effect earlier, since the end of World War II.

It needs to be emphasized that this trend has emerged not only in the United States but throughout Western Europe. It is most conspicuous in Great Britain, the Netherlands, Belgium, and Denmark. It has been chronic in Italy and in varying degrees has come into being in Sweden and even in the Federal Republic of West Germany. France has its own tradition of chronic electoral instability, but the contemporary trend conforms to those of other Western industrialized nations.

Political parties and the periodic national elections are not able to perform the self-regulating tasks of social control. It is possible to examine and focus on the internal structure of the political parties, their social composition, their processes of leadership recruitment, their financial bases, and their internal decision-making process as elements in an explanation of this secular trend. While such an elite and institutional analysis helps clarify the weakness of contemporary parliamentary regimes, this analysis focuses on the changing character of the social structure. The tensions and conflicts that the political elites and political organizations must confront reflect not only the altered mode of large-scale industrial production but also the development of the welfare expenditures managed by the state. In other words, the necessities of industrial development create the welfare state; and, in turn,

From *Social Control of the Welfare State* (New York: Elsevier Scientific Publishing Co., 1976), pp. 85–88, 90–99. Reprinted by permission of Gayle Janowitz.

139

the welfare state generates a set of economic equity claims that are complex, diffuse, and even mutually contradictory.

Moreover, welfare expenditures do not necessarily generate partisan loyalties. To the contrary, these allocations are more and more considered a matter of law and citizen right. This orientation serves to weaken or undermine partisan attachments.

The argument offered is that these welfare benefits change the patterns of social stratification and economic inequality, which in turn condition political participation and party orientation and help to explain the emergence of weak political regimes. Thus, popular electoral behavior can be taken as an index of social control, that is, voting patterns as indicators of the relative level of effectiveness of contemporary mechanisms of social and political control.

Critical Elections

One can assert that in the past socioeconomic change in the United States and the emergence of the welfare state created the need for political change. The political arrangements that facilitated industrial growth had to be adapted to the welfare state. The effectiveness of the process of adaptation and its limitations can be assessed by the key notion of the critical or realignment election. In the research literature, the elections of 1896 and 1932 are offered as such critical elections because they served to restructure political alternatives and produce important political decisions.[1] Three elements are operative in a critical election. First, the critical election produces a new majority—that is, there is a marked realignment in the sociopolitical basis of the majority and minority blocs. Second, the shift is sharp and relatively durable. Third, these two elements imply that the restructuring of the patterns of voting creates a decisive political majority, which has important and persistent political consequences. Thereby, the realignment election represents a decisive accomplishment in terms of self-regulation and social control. Each occurrence of a critical election is apparently foreshadowed. This was so in the emergence of a "Populist" vote in 1894 in advance of the critical election of 1896. Again, the campaign of Alfred Smith represented the preliminary step in reorienting the Democratic party in 1928 and was the essential precondi-

1. V. O. Key, Jr., "A Theory of Critical Elections," *Journal of Politics* 17 (February 1955): 3–18; W. D. Burnham, "The Changing Shape of the American Political Universe," *American Political Science Review* 54 (March 1965): 7–28; W. D. Burnham, *Critical Elections and the Mainsprings of American Politics* (New York: Norton, 1970).

tion for the Franklin D. Roosevelt political coalition of 1932 and thereafter.

It may well be that the passage of time and the limited empirical data help create, in retrospect, the image of a realignment election. Therefore, more time is required to identify the critical elections after 1932. However, in view of the weak political regimes that have emerged and the contemporary "crisis" of political legitimacy, there may well have been no subsequent critical election. Since 1945, there has been no critical election in the United States that has produced an effective and fairly enduring parliamentary majority in response to the emerging issues of the post–World War II period. Instead, there has been continuous, marginal, and unstable political aggregation. In other words, the election of 1932 was the last critical election. There is no reason to assume that another critical election will not take place, but the changes in the patterns of social stratification and inequality under the welfare state complicate the process of electoral transformation.

In any case, the concept of the critical election sets the historical framework for the trend analysis of the emergence of weak political regimes. For this purpose, the periods 1920 to 1948 and 1948 to 1972 are appropriate for comparison. . . .

To work effectively, a competitive election must create a stable majority that is able to rule. The balance between the majority and the minority must be such that the minority—by itself or in coalition with other political elements—maintains a reasonable chance of success in forthcoming elections. If the majority becomes excessively preponderant, viability of the electoral system as a mechanism of self-regulation is weakened. But the opposite situation has come to characterize the pattern of electoral behavior both in the United States and generally in Western Europe. The outcome of the national election, in one form or another, is such that an effective and stable political regime is not created. There has been a growth of "weak," or minority, governments. The forms and patterns are diverse. The margin of victory for the leading party may be slim; or, in fact, the victorious party may obtain only a minority of the vote; likewise, its parliamentary majority may be too narrow to be considered a governing party. In the presidential system, the chief executive may find himself with the opposition party in command of the legislative majority. The result of these outcomes is hardly an effective system of checks and balances; rather it is political fragmentation or disarticulation and a variety of forms of stalemate, because there has not been a critical or realignment election which has constructed an effective political majority.

For the United States, in the period 1920 to 1928, the electoral system created a relatively stable majority political regime that was Republican and that endured for three presidential terms. It was replaced in 1932 by a stable Democratic majority political regime, which persisted for an even longer period of time, namely five presidential terms. However, since 1948 the outcome has been neither a relatively stable political regime nor, with one single exception in 1964, even a single term of control of both the presidency and both legislative houses by the same party; instead, the results have been disarticulated.

While the political historians do not identify the post–World War I election of 1920 as a critical election, it did replace the Wilson administration and create a Republican majority that persisted until 1932. The electoral competition gave the Republican presidents decisive popular mandates (ranging from an advantage of 26.3 percent in 1920 to 7.3 percent in 1928); moreover, these presidents had working majorities in both houses of Congress throughout the period.

In 1928, the first element of a movement toward a critical election could be seen—that is, seen in retrospect. The drop in the popular vote for the president was noteworthy but limited; it was the decline in senatorial seats for the Republicans that signaled the emergence of the new Democratic party with its new strength and base in the North. The 1932 election has been defined by political historians as a critical election because it created the new Democratic party majority, a decisive majority, which persisted both in the popular vote for the president and in the composition of both houses of Congress. The high point was reached in 1936 when Roosevelt gained a plurality of 24.3 percent. The trend in the popular presidential majority was consistently downward after 1936 but still reached 7.5 percent in 1944. The popular Democratic presidential position was paralleled by a consistent majority in both houses, which was tempered at critical points because of the importance of the North-South political split. However, from 1920 through the election of 1944 the electoral system created relatively clear-cut political regimes.

In retrospect, the election of 1948 had the elements of an election antecedent to a critical election of realignment. The popular advantage of the Democratic president continued to decline; it reached the level of 4.5 percent. While the House of Representatives returned a decisive majority of Democratic legislators, the majority in the Senate was reduced to two members. The elements of emerging political disarticulation were beginning to appear.

The outcome of the 1952 election was not that of a critical election of realignment. Instead, the post–World War II pattern of executive dominance—unstable dominance at that—and a stalemated or divided legislative balance emerged. In contrast to the majority political regimes of the period 1920 to 1944, the elements of the "weak" system of parliamentary rule had their origins not in the particular political events of the 1968 to 1972 period but in the results already foreshadowed in the election of 1952. The long-term trend from 1952 to 1972 can be described in part as a period of decline in the national legislative strength of the Republican party. However, we are dealing with more than the relative electorate strength of the major parties. We are dealing with basic changes in the structure of electoral behavior.

In 1952, General Dwight D. Eisenhower was elected by a decisive majority (10.7 percent advantage) but not by a margin of the magnitude accorded Republican presidents in the post–World War I period or to Roosevelt in the first two elections of the New Deal period. Moreover, Eisenhower did not have a formal (and certainly not a working) majority in the legislature as a whole. The distribution was balanced in the House of Representatives, and the number of Republican senators only exceeded the number of Democrats by one. For the first time since 1920, the United States government was not based on a unified political regime. In 1956, General Eisenhower increased his popular vote so that the percent advantage reached 15.4 percent; but the pattern of unstable disarticulation was becoming institutionalized. In both houses of Congress, the Democratic party was in the formal majority—with only two seats more than the Republicans in the Senate, but more markedly in the House of Representatives with thirty-three seats more. The weak government in the United States is not the result of the Vietnam era but has been operative increasingly throughout the post–World War II period.

The pattern of national elections continued essentially in this format through the 1972 election. In 1960, the Democratic president was elected without an effective popular mandate, although he had a working majority in both houses of Congress (thirty in the Senate, and eighty-nine in the House of Representatives). Only in the 1964 election did Lyndon B. Johnson create the conventional pre–World War II majority political regime with a landslide popular mandate and a marked increase in the Democratic majority in both houses of Congress. However, the result of the 1964 election could not be taken as a critical election of realignment since by 1968 Richard Nixon was elected as the head of a minority political regime. He collected only a plurality of the popular presidential vote (43.4 percent) and his advantage over the Democratic candidate was limited to 0.7 percent. The strength of the George Wallace vote, which totaled 13.6 percent of the vote, rendered him, in effect, a minority president. Moreover, the Democratic party held a working majority in both houses of Congress (fourteen in the Senate and fifty-one in the House of Representatives). The pattern of a divided political regime or a disarticulated outcome was even more pronounced in the 1972 election in which Richard Nixon achieved a landslide popular majority—a 23.2 percent advantage over the Democratic contender—but the dominance of the Democratic legislators in both houses of Congress remained.

The implications for the social control perspective are clear. If one assumes that the election outcome is a manifestation of the relative ability of a society to regulate itself, then the absence of a stable majority political regime implies that this indicator reflects significant limitations in the patterns of effective control. Moreover, the election is more than an indicator of social control—it is a mechanism for achieving social control. Thus, these data highlight the strain on the central institution for implementing effective social control.

Trends in Electoral Behavior

The available data on citizens' participation in the national elections help clarify the emergence of weak political regimes. Four specific trends in electoral participation can be examined which extend from 1920 to 1975 and highlight the transformation of electoral participation. The patterns of transformation give meaning to the increasing inability of the electoral process since the election of 1948 to generate stable and majority political regimes. We are dealing with relatively long-term trends and not the particular manifestation of the elections of 1968 and 1972. These specific trends deal with (a) the level of voting participation, (b) fluctuations in voting preference, (c) shifts in patterns of party affiliation, and (d) beliefs about the legitimacy and effectiveness of the electoral process and elected officials. As in the analysis of critical elections, the election of 1952 is a useful dividing point for the period after 1920.

First, the trend in voting participation indicates that since 1952 the long-term increase after the turn of the century has not been effectively maintained. Given the increasing levels of education, wide exposure to the mass media, and the politicization of minority groups, the failure of voting participation to increase is particularly noteworthy. During the period after 1920 and especially after 1930, competitive politics directly influenced the turnout and increased voting participation. The trend is not consistently upward, since in 1944 and 1948 the turnout failed to reach the level reached in 1940. In terms of secular trends, the election of 1952 produced one high point in the presidential turnout. Since 1952, the new pattern of a disarticulated political result in the national election has been accompanied by no further increases in voting participation. In fact, from 1952 to 1968 the overall turnout remained fairly stable (varying from 59 to 62 percent), while in the election campaign of 1972 between Richard Nixon and George McGovern, voter participation dropped markedly to 55.7 percent. Thus, from 1960 to 1972 and especially in 1972 in the United States, competitive politics, which remained intense, did not produce increased levels of electoral participation.

Second, since 1952 there has been an increase in the magnitude of shifts in voting patterns from one election to the next. In other words, the post–World War II period has not been characterized by a system composed of large voting blocs with the outcome, from one election to the next, being determined by rather small shifts in voter preference. To the contrary, the structure of the electorate reveals an increasingly important segment that is prepared to shift from one pattern of voting to another with its members changing their preference for president and engaging in an increasing amount of ticket splitting. Higher levels of education and more extensive political sophistication as a result of the mass media facilitate this trend. But the underlying explanation must be sought in the changing social basis of political participation and the citizens' resulting definition of their political self-interest.

If one examines the period from 1920 to 1948, omitting the realignment election of 1932, one finds that the pattern of voting shifts from one election to the next is moderate. The average two-party shift for the six presidential elections was 5.0 percentage points. However, from 1948 to 1972 electoral behavior was much more volatile. In fact, the average two-party shift was three times as great. For the seven presidential elections, the average shift was 17.1 percentage points.

Along with increased volatility, there has been a growth in ticket splitting. The documentation showing this trend is indeed impressive. Paul T. David has demonstrated the continuous and persistent increase in ticket splitting from 1872 to 1970.[2] His analysis is based on the difference in six pairs of voting decisions involving the offices of president, governor, senator, and representatives. It is striking that there is no reversal in the long-term trend of a century in the increased ticket splitting.

Third, the number of citizens who describe themselves as indepen-

2. Paul T. David, *Party Strength in the United States, 1872–1970* (Charlottesville, Va: University Press of Virginia, 1972).

dents or as having no basic party affiliation has increased since 1952, and especially among young voters. The specific observation that there has been a shift in the characteristics of those citizens who call themselves independent is especially important. As of 1952, the bulk of the independents had weak involvements in politics and marginal political preferences. The trend has been one in which independents are increasingly persons with more education and with strong interests in politics and articulated political demands. Thus, the growth of the concentration of independents does not imply a decline in political interest and involvement, since an important number of them think of themselves as politically responsible and involved.[3]

According to Gallup surveys, the trend in the electorate of those who consider themselves independents ranges from a low of 20 percent in 1940 to 34 percent in 1974. From October 1952 to November 1970, the findings of the Survey Research Center, University of Michigan, confirm these trends. Both these sources also point out that the trend toward "independent" affiliation is even more pronounced among young people. In fact, among college students, by 1974 almost one-half called themselves independents.

Fourth, since 1964 there has been a trend toward a marked reduction in trust and confidence in the electoral system and the outcome of elections. This trend is no doubt linked to the specific impact of military intervention in Vietnam and has been strengthened by the events surrounding the Watergate investigation. However, it antedates the first years of the 1970s and reflects underlying changes in the social structure and in the organization of politics.[4]

None of these trends can be taken as a measure per se of political apathy or depoliticization of the citizens of the United States; they are manifestations of the tension between political goals and available political means. They reflect underlying changes in social stratification and inequality and the ineffectiveness of the political process as a mechanism of social control. In particular, these electoral trends highlight the long-term pattern of attenuation of stable affiliation with the two major parties. In the absence of decisive electoral realignments, extraparliamentary mechanisms for social control of the welfare state become of increasing importance. Nevertheless, whether one charts long-term trends in electoral participation and attitudes or uses the notion of critical elections, the emergence of weak political regimes (in

3. Philip E. Converse, "Change in the American Electorate," in Angus Campbell and Philip E. Converse, eds., *The Human Meaning of Social Change* (New York: Russell Sage Foundation, 1972), pp. 263–338.
    4. Ibid., pp. 322–30.

the United States and in the nations of Western Europe) is significantly conditioned by changes in social stratification and patterns of inequality created by the expansion of the welfare state.[5] In other words, it is the combined impact of the shifts in social stratification plus the impact of a welfare budget based on the decline of economic surplus that strains the electoral and parliamentary institutions.

5. The extensive use of public opinion polling has not served to strengthen the electoral process as some experts had anticipated. The results of surveys have been to frame issues in such a fashion as to fragment the electoral process rather than to encourage public concern with the coherence and legitimacy of contending political parties. Surveys create the impression in segments of the citizenry of mass manipulation as well and serve at times to shift the context from competition about issues to that between personalities. Mark Abrams, "Political Parties and the Polls," in Paul F. Lazarsfeld, William H. Sewell, and Harold L. Wilensky, eds., *The Uses of Sociology* (New York: Basic Books, 1967), pp. 427–36.

III

PRIMARY GROUPS AND PERSONAL CONTROL

8

Social Personality and Personal Control

The logic of systemic analysis includes a safeguard against excessive, rigid sociological reductionism. Instead, in the systemic analysis of social change and social control, it is both desirable and essential at points to interject conceptions of personality or, more to the point, conceptions of social personality. This is appropriate because the social control perspective focuses on the mechanisms of socialization and on the processes of internalization of norms or, in the older language, on the degree to which the person accepts values guided by "higher moral principles" rather than merely by the pursuit of self-interest.

Despite the modest research accomplishment, the formulations of personality and culture offer one point of departure.[1] This type of social psychology has enduring relevance because it focuses on authority and the subjective dimensions of authority. The students of personality and culture have sought to incorporate into their analysis the realistic constraints on institutional authority. They have also been sensitive to the historical setting; one cannot speak of culture without appropriate time referents. But one remains uneasy about the problems of empirical investigation, for all too often the results still appear too oversimplified.

It is no fatal flaw; but the "outside" observer rather than the "inside" participant appears best prepared to undertake such investigations, for in fact they may require considerable personal and social distance. As a result social-psychological reactions to authority are reported by Ruth Benedict for the Japanese; by Margaret Mead for the Russians; by Henry V. Dicks for the Germans; by Lucien Pye for the Chinese.[2] The insider appears reluctant or inhibited. At best Michel

From *The Last Half-Century*, pp. 320–29. ©1978 by The University of Chicago. All rights reserved.

1. Alex Inkeles and Daniel Levinson, "National Character: The Study of Modal Personality and Sociocultural Systems," in *The Handbook of Social Psychology*, vol. 4, ed. Gardner Lindzey and Elliot Aronson (Reading, Mass.: Addison-Wesley Publishing Co.), pp. 418–506; Clifford Geertz, "A Study of National Character," *Economic Development and Cultural Change* 12 (January 1964): 205–9.

2. Ruth F. Benedict, *The Chrysanthemum and the Sword* (Boston: Houghton Mifflin, 1946); Margaret Mead, *Soviet Attitudes toward Authority* (New York: McGraw-Hill,

Crozier, the French sociologist, has presented specific themes in his analysis of authority relations in French bureaucratic settings; and the same approach is pursued in the analysis by Geoffrey Gorer, the English anthropologist, of English character structure.[3] Most telling, from the point of view of the tasks at hand, the intellectual apparatus and methodology of the study of personality and social structure have not been energetically and extensively applied to the citizenry of the United States. No doubt the very heterogeneity of the United States resists such an intellectual enterprise. The massive study of *The Authoritarian Personality,* stimulated by the "Frankfurt school" while residing in the United States, is highly selective because of ideological considerations.[4] It deals only with authoritarianism of the "right" and omits that of the "left." The fundamental finding that tolerant attitudes toward minority groups are concentrated among those who are "antiauthoritarian"—in opposition to the existing authority structure—is a serious oversimplification. Nevertheless, one can "measure" authoritarian attitudes and they do relate to political attitudes and political behavior.

But the exploration of social control does not rest on the search for a general theory of action which fuses sociological and personality theories. Instead I believe that sociological analysis of social change and social control in a specific historical period both requires and is enriched by the incorporation of particular conceptions and variables of social personality. This is merely a continuation of the intellectual heritage of sociology, which includes a persistent emphasis on the distinction between personal and social disorganization.[5] The important consideration is that we are dealing not with exclusively infantile socialization but with the formation of personality throughout the entire life cycle.

Nor does the inclusion of personality dimensions imply that the so-

1951); Henry V. Dicks, "Personality Traits and National Socialist Ideology," *Human Relations* 3 (1950): 111–54; Lucien Pye, *The Spirit of Chinese Politics: a Psychocultural Study of the Authority Crisis in Political Development* (Cambridge: MIT Press, 1968).

3. Michel Crozier, *The Bureaucratic Phenomenon* (Chicago: University of Chicago Press, 1964); Geoffrey Gorer, *Exploring English Character* (London: Cresset Press, 1955).

4. Theodor Adorno et al., *The Authoritarian Personality* (New York: Harper, 1950); Edward Shils, "Authoritarianism: 'Right' and 'Left,'" in *Studies in the Scope and Method of the Authoritarian Personality,* ed. Richard Christie and Marie Jahoda (Glencoe, Ill.: Free Press, 1954), pp. 24–49.

5. Morris Janowitz, ed., *W. I. Thomas: On Social Organization and Social Personality* (Chicago: University of Chicago Press, 1966), pp. 11–36.

ciologist must constantly shift or enlarge his frame of reference. It does imply that the analysis of the changing patterns of social control in an advanced industrial society is assisted by such incorporations even though the result is to undermine, or at least retard, the search for paradigmatic models. Moreover, if one holds a perspective which requires the enlargement of both voluntarism and rationality in the management of societal institutions, an interface with the elements of social personality and motivation becomes inescapable.

Theories of personality abound and are constantly being explicated. But there is a basic meaning—a primitive meaning—which has emerged and which impinges directly on the study of social control. When one talks about personality, one refers to relatively enduring predispositions—emotive and attitudinal—to behave; they are the externalization of internal "psychic states" which carry over from one interpersonal and social setting to the next. This line of reasoning can be found in diverse sources, such as W. I. Thomas, who spoke of the "organization of attitudes" and the resulting "definition of the situation" as he made use of an interactional psychology.[6] It is equally present in Erik H. Erikson's emphasis on the "stages of man" and the resulting modalities of social life.[7] To ground one's perspective toward personality in psychoanalytical theories produces a very different set of intellectual priorities.[8] But these and related formulations work against belabored sociological reductionism, on the one hand, and general systems theories, on the other hand. I use the term "social personality" to encompass the convergence in these orientations toward personality which sees the organization of attitudes as (1) rooted in intrapsychic states, (2) strongly impacted during childhood, and (3) nevertheless capable of being refashioned throughout the life cycle.

There is another simple but overriding element in the incorporation of social personality into the analysis of social control. A person's attachment to and participation in the more remote societal institutions are not only mediated by intimate and primary groupings and local social organizations. The connections between the person and the so-

6. W. I. Thomas, *The Child in America: Behavior Problems and Programs* (New York: Knopf, 1928).

7. Erik H. Erikson, *Childhood and Society* (New York: Norton, 1950), chap. 7.

8. Harold Lasswell, *Psychopathology and Politics* (Chicago: University of Chicago Press, 1930), pp. 261–63; Alexander Goldenweiser, "Some Contributions of Psychoanalysis to the Interpretation of Social Facts," in *Contemporary Social Theory*, ed. Harry Elmer Barnes, Howard Becker, and Francis Becker (New York: Appleton-Century, 1940), pp. 391–430.

ciety (and the state) have more direct dimensions of great symbolic content.[9] These more direct linkages among the mass of the citizenry and elite groups cannot be explored without references to social-psychological and personality content. Thus, it is necessary to distinguish the processes of microsocialization and local socialization from those of societal socialization. . . .

The substantive meaning of social control is grounded in persuasion, although . . . the mechanisms of social control assume a minimum—an irreducible minimum—of legitimate coercion and physical sanctions. However, the terms "persuasion" and "coercion" have their common-sense and their "primitive" social-science meanings by reference to the personality concept. Persuasion is "to induce by arguments," and to "affect beliefs." It is not possible to think about social control without assuming that the person is engaged in periodic modification of his beliefs on the basis of persuasion, both interpersonal and mass.

On the other hand, coercion is the "use of physical force to control a person or a group." The brute efforts to negate a person's "will" imply that there is a a core of attitudes and predispositions to behave which characterize the person and his social groupings. The goal of coercion—even of legitimate coercive sanction—is not only to modify behavior but to condition underlying personality as well.

Systemic analysis seeks to emphasize and clarify the distinction between persuasion and coercion. The value orientation of the social control perspective works to this end. However, in reality, aspects of persuasion, especially mass persuasion, and coercive sanctions become fused and difficult to separate. The term "coercive persuasion" is a linguistic barbarism but it is not a sociological contradiction. It refers to direct use of symbols to achieve coercive controls. Coercive persuasion is to be found in social mechanisms, from the intensive small group"encounters" which have been called brainwashing to particular forms of behavior modification.[10] In effect, the elements of meaningful

9. The direct relation between the person and the nation-state is epitomized by the not infrequent response of well-educated and highly politically involved voters in the 1976 presidential election who resolved their indecisions only when actually in the voting booth. As reported by one respondent, "I entered the voting booth committed to the idea that I would not vote for President. But when I saw the label, 'President,' I knew I had no option but to vote for the highest office in the land, and then I finally gave in and voted for Carter."

10. H. Schein, Coercive Persuasion: A Socio-Psychological Analysis of American Civilian Prisoners of the Chinese Communists (New York: Norton, 1961).

persuasion have been removed, and from the perspective of social control we are dealing with an essential reliance on coercive control.

On the other hand, we also have the idea of and actuality of symbolic force or symbolic coercion. From the writings of Georges Sorel until those of Frantz Fanon, these notions have attracted attention, especially among university-based intellectuals.[11] Violence and the various forms of coercion are characterized, not in terms of the physical element and physical consequences, but rather in terms of their symbolic content and manifestation. The resort to violence sets in motion, for the person and the group, social-psychological processes of personal emancipation and social development. In this view, the application of coercion is to be seen as an educative process. From the perspective of social control, such a formulation is at best a play on words. The definition and the application of symbolic violence are to be seen as a specialized form of violence and coercion.

By contrast, . . . the goal of social control is the reduction of violence and coercion, by strengthening group self-regulation. Such self-regulation is enhanced by the strength of personal control. . . . Personal control means a person's capacity to channel his energies and to satisfy his needs and impulses while minimizing damage to himself and to others.[12] Personal control—to the extent that it operates—cannot be only the result of intimate or local or metropolitan socialization. Personal control and the resulting contributions to social control involve macrosociological or societal-wide mechanisms of socialization. In this sense the social organization of an advanced industrial society rests on a national system of persuasion and legitimate coercion, and the resultant internalization of the operative norms. Thus it is not metaphysical to assert that the person has direct connections with the nation-state. . . .

Our task is not limited to making use of "psychological" variables to explain differences in attitudes and values within particular social groups or social segments. Instead, personal control emerges as an equivalent conception to social control, which has particular relevance in exploring a person's attachment or lack of it to the larger societal collectivity.

There are value judgments involved in relating social control to personal control; but we are not dealing with a set of personal prefer-

11. Georges Sorel, *Réflexions sur la violence* (Paris: Rivière, 1946).
12. See Bruno Bettelheim and Morris Janowitz, *Social Change and Prejudice* (New York: Free Press, 1964), pp. 198–244.

ences. We are dealing with the subjective dimension of changing patterns of institutional authority. In a competitive political democracy, the mass electorate—even those members of limited education—must be able, in theory and practice, to choose deliberately between political candidates. This deliberate choice can be heavily influenced by communal traditions and concern for the personalities of the contenders, but there must be, over the long run, a component of autonomy in the decision.

The idea of personal control is not based on an "oversocialized" human being for whom the exercise of autonomy creates "destructive" strain and personal conflict.[13] In the most fundamental terms, personal control implies that there is acceptance of external authority, not mere submission to authority. In turn, the person's social personality has been molded to permit some degree of autonomy with respect to external authority, or at least to have some element of psychological distance or realistic awareness about authority processes.

An elaboration of the language of psychoanalysis at this point articulates with the institutional approach which has been pursued. It is possible to identify three types of psychological control which relate the person to the institutions of social control; *external, superego,* and *ego* (or personal) control. These relations reflect the accumulated outcome of socialization, local and societal.

External control or the submission to external authority reflects a minimum of internalization and the minimum of development of personal autonomy. It must therefore be based on the immediate physical or symbolic presence of external authority, and extensive reliance on coercive authority. It reflects the subjective dimension of authority based on domination, and requires a pervasive component of physical coercion or a coercive psychological climate; submission to external authority is in effect the opposite to personal control. In contrast, *superego control,* or conscience control, reflects a concern with moral principle—that is, with collective responsibility and with the means for achieving group goals. Superego control implies that the person recognizes that a narrow, blind pursuit of self-interest is not an effective basis for a moral order. (Group goals can be formulated and expressed in terms of the importance of enlightened self-interest.) But the essential psychological aspect of superego control is that it relies on the availability of particular external agents—parents, teachers, reli-

13. Dennis Wrong, "The Oversocialized Conception of Man in Modern Sociology," *American Sociological Review* 26 (April 1961): 182–93.

gious leaders, political officials—to reassert and reinforce the relevance of the "higher moral" principles.

If superego control depends on continuous and continued external reinforcement, *ego control*—that is, personal control—has a critical element of self-generation and self-regulation. The antisocial and irrational tendencies of the person are moved to some extent into the sphere of consciousness and therefore become accessible to rational intervention. But there is no need to assert a sharp distinction or inherent opposition between emotional predisposition and ego control; rather, their complex interpenetration must be recognized. Again a wide range of psychological theories converge; personal control and rational behavior are not self-sustained but require emotive interaction and group attachments.

These forms of psychological control relate directly to the changed character of institutional authority and to the long-term shift from authority based on domination to authority incorporating manipulation—or authority based on consent, if one cannot use "manipulation" in a nonpejorative sense. Thus it is obvious that the trends in the social organization of the United States require stronger, more extensive reliance on personal control if effective social control is to be achieved. It is equally obvious that the strengthening of personal controls has not proceeded at a sufficiently rapid pace to achieve this goal.

Since the social control perspective rejects the "rational man" conception, it recognizes that even under the optimum social conditions, acceptance of external control would operate in wide areas of social behavior. In the process of socialization, the limits of personal control, that is, ego control, are manifested in particular in the person's direct attachment to the nation-state and his sense of nationality. Acceptance of external authority in varying degrees is dictated by the reality of the boundaries, both functional and symbolic, of the nation-state.[14] The limited growth of supranational institutions hardly alters the fundamental fact that the nation-state remains the organizing unit of the world community.

The strength of national attachments does not mean that local attachments become extinct; we have emphasized that local attachments become more specialized. Likewise, it is hoped that the growth of a world community perspective does not necessarily require the atrophying of national sentiments but rather a modification of their con-

14. Leonard W. Doob, *Patriotism and Nationalism: Their Psychological Foundations* (New Haven: Yale University Press, 1964).

tent and scope. There is no reason to assume that we are dealing with a zero sum game. In fact, it would be more appropriate to assert that the maturation of personal and social control increases a person's capacity to relate himself to more and more encompassing systems of authority.

Ethnicity, religion, regionalism, and the like are the intervening dimensions in a sense of nationality. Harold D. Lasswell's phrase "world politics and personal insecurity" highlights the immediate interaction of social personality and national identifications. A sense of nationality reflects inner feelings which through socialization become externalized attitudes. In this process, the person, for better or for worse, manifests an acceptance of external authority and even of submission to external authority.

We do not have a body of trend data on the increase or decrease in the strength of national sentiments in the United States for the period since World War I. Social scientists have failed to include questions on this central topic in their sample surveys. It could be that social scientists' highly critical attitudes and indifference to national symbols account for this lack. But it would be in error to infer that the limited number of trend data reflect an atrophying of national sentiment and patriotism in the United States.

There *has* been a growth of indifference, even of hostility, toward the symbols of nationalism among a very limited part of the population. This includes persons with extensive higher education and with strong oppositional attitudes. The events of Vietnam supplied the justification for the expression of such sentiments. Representatives of this segment are very visible and include persons in the mass media.

On the other hand, there has been a long-term countertrend in the growth of nationalism since 1920. One might even speak of the shift from "old-fashioned" patriotism into a more elaborate sense of national "spirit." The decline of ethnic nationalist sentiments and the incorporation of submerged groups into the social and political structure of the society mean that a larger proportion of the population feel that they are "Americans." For a small portion whose size is difficult to estimate, nationalist attitudes are defensive and stereotypic, a form of reactive nationalism. The nationalist feelings do not articulate with the realities of the position of the United States in the world community. However, for most of the population, World War II transformed or extended the meaning of nationalism. In contrast to the period after World War I, the new nationalism was compatible with extensive international perspectives and interests. The frustrations of the Vietnam War and the impact of domestic and economic tensions began to constrict the "enlightened" nationalism. Likewise, the persistent criticism of the United States in the mass media by oppositionist spokesmen and journalists contributed to the mobilization of defensive and stereo-typic nationalism and old-fashioned "patriotism."

On balance, as of 1976, nationalist identifications in the United States remain pervasive and are central in the organization of citizen attitudes. However, we are dealing with a complex and unstable ad-mixture of "enlightened nationalism" and strong components of "re-active patriotism." It is within this nationalistic context that societal socialization takes place and in which the following hypotheses about the consequences of the instrumentalities of the media and legitimate coercion are offered.

It is our general assumption that the mass media over a half-century have become more important in the process of societal socialization and accordingly in influencing specific political and electoral behavior of the citizenry. Again, this is not a predetermined, inevitable, or linear trend. There are built-in limitations and the possibility of a reversal. The increased importance of the mass media reflects fundamental changes in the social organization of an advanced industrial society. In our analysis, in particular, the increased disarticulation between the hierarchical bureaucracies of work and occupation and the structure of residential communities are the preconditions.

We are dealing not only with the traditional arguments about the increased complexity of the division of labor and enlarged magnitude of scale, but also with the result of the growth of the welfare state, which complicates a person's enlightened pursuit of his self-interest in the political arena. The interest groups, voluntary associations, and political institutions reflect the disarticulation between work and com-munal attachment. As a result, advanced industrial society requires higher levels of personal controls both to link the person to the nation-state and to contribute to the quality of citizen participation. . . .

9

Cohesion and Disintegration in the Wehrmacht in World War II

The Army as a Social Group

This study is an attempt to analyze the relative influence of primary and secondary group situations on the high degree of stability of the German Army in World War II. It also seeks to evaluate the impact of the Western Allies' propaganda on the German army's fighting effectiveness.[1]

Although distinctly outnumbered and in a strategic sense quantitatively inferior in equipment, the German army, on all fronts, maintained a high degree of organizational integrity and fighting effectiveness through a series of almost unbroken retreats over a period of several years. In the final phase, the German armies were broken into unconnected segments, and the remnants were overrun as the major lines of communication and command were broken. Nevertheless, resistance which was more than token resistance on the part of most divisions continued until they were overpowered or overrun in a way which, by breaking communication lines, prevented individual battalions and companies from operating in a coherent fashion. Disintegration through desertion was insignificant, while active surrender, individually or in groups, remained extremely limited throughout the entire Western campaign.

In one sense the German High Command effected as complete a defense of the "European Fortress" as its own leadership qualities and the technical means at its disposal permitted. Official military analyses, including General Eisenhower's report, have shown that lack of manpower, equipment, and transportation, as well as certain strate-

Coauthored with Edward A. Shils. From *Public Opinion Quarterly* 12 (summer 1948): 280–92. © 1948 by The University of Chicago. All rights reserved.

1. For a further treatment of these problems see Henry V. Dicks, "Personality Traits and National Socialist Ideology," *Human Relations* (June 1950: 3:1 111–55.

gical errors, were the limiting factors.[2] There was neither complete collapse nor internally organized effort to terminate hostilities, such as signalized the end of the first world war.

This extraordinary tenacity of the German army has frequently been attributed to the strong National Socialist political convictions of the German soldiers. It is the main hypothesis of this paper, however, that the unity of the German army was in fact sustained only to a very slight extent by the National Socialist political convictions of its members, and that more important in the motivation of the determined resistance of the German soldier was the steady satisfaction of certain *primary* personality demands afforded by the social organization of the army.

This basic hypothesis may be elaborated in the following terms.

1. It appears that a soldier's ability to resist is a function of the capacity of his immediate primary group (his squad or section) to avoid social disintegration. When the individual's immediate group, and its supporting formations, met his basic organic needs, offered him affection and esteem from both officers and comrades, supplied him with a sense of power, and adequately regulated his relations with authority, the element of self-concern in battle, which would lead to disruption of the effective functioning of his primary group, was minimized.

2. The capacity of the primary group to resist disintegration was dependent on the acceptance of political, ideological, and cultural symbols (all secondary symbols) only to the extent that these secondary symbols became directly associated with primary gratifications.

3. Once disruption of primary-group life resulted through separation, breaks in communications, loss of leadership, depletion of personnel, or major and prolonged breaks in the supply of food and medical care, such an ascendancy of preoccupation with physical survival developed that there was very little "last-ditch" resistance.

4. Finally, as long as the primary-group structure of the component units of the Wehrmacht persisted, attempts by the Allies to cause disaffection by the invocation of secondary and political symbols (e.g., about the ethical wrongfulness of the National Socialist system) were mainly unsuccessful. By contrast, where Allied propaganda dealt with primary and personal values, particularly physical survival, it was more likely to be effective.

Long before D-Day in Western France, research was undertaken in the United Kingdom and North Africa on these social psychological

2. Report by the Supreme Commander on operations in Europe by Allied Expeditionary Force, June 6, 1944, to May 8, 1945.

aspects of the enemy's forces. These studies were continued after D-Day by the Intelligence Section of the Psychological Warfare Division of SHAEF. Although of course they are subject to many scientific strictures, they provide a groundwork for the evaluation of the experiences of the German soldier and for the analysis of the social organization of the German army. Methods of collecting data included front-line interrogation of prisoners of war (Ps/W) and intensive psychological interviews in rear areas. Captured enemy documents, statements of recaptured Allied military personnel, and the reports of combat observers were also studied. A monthly opinion poll of random samples of large numbers of Ps/W was also undertaken. This paper is based on a review of all these data.

Modes of Disintegration

Preliminary to the analysis of the function of the primary group in the maintenance of cohesion in the German army, it is necessary to classify the modes of social disintegration found in any modern army:

  1. Desertion (deliberately going over to the enemy lines)
     a) by individual action
        (1) after discussion with comrades
        (2) without prior discussion with others
     b) by groups acting in concert
  2. Active surrender (deliberate decision to give up to the enemy as he approaches and taking steps to facilitate capture, e.g., by sending emissaries, by calling out, by signaling, etc.)
     a) by single individuals
     b) by group as a unit
        (1) by mutual agreement
        (2) by order of or with approval of NCO or officer
     c) by plurality of uncoordinated individuals
  3. Passive surrender
     a) by individuals acting alone
        (1) nonresistance (allowing oneself to be taken prisoner without taking effective steps to facilitate or obstruct capture; passivity may be a means of facilitating surrender)
        (2) token resistance (allowing oneself to be taken prisoner with nominal face-saving gestures of obstruction to capture)
     b) by plurality of uncoordinated individuals
  4. Routine resistance: rote or mechanical, but effective, execution of orders as given from above with discontinuance when the enemy be-

comes overwhelmingly powerful and aggressive.

5. "Last-ditch" resistance which ends only with the exhaustion of fighting equipment and subsequent surrender or death. (This type of soldier is greatly underrepresented in studies of samples of Ps/W. Therefore the study of Ps/W alone does not give an adequate picture of the resistive qualities of the German soldier.)

A more detailed description of each of the above classes will be useful in the following analysis:

Desertion involved positive and deliberate action by the German soldier to deliver himself to Allied soldiers for capture by crossing the lines, e.g., by planfully "losing himself" while on patrol and "blundering" into the enemy's area of control or by deliberately remaining behind during a withdrawal from a given position so that when the Allied troops came up they could take him.

In *active surrender* by the group as a unit, the positive act of moving across to enemy lines was absent but there was an element common with desertion in the deliberate attempt to withdraw from further combat. Like many cases of desertion, the decision to surrender as a group was arrived at as a result of group discussion and mutual agreement. The dividing line between active surrender and desertion brought about by lagging behind was shadowy. There were other forms of group surrender which were clearly different from desertion, e.g., the sending of an emissary to arrange terms with the enemy; the refusal to carry out aggressive orders, or to fight a way out of encirclement.

In *passive surrender,* the intention of a soldier to remove himself from the battle was often not clear even to himself. The soldier who was taken prisoner by passive surrender might have been immobilized or apathetic due to anxiety; he might have been in a state of bewildered isolation and not have thought of passive surrender until the perception of an opportunity brought it to his mind. Nonresistant passive surrender frequently occurred in the case of soldiers who lay in their foxholes or hid in the cellars or barns, sometimes self-narcotized by fear, or sometimes deliberately waiting to be overrun. In both cases, they made only the most limited external gestures of resistance when the enemy approached. In the second type of passive surrender—token resistance—the surrendering soldier desired to avoid all the stigma of desertion or surrender but nevertheless showed reluctance to undertake aggressive or defensive actions which might have interfered with his survival.

An examination of the basic social organization of the German army, in terms of its primary-group structure and the factors which strengthened and weakened its component primary groups, is first required in order to account for the stability and cohesion of resistance, and in order to evaluate the impact of Allied propaganda.

The Function of the Primary Group[3]

> "The company is the only truly existent community. This community allows neither time nor rest for a personal life. It forces us into its circle, for life is at stake. Obviously compromises must be made and claims be surrendered. . . . Therefore the idea of fighting, living, and dying for the fatherland, for the cultural possessions of the fatherland, is but a relatively distant thought. At least it does not play a great role in the practical motivations of the individual."[4]

Thus wrote an idealistic German student in the first world war. A German sergeant, captured toward the end of the second world war, was asked by his interrogators about the political opinions of his men. In reply, he laughed and said, "When you ask such a question, I realize well that you have no idea of what makes a soldier fight. The soldiers lie in their holes and are happy if they live through the next day. If we think at all, it's about the end of the war and then home."

The fighting effectiveness of the vast majority of soldiers in combat depends only to a small extent on their preoccupation with the major political values which might be affected by the outcome of the war and which are the object of concern to statesmen and publicists. There are of course soldiers in whom such motivations are important. Volunteer armies recruited on the basis of ethical or political loyalties, such as the International Brigade in the Spanish Civil War, are affected by their degree of orientation toward major political goals. In the German army, the "hard core" of National Socialists were similarly motivated.

But in a conscript army, the criterion of recruitment is much less specialized and the army is more representative of the total population liable to conscription. Therefore the values involved in political and

3. Charles Horton Cooley, in *Social Organization* (New York, 1909), defines primary groups: "By primary groups I mean those characterized by intimate face-to-face association and cooperation . . . it is 'we'; it involves the sort of sympathy and mutual identification for which 'we' is the natural expression. One lives in the feeling of the whole and finds the chief aims of his will in that feeling" (p. 23). "The most important spheres of this intimate association and cooperation—though by no means the only ones—are the family, the play group of children, and the neighborhood or community group of elders" (p. 24). "The only essential thing being a certain intimacy and fusion of personalities" (p. 26).

4. *Kriegsbriefe gefallener Studenten*, 1928, pp. 167–72. Quoted by William K. Pfeiler, *War and the German Mind* (New York, 1941), p. 77.

social systems or ethical schemes do not have much impact on the determination of a soldier to fight to the best of his ability and to hold out as long as possible. For the ordinary German soldier the decisive fact was that he was a member of a squad or section which maintained its structural integrity and which coincided roughly with the *social* unit which satisfied some of his major primary needs.[5] He was likely to go on fighting, provided he had the necessary weapons, as long as the group possessed leadership with which he could identify himself, and as long as he gave affection to and received affection from the other members of his squad and platoon. In other words, as long as he felt himself to be a member of his primary group and therefore bound by the expectations and demands of its other members, his soldierly achievement was likely to be good.

Modern social research has shown that the primary group is not merely the chief source of affection and accordingly the major factor in personality formation in infancy and childhood. The primary group continues to be the major source of social and psychological sustenance through adulthood.[6] In the army, when isolated from civilian primary groups, the individual soldier comes to depend more and more on his military primary group. His spontaneous loyalties are to its immediate members whom he sees daily and with whom he develops a high degree of intimacy. For the German soldier in particular, the demands of his group, reinforced by officially prescribed rules, had the effect of an external authority. It held his aggressiveness in check; it provided discipline, protection, and freedom from autonomous decision.[7]

Army units with a high degree of primary-group integrity suffered little from desertions or from individually contrived surrenders. In the Wehrmacht, desertions and surrenders were most frequent in groups of heterogeneous ethnic composition in which Austrians, Czechs, and Poles were randomly intermixed with each other. In such groups the difficulties of linguistic communication, the large amount of individual

5. On the relations between the *technical* group and *social* group, cf. T. N. Whitehead, *Leadership in a Free Society* (Cambridge, Mass., 1936), chap. 4.

6. Cooley, *Social Organization*, part 1, pp. 3–57; S. Freud, *Group Psychology and the Analysis of the Ego*, chap. 4; Elton Mayo, *The Human Problems of an Industrial Civilization* (New York, 1933); A. T. M. Wilson, "The Service Man Comes Home," *Pilot Papers: Social Essays and Documents* 1:2 (April 1946): 9–28; R. R. Grinker and J. P. Spiegel, *Men under Stress* (Philadelphia, 1945), chap. 3; T. N. Whitehead, *Leadership in a Free Society,* chaps. 1, 7, 10; also A. D. Lindsay, *The Essentials of Democracy* (Oxford, 1935), pp. 78–81.

7. German combat soldiers almost always stressed the high level of camaraderie in their units. They frequently referred to their units as "one big family."

resentment and aggressiveness about coercion into German service, the weakened support of leadership due to their inability to identify with German officers—all these factors hampered the formation of cohesive groups.

Sample interviews with Wehrmacht deserters made in North Africa in 1943 and in France and Germany in 1944 and 1945 showed an overwhelmingly disproportionate representation of elements which could not be assimilated into primary groups. A total of 443 Wehrmacht Ps/W captured toward the end of the North African campaign, consisting of 180 Germans, 200 Austrians and 63 others (Czechs, Poles, Yugoslavs, etc.), had very markedly different tendencies toward desertion: 29 percent of the Germans were deserters or potential deserters; 55 percent of the Austrians fell into these two classes, as did 78 percent of the Czechs, Poles, and Yugoslavs. Of the 53 German deserters, only one declared that he had "political" motives for desertion. In the Western European campaign, the bulk of the deserters came from among the "Volksdeutsche,"[8] Austrians, Poles, and Russians who had been coerced into German military service. It was clear that in view of the apolitical character of most of the deserters, the grounds for their desertion were to be sought among those variables which prevented the formation of close primary-group bonds, the chief of which were insuperable language differences, bitter resentment against their coerced condition, and the unfriendliness of the Germans in their units.

Among German deserters, who remained few until the close of the war, the failure to assimilate into the primary-group life of the Wehrmacht was the most important factor, more important indeed than political dissidence. Deserters were on the whole men who had difficulty in personal adjustment, e.g., in the acceptance of affection or in the giving of affection. They were men who had shown these same difficulties in civilian life, having had difficulties with friends, work associates, and their own families, or having had criminal records. Political dissidents, on the other hand, when captured justified their failure to desert by invoking their sense of solidarity with their comrades and expressed the feeling that had they deserted when given a post of responsibility their comrades would have interpreted it as a breach of solidarity. For the political dissident, the verbal expression of political dissent was as much antiauthoritarianism as he could afford, and submission to his group was the price which he had to pay for it.

The persistent strength of primary-group controls was manifested

8. Individuals of German extraction residing outside the boundaries of Germany.

even in the last month of the war, when many deserters felt that they would not have been able to have taken the initial step in their desertion unless they had discussed the matter with their comrades and received some kind of legitimation for the action, such as a statement of approval.[9] And, on the other hand, the same ongoing efficacy of primary-group sentiment was evident in the statements of would-be deserters who declared they had never been able to cross the threshold because they had been told by their officers that the comrades who remained behind (i.e., the comrades of the men who had deserted) would be shot. Hence, one of the chief forms of disintegration which occurred in the last stages of the war took the form of group surrender, in which, after ample discussion within the unit, the authorization of the leading personalities and often of the NCO's had been granted for the offering of token resistance to facilitate capture, or even for outright group surrender.

Factors Strengthening Primary-Group Solidarity
The Nazi Nucleus of the Primary Group: The "Hard Core"

The stability and military effectiveness of the military primary group were in large measure a function of the "hard core," who approximated about 10 to 15 percent of the total of enlisted men; the percentage was higher for noncommissioned officers and was very much higher among the junior officers.[10] These were, on the whole, young men between 24 and 28 years of age who had had a gratifying adolescence in the most rewarding period of National Socialism. They were imbued with the ideology of gemeinschaft (community solidarity),[11] were enthusiasts for the military life, had definite homoerotic tendencies and accordingly placed a very high value on "toughness," manly comradeliness, and group solidarity.[12] The presence of a few such men in the group, zealous, energetic, and unsparing of themselves, provided models for weaker men, and facilitated the process of identification. For those for whom their charisma did not suffice and who were ac-

9. Approval of desertion by a married man with a large family or with heavy familial obligations was often noted near the war's end. For such men, the stronger ties to the family prevented the growth of insuperably strong ties to the army unit.

10. The "hard core" corresponds to opinion leaders, as the term is currently used in opinion research.

11. Herman Schmalenbach, "Die soziologische Kategorien des Bundes," *Die Dioskuren* 1 (München, 1922), pp. 35–105; and Hellmuth Plessner, *Grenzen der Gemeinschaft* (Bonn, 1924).

12. Hans Bluher, *Die Rolle der Erotik in der männlichen Gesellschaft* (Jena, 1921), vol. 2, part 2, especially pp. 91–109, 154–77.

cordingly difficult to incorporate fully into the intimate primary group, frowns, harsh words, and threats served as a check on divisive tendencies. The fact that the elite SS divisions and paratroop divisions had a larger "hard core" than other divisions of the army—so large as to embrace almost the entire group membership during most of the war—accounted for their greater fighting effectiveness. And the fact that such a "hard core" was almost entirely lacking from certain *Volksgrenadier* divisions helped to a considerable extent to account for the military inferiority of these units.

One of the functions of the "hard core" was to minimize the probability of divisive political discussions. There was, of course, little inclination to discuss political matters or even strategic aspects of the war among German soldiers. For this reason widespread defeatism concerning the outcome of the war had little consequence in affecting behavior (until the spring of 1945) because of the near impossibility—objective as well as subjective—of discussing or carrying out alternative plans of action.

In contrast with the "hard core," which was a disproportionately large strengthening factor in the integrity of the military primary group, the "soft core" was a source of infection which was by no means comparable in effectiveness. Unlike the first world war experience in which antiwar attitudes were often vigorously expressed and eagerly listened to by men who were "good comrades," in the second world war the political antimilitarist or anti-Nazi who expressed his views with frequency and vigor was also in the main not a "good comrade." There was a complete absence of soldiers' committees and organized opposition, even in March and April 1945 (except for the Bavarian Freiheitsaktion, which was constituted by rear-echelon troops). On isolated occasions, the Western Allies were able to exploit a man who had been a "good comrade" and who, after having been captured, expressed his defeatism and willingness to help end the war; he was thereupon sent back into the German line to talk his comrades into going over with him to the Allied lines. Here the "soft core" man exploited his comradely solidarity, and it was only on that basis that he was able to remove some of the members of his group from the influence of the "hard core."

Community of Experience as a Cohesive Force

The factors which affect group solidarity in general were on the whole carefully manipulated by the German general staff. Although during the war Germany was more permeated by foreigners than it had ever been before in its history, the army was to a great extent carefully protected from disintegrating influences of heterogeneity of ethnic and national origin, at least in crucial military situations. German officers saw that solidarity is fostered by the recollection of jointly experienced gratifications and that accordingly the groups who had gone through a victory together should not be dissolved but should be maintained as units to the greatest degree possible.

The replacement system of the Wehrmacht operated to the same end.[13] The entire personnel of a division would be withdrawn from the front simultaneously and refitted as a unit with replacements. Since new members were added to the division while it was out of line they were thereby given the opportunity to assimilate themselves into the group then the group as a whole was sent forward. This system continued until close to the end of the war and helped to explain the durability of the German army in the face of the overwhelming numerical and material superiority of the Allied forces.

Deterioration of group solidarity in the Wehrmacht which began to appear toward the very end of the war was most frequently found in hastily fabricated units. These were made up of new recruits, dragooned stragglers, air force men who had been forced into the infantry (and who felt a loss of status in the change), men transferred from the navy into the infantry to meet the emergency of manpower shortage, older factory workers, concentration camp inmates, and older married men who had been kept in reserve throughout the war and who had remained with the familial primary group until the last moment. The latter, who were the "catch" of the last "total mobilization," carried with them the resentment and bitterness which the "total mobilization" produced and which prevented the flow of affection necessary for group formation. It was clear that groups so diverse in age composition and background, and especially so mixed in their reactions to becoming infantrymen, could not very quickly become effective fighting units. They had no time to become used to one another and to develop the type of friendliness which is possible only when loyalties to outside groups have been renounced—or at least put into the background. A preview of what was to occur when units became mixed was provided by the 275th Fusilier Battalion, which broke up before

13. This policy sometimes created a serious dilemma for the Wehrmacht. Increasingly, to preserve the sense of group identity and the benefits of solidarity which arose from it, regiments were allowed to become depleted in manpower by as much as 50 to 75 percent. This, however, generated such feelings of weakness that the solidarity gains were canceled.

the First U.S. Army drive in November. Thirty-five Ps/W interrogated from this unit turned out to have been recently scraped together from fifteen different army units.

The most ineffective of all the military formations employed by the Wehrmacht during the war were the Volkssturm units. They ranged in age from boys to old men, and were not even given basic training in the weapons which they were supposed to use. Their officers were Nazi local functionaries who were already objects of hostility and who were therefore unable to release a flow of affection among equals. They had moreover not broken their family ties to the slightest extent. They still remained members of a primary group which did not fuse into the military primary group. Finally, they had no uniforms. They had only brassards to identify them and through which to identify themselves with one another. The mutual identification function of the uniform which plays so great a role in military units was thereby lost. As soon as they were left to their own devices, they disintegrated from within, deserting in large numbers to their homes, hiding, permitting themselves to be captured, etc.

Factors Weakening Primary-Group Solidarity
Isolation

The disintegration of a primary group depends in part on the physical and spatial variables which isolate it from the continuous pressure of face-to-face contact. The factor of spatial proximity in the maintenance of group solidarity in military situations must not be underestimated. In February and March of 1945, isolated remnants of platoons and companies were surrendering in groups with increasing frequency. The tactical situation of defensive fighting under heavy American artillery bombardment and the deployment of rear outposts forced soldiers to take refuge in cellars, trenches, and other underground shelters in small groups of three and four. This prolonged isolation from the nucleus of the primary group for several days worked to reinforce the fear of destruction of the self, and thus had a disintegrative influence on primary-group relations.[14] A soldier who was isolated in a cellar or in a concrete bunker for several days and whose anxieties about physical survival were aggravated by the tactical hopelessness of his situation was a much more easily separable member of his group than one who, though fearing physical destruction, was still bound by the con-

14. This proposition is in opposition to the frequently asserted view that social solidarity of an intense sort is positively and linearly related to fear of threat from the outside.

tinuous and vital ties of working, eating, sleeping, and being at leisure together with his fellow soldiers.

This proposition regarding the high significance of the spatial variable for primary-group solidarity and the maintenance of the fighting effectiveness of an army is supported by the behavior of the retreating German army in North Africa in 1943, and in France and Germany in September–October 1944 and March 1945. As long as a retreat is orderly and the structure of the component units of an army is maintained, strategic difficulties do not break up the army. An army in retreat breaks up only when the retreat is poorly organized, when command is lost over the men, so that they become separated from their units and become stragglers, or when enemy penetrations isolate larger or smaller formations from the main group.[15]

Stragglers first became a moderately serious problem in the German army in October 1944. On October 22, 1944, General Keitel ordered that a maximum of one to three days be allowed for stragglers to reattach themselves to their units. The previous limit had been five days. The aggravation of the straggler problem was further documented by General Blaskowitz's order of March 5, 1945, according to which the category of stragglers was declared to have ceased to exist. Soldiers who lost contact with their own units were directed to attach themselves immediately to the "first troops in the line which [they] can contact. . . ."

Familial Ties and Primary-Group Disintegration

Prisoners of war remarked with considerable frequency that discussions about alternative paths of action by groups of soldiers who were entirely defeatist arose not from discussions about the war in its political or strategic aspects, but rather from discussions about the soldiers' families.[16] The recollection of concrete family experiences reactivated sentiments of dependence on the family for psychological support and correspondingly weakened the hold of the military primary group. It was in such contexts that German soldiers toward the end of the war were willing to discuss group surrender.

15. The Germans in the Channel ports were able to resist so long partly because the men remained together where they were constantly in each other's presence. Thus the authority of the group over the individual was constantly in play.

16. A 36-year-old soldier—a Berlin radio worker—who surrendered prematurely, said: "During one month in a bunker without light and without much to do, the men often discussed capture. Conversation usually started about families: who was married and what was to become of his family? The subject became more acute as the Americans approached."

To prevent preoccupation with family concerns, the families of German soldiers were given strict instructions to avoid references to family deprivations in letters to the front. In the winter and spring of 1945, when Allied air raids became so destructive of communal life, all telegrams to soldiers at the front had to be passed by party officials in order to insure that no distracting news reached the soldiers. On the other hand, care was taken by party and army authorities that soldiers should not be left in a state of anxiety about their families, and to this end vigorous propaganda was carried on to stimulate correspondence with soldiers at the front. For those who had no families and who needed the supplementary affection which the army unit could not provide, provisions were made to obtain mail from individuals (including party officials) who would befriend unmarried or family-less soldiers, with the result that the psychic economy of the soldier was kept in equilibrium.

There was, however, a special type of situation in which the very strength of familial ties served to keep the army from further disintegration. This arose toward the end of the war, when soldiers were warned that desertion would result in severe sanctions being inflicted on the deserter's family.[17]

Toward the end of the war, soldiers tended to break away from the army more often while they were on leave and with their families, and therefore isolated from personal contact with their primary-group fellows. When soldiers returned to visit their families, then the conflict between contradictory primary-group loyalties became acute. The hold of the military primary group became debilitated in the absence of face-to-face contacts. The prospect of facing, on return to the front, physical destruction or a prolonged loss of affection from the civilian primary group, especially the family, prompted an increasing number of desertions while on furlough.

All of these factors contributed to loosen the solidarity of the German army, especially when the prospect of physical destruction began to weigh more heavily. Severe threats to the safety of the civilian primary group created anxiety which often weakened the hold of the military primary group. When the area of the soldier's home was occupied by the enemy or when the soldier himself was fighting in the area, there

17. This threat was never actually carried out. Furthermore, the *Sicherheitsdienst* (Security Service) admitted the impossibility of taking sanctions against the deserter's family because of the difficulty of locating them in the disorder of German civilian life. As the German soldiers became aware of the impotence of the SD in this respect, this barrier against desertion weakened.

was strong disposition to desert homeward. One such soldier said: "Now I have nothing more for which to fight, because my home is occupied."

The strong pull of the civilian primary group became stronger as the coherence of the army group weakened. But sometimes the former worked to keep the men fighting in their units, i.e., when they reasoned that the shortest way home was to keep the group intact and to avoid capture or desertion. Otherwise there would ensue a long period in an enemy P/W camp. On the other hand, in the event of the defeat of a still intact army, there would be only a short period of waiting before demobilization.

Demand for Physical Survival

The individual soldier's fear of destruction ultimately pressed to weaken primary-group cohesion; nevertheless it is striking to note the degree to which demands for physical survival could be exploited by Wehrmacht authority to the end of prolonging resistance. Where the social conditions were otherwise favorable, the primary bonds of group solidarity were dissolved only under the most extreme circumstances of threat to the individual organism—in situations where the tactical prospects were utterly hopeless, under devastating artillery and air bombardment, or where the basic food and medical requirements were not being met. Although aware for a long time of the high probability of German defeat in the war and of the hopelessness of the numerous individual battles, very many German soldiers continued to resist without any serious deterioration in the quality of their fighting skill. But where the most basic physiological demands of the German soldier were threatened with complete frustration, the bonds of group solidarity were broken.

Concern about food and about health always reduces the solidarity of a group. Throughout the war, and until the period just before the end, German army medical services were maintained at a high level of efficiency; the decline in their efficiency coincides with the deterioration in the morale of the men. Special care was also observed in the management of the food supply, and accordingly few German soldiers felt that the food supplies were inadequate. Indeed, as late as October 1944, only 15 percent of a sample of 92 Ps/W declared that they were at all dissatisfied with army food. By January, however, the situation changed and Ps/W reported increased preoccupation with physical survival, with food, and the shortage of clothing. Soldiers in certain units were beginning to "scrounge." The extreme cold of the winter of

'44–'45 also began to tell on the men, whose military self-esteem was being reduced by the raggedness of their uniforms and the failure to obtain replacements for unsatisfactory equipment.

Thus, to keep groups integral, it was necessary not only to provide positive gratifications but also to reduce to a minimum the alternative possibilities of increasing the chances for survival by leaving the unit. For this reason the Nazis sought to counteract the fear of personal physical destruction in battle by telling the men that accurate records were kept on deserters and that not only would their families and property be made to suffer in the event of their desertion, but that after the war, upon their return to Germany, they, too, would be very severely punished. They were also told by their officers that German agents were operating in American and British P/W cages in order to report on violations of security and on deserters. A Wehrmacht leaflet to German soldiers mentioned the names of two deserters of the 980th Volksgrenadier who were alleged to have divulged information and stated that not only would their families be sent to prison and suffer the loss of their property and ration cards, but the men themselves would also be punished after the war. In actuality, they were often punished in the P/W camps by the extreme Nazis who exercised some control in certain camps.

For the same reason, as long as the front was relatively stable, the Wehrmacht officers increased the natural hazards of war by ordering mine fields to be laid, barbed wire to be set up, and special guards to be posted to limit the freedom of movement of isolated and psychologically unattached individuals who, in situations which offered the chance of safely withdrawing from the war, would have moved over to the enemy's lines. Although the number of avowedly would-be deserters remained very small until near the end of the war, even they were frequently immobilized for fear of being killed by the devices set up to prevent their separation from the group. The danger of destruction by the Allies in the event of desertion also played a part in keeping men attached to their military units. As one P/W who had thought of desertion but who never took action said, "by day our own people shoot us, by night yours do."

Another physical narcissistic element which contributed somewhat to resistance on the Western front was fear of castration in event of the loss of the war. (This was effective only among a minority of the German soldiers.) The guilt feelings of the Nazi soldiers who had slaughtered and marauded on the Eastern front, and elsewhere in Europe, and their projection onto the enemy of their own sadistic impulses, heightened their narcissistic apprehensiveness about damage to their vital organs and to their physical organism as a whole. Rumors of castration at the hands of the Russians circulated in the German army throughout the last three years of the war and it is likely that they were largely the result of ruthless methods on both sides.

The Nazis perceived the function of fear of personal destruction in the event of capture as a factor in keeping a group intact after the internal bonds had been loosened. There were accordingly situations in which SS detachments deliberately committed atrocities on enemy civilians and soldiers in order to increase the anxieties of German soldiers as to what would befall them in the event of their defeat and capture. This latter policy was particularly drastically applied by the Waffen-SS in the von Rundstedt counteroffensive. It appears to have been an effort to convince German soldiers that there were no alternatives but victory or resistance to the very end and that surrender or desertion would end with slaughter of the German soldiers, as it had in the cases of the Allied soldiers. This was not effective for the mass of the German soldiers, however, who were becoming convinced that the law-abiding British and Americans would not in most situations harm them upon capture.

The dread of destruction of the self, and the demand for physical survival, while breaking up the spontaneous solidarity of the military primary group in most cases, thus served under certain conditions to coerce the soldier into adherence to his group and to the execution of the orders of his superiors. . . .

10

Ethnic Intolerance and Hostility

... If ethnic intolerance is rooted in the intolerant individual's personality, then we must ask ourselves what in this society shapes personality in such a way that ethnic intolerance seems a frequent, if not a favorite, outlet for hostility. While it is not true, as the Marxist maintains, that ethnic intolerance is a consequence of the capitalist system, ethnic intolerance occurring within a capitalist society will nevertheless be deeply influenced in character by that society.

Intolerance is always an outlet for hostility, but ... it depends for its intensity on the degree of hostility accumulated, and on the strength of the controls which restrain it. While hostility against outgroups is probably as old as society, the particular form in which hostility occurs is particular to the society in which it appears. Although anti-Semitism has been present in slave societies, feudal societies, capitalist societies, and recently too in communist society, it appears in each case to have been a different social phenomenon. What is historically permanent in anti-Semitism, for example, is only that members of a particular religious or ethnic group have been persecuted. The German-Jewish scientist, banker, physician, or laborer whom Hitler persecuted was as different from the medieval Jewish ghetto pawnbroker as was the German SS man from the German peasant or master craftsman who persecuted Jews in the Middle Ages. And as different as they were from one another, so also were their persecutions. Their differences originated in the different forms of society in which they lived—societies which shaped their personalities, outlooks, motives, and actions, which aroused their hostility, created frustration, and controlled its discharge. Hence their motives in persecuting the Jews were equally different, and equally rooted in the structure of their society. ...

In a slave society in which one ethnic group rules another, the ruling group does more than simply tolerate the life—and even to some degree the well-being—of the discriminated group. The presence of this

From *Dynamics of Prejudice*, by Bruno Bettelheim and Morris Janowitz, pp. 162–73. Reprinted by permission of The Free Press, a division of Macmillan, Inc. © 1950 by The American Jewish Committee. © 1964 by The Free Press.

group is not only desired, it is vital to the working of society, and the latter, in case of need, must assure itself by warfare of securing new slaves. Some remnants of the attitudes originating in the needs of a slave society might account in part for observations made ... that while the very intolerant men asked for the deportation of Jews, almost none of them requested deportation of Negroes, but requested instead that they be kept in their "place." The reason may well be that the Negro, although discriminated against, is nevertheless experienced as an important member of society, or at least as a person who serves a useful function. If the Negro were to leave, it would be left to the white man to perform those less desirable tasks which are now relegated to the Negro. Thus ethnic intolerance in its modern form was unthinkable in a society whose ethnic outgroups actually provided the economic base, as in a slave society. As a matter of fact, there are many ways in which modern ethnic intolerance tends to reestablish settings which were characteristic of slave society—the Negro must know and keep in his "place"; the Jew and members of other inferior races must labor in the concentration camp.

Ethnic intolerance as a social phenomenon takes on markedly different aspects depending on the social structure in which it occurs, and can be comprehended only when viewed in the context of that society. The example of medieval anti-Semitism may serve as an additional illustration. Jewish persecution in the Middle Ages charged the Jews with enjoying ill-begotten wealth—and the desire to gain, through plundering their riches, was an important incentive. But in medieval anti-Semitism these seemed only random phenomena. What seemed to excite real ire in the populace was that the Jews refused to be saved, thus reviving and enforcing in the Christians repressed doubts about their own salvation. (Without firsthand knowledge, all statements about the inner psychological processes of individuals who lived during the medieval period must remain conjecture. Still it might be reasonable to assume that his id, superego, and ego served similar functions in the psychological apparatus, but were differently constituted than those of modern man. Cleanliness was considered vain, if not unhealthy; the content of the superego was ordained by the Church; and the priest and the Church provided the most powerful superego representation. The superego had no need to evoke symbols of self-respect or individual conscience for restraining ego and id—the fear of hell and damnation were much more powerful incentives. Moreover, the ego was not confronted with an abundance of choices, and a relatively weak ego sufficed for mastering the tasks of life. Life activities were more rigidly organized and less subject to freedom of choice than they are today and the ego was less taxed in its need to synthesize opposing tendencies. Which of these tendencies, and in which ways they might be satisfied was more or less ordered by rules and tradition.)

It seems reasonable to assume that the ego of medieval man was at least as much concerned with saving his immortal soul as it was with making his temporal life successful. It is difficult to decide where his individual superego began, and where the Church and its teaching served him in its stead. Even the true medieval heretics (St. John of the Cross, etc.) bowed to the authority of popes, of whose individual shortcomings they were not unaware.[1]

What the individual during the Middle Ages appears to have feared most was not loss in status or economic security, but loss of grace. Much as he might have cherished the former, it was far more important, and a much greater threat, to fear damnation and the loss of eternal life. But it was not always easy to live by the rules of the superego-Church. (That the Church permitted considerable id gratification may be disregarded for the purpose of this discussion.) The id pressed for a gratification that was not always sanctioned by the Church, so that the ego and individualized superego may often have joined forces in doubting salvation through religious conformity. Such doubts had to be done away with, had to be persecuted and extinguished. They were the greatest threat to the individual's integration. One way to eliminate this threat was to project the conflict onto the Jews. In the Middle Ages, the most frequent accusation made against Jews, and the one which aroused the greatest hatred, was that they had desecrated the host. Closely related was the other accusation that they had committed ritual murders, used children they had killed to say a black mass.

The example of the Marannos (Spanish Jews converted to Catholicism) shows that these accusations reflected a very probable origin of anti-Semitism at that time, namely the Christian's fear of being a bad Catholic (more so, at least, than modern accusations indicate the real reasons for modern anti-Semitism). These Spanish Jews were notoriously wealthy as well as culturally and politically influential, and

1. Thus the superego which forced them to take a stand against the temporary Church was not strong enough to assert its absolute independence. On the other hand, the Protestant reformers, and their forerunners from Wycliffe on, seem to have had more individualized superegos which permitted them to supplement faith with their own observations in taking a stand against Church and pope. But in this sense they were rather precursors of modern man than typically medieval and once the reforms they inaugurated were established, modern times had begun.

aside from religious accusations, their wealth, too, was held against them.[2] Still a change of religion put an end to their persecution, provided they really meant it. As soon as Spanish Jews became Catholics, they were not only permitted to retain status and wealth, but were frequently known to increase in both.

In modern times when religious appeals have been introduced as a basis for the persecution of Jews, they have nearly always fallen flat.[3] Religious fear, or such inner conflicts as are based on it, is just no longer important enough to motivate large masses. Again and again ritual murder stories have been circulated, but have never been widely believed, or at least not in urban centers. The only places where they were lent some credence and led to persecutions were in eastern Europe, where economic, political, and religious organization was still very similar to that of the Middle Ages (the last time in the notorious Beilis case of 1911). Religious conversion which protected Spanish Jews was ultimately of little help to Jews in Germany. Thus although in the two examples, the German and the Spanish, both religious and economic accusations were used, the religious was more basic in the Middle Ages, while it is insignificant in modern times. On the other hand, the economic accusation seems all-important in modern times. The racial issue raised in National Socialist Germany seems but a return to the Middle Ages with racialism taking the place of religion. But into this new "religion" one cannot be "admitted"—the infidel, the man of a lower race, must be extinguished.

While the ethos of medieval society was largely religious, that of the men studied was largely economic. By and large, the latter considered income as the main status-providing factor. Security itself was experienced mainly as economic—as job or income security—and even those men who valued intellectual achievement viewed it chiefly as an economic asset.

The men strove little for religious salvation, but they certainly wished for economic security, which was even more important to them than higher income, as some of them stated themselves. But economic security is not easily achieved in a competitive society. Moreover, the notion is widespread that in a competitive society everyone can better his status if he tries hard enough. This, of course, puts an added psy-

2. The modern accusation of clannishness (the one most frequently used by the men in the sample) was absent in medieval anti-Semitism, probably because the modern sense of isolation and the fear of alienation were not then prevalent.

3. Throughout the interviews when reasons for the dislike of Jews were mentioned, references to religion were almost totally absent.

chological burden on the man who does not even achieve an occupational position which he thinks will assure his economic well-being. In addition to not attaining needed security, he also experiences a blow to his self-esteem.

Thus the person who experiences a lowering of income is doubly deprived. He is dissatisfied with himself and in addition must fear for his economic welfare. Frustration therefore accumulates and presses for discharge in those men who experience downward mobility. To such men, ethnic discrimination offers a convenient outlet. But . . . it was not only those who experienced a lowering of economic status who were prejudiced, but also those who were stationary in that respect, although there was a significant difference in the intensity of intolerance between these two groups. In terms of existing society even the men whose status was unchanged had reason to be fearful, although they needed, in general, to be less anxious than those on the downgrade. The no-mobility group had failed to live up to the challenge that one better oneself which is inherent in competitive society. Although many social scientists would agree that to remain stationary in our society often indicates that a man has made good in competition, such an attitude is not yet part of the economic ethos. Therefore such men are not really at peace; their self-esteem, too, is threatened, though considerably less so than that of a member of the downwardly mobile group. Thus, among other reasons, even the stationary group took advantage of ethnic discrimination as a channel for the discharge of accumulated hostility. On the other hand, the upwardly mobile group, for their part, had gained enough courage from recent successes to feel they might weather a future depression which they, too, nevertheless feared.

. . . The intolerant men felt that the Jews were successful in those areas where they themselves had failed to make good. Their superegos—in line with the economic ethos of society—required that they increase their earnings and rise in the hierarchy of status. Against these demands, which they could not fulfill, the stationary and particularly the downwardly mobile group defended their egos by pointing to the Jews. It was the Jews, they claimed, who exercised undue control, possessed the money, and thus prevented their own success.

But these same groups among the sample were also the ones who were considerably more intolerant of Negroes than were the men who had risen economically. They could hardly accuse the Negroes of controlling them and thus blocking their advance, nor could they accuse them of possessing the money. Moreover, it has been pointed out that unacceptable id tendencies were most frequently projected onto Negroes, and these tendencies were certainly not required by the social ethos. If the specific form of intolerance in a given society is a function of that social structure and if the character of modern anti-Semitism is conditioned by the structure of modern society, the same must also hold true for intolerance toward the Negro. While the economic and social ethos which was evident among the sample generally required that a man should work hard, earn good money, and in that way better his status, by the same token it rejected tendencies toward laziness, lack of orderliness and cleanliness, unreliability, immorality, and loss of property through neglect.[4]

The type of accusations directed against the Negroes and the manner in which individual tendencies are projected onto that group are highly influenced by social mores. These mores decree which tendencies are unacceptable and which must be integrated and, if that is not possible, which must be eliminated. Those men who had risen occupationally (and to some degree those who had remained stationary) seem to have felt they had complied with the social ethos and thus felt less threatened by their instinctual desires. With their achievement they showed both the world and themselves that their rejected id tendencies interfered in no way with their doing their "duty." Their wish to "take things easy" was obviously no hindrance to their well-being and therefore implied considerably less of a threat to their integration than it did to the no-mobility or downwardly mobile groups. . . .

Obviously a man who is convinced that his stationary or even downward socioeconomic position is only temporary can view his position with greater equanimity than one who is more or less convinced it is permanent. He will be able to maintain his integration despite superego pressure for greater achievement. On the other hand, a person who views his occupational potential with pessimism, who fears that an impending change in the business cycle will lead to a loss of his present earning power, will be unable to integrate his superego's pressure and less able to permit himself even those id gratifications which someone more relatively secure can afford to enjoy with ease.

The degree to which a person is haunted by fear depends in good measure on what he feels is expected of him, either by himself or by others. Perhaps in the Middle Ages the man who felt sure he was saved was relatively free from fear and could therefore integrate the comparatively small amounts of aggression he might otherwise have dis-

4. The accusation that the presence of Negroes depreciates the value of property usually carries the definite connotation that such depreciation is due to willful neglect. To lose money or to occasion depreciation through chance rarely arouses the disgust which is created by supposedly willful negligence.

charged in ethnic hostility. On the other hand, by persecuting the un-
believers the man who feared his damnation might have tried to
demonstrate to himself, to others—and, he may have hoped, to God—
that he was not as bad a Christian as he feared. He, too, might have
been persecuting another "doubting" man so that he might temporarily forget his own doubts. At the same time such persecution allowed
him to discharge some of the hostility which was partially created by
his fear of damnation, a fear which arose from his doubts. According
to this study, many fears now related to intolerance are of an economic
nature, hence can be approached rationally and, perhaps, dissolved. In
many ways the situation is better in modern times, where few fears are
related to the inaccessible supernatural. There are still ways to demonstrate to a person that he may feel secure about his economic future—or there would be if a constant increase in earning power, and
success in competition were no longer a feature of economic security—while there was no way, in the Middle Ages, of assuring a man
of salvation. Of course, this holds true only in so far as, and as long as,
the economic system with its vastness, complexity, and lack of individual responsibility or comprehension of the consequences of economic
actions is not experienced by the individual as equally incomprehensi-
ble and overpowering as the supernatural appeared to the man of the
Middle Ages.

The Individual

After so much has been said about the economic concomitants of intolerance it should again be stressed . . . that objective reality seemed
comparatively less important in shaping interethnic attitudes than the
personal frame of reference within which objective reality is experienced. Despite the insecurities of the present day, quite a number of the
veterans had egos which were adequate enough to master economic
anxieties so that they were not forced to evaluate past, present, and
future experiences as deprivational. They were relatively free of fear
and found it possible to be optimistic even in adverse circumstances
(combat, threat of depression, etc.). Such optimism and the self-
confidence and self-respect which go with it, as well as the parallel
ability to control hostility, all originate in fortunate childhood experiences. Positive relationships to parents and other members of the primary group and sufficient gratification of instinctual needs during
childhood seem to equip a child with sufficient emotional strength to
grow into an adult who feels able to master the difficulties of contem-

porary life.⁵ Thus, in more than one way, anxiety about the future and the discharge of aggression in hostile action is a two-generation problem. The individual who has experienced even relative security in childhood will probably have acquired a personality structure which permits him to weather even relatively great frustrations and insecurities without experiencing them as a threat to his personal integration. He will not need to bolster his integration through the mechanism of projection, or the explosive and irrational discharge of hostility against members of an outgroup. On the other hand, a child born into a family which experiences actual deprivation during the child's most formative years will, in addition to actual deprivation, most probably be raised in an atmosphere of emotional insecurity. He will be unable to view his life experiences optimistically and thus every positive experience will lose much of its reassuring, ego-strengthening value. Conversely, every negative experience will seem according to expectation and thus even more deprivational and overpowering.⁶

5. Clinical observations of severely disturbed children permit several interesting inferences on the consequences of actual and emotional deprivation during infancy and childhood. Children who on initial examination showed comparable degrees of disturbance, nevertheless showed marked differences in improvement during psychiatric treatment, depending chiefly on their past life experiences. Children who had suffered severe actual deprivation because they had been raised in submarginal families or in orphanages soon improved markedly. The abundant gratification of instinctual and interpersonal needs, as provided by the new environment, during treatment—they lived in a psychiatric institution—permitted them to modify their outlook on life quite rapidly. They learned soon enough that past deprivations were only one of many possible kinds of experiences and realized that life has more to offer than they had once thought. Hence, they did their best to adjust to it. On the other hand, children of well-to-do families who had always enjoyed abundance with regard to food and shelter—children who, as a matter of fact, had often been resentfully "overprotected" and in whose case "good" care covered up for intense rejection—these children took very much longer to conceive of the gratification offered at the treatment institution as anything desirable. Clinically speaking, their task was much more complex when compared to that of the "orphans." It was easier for the economically deprived children to change their outlook on life once—contrary to previous expectations—abundant gratification was regularly available. The same offer, and even its acceptance, remained ungratifying to the emotionally deprived children of well-to-do parents. Such offerings and whatever else was done for them were evaluated in terms of their old, pessimistic frame of reference and were, hence, of no positive value.

6. In Germany, it was not the middle-aged group of men who had served in the first World War, and many of whom had experienced great losses in the after-war years, who furnished Hitler with his most ardent followers, although the leader himself and his officers came from that group. The bulk of the middle-aged men, despite the downward mobility they had generally experienced, manned the *Reichsbanner* and the *Stahlhelm* (the liberal and the conservative military organizations) and not the SS. In part, this can

... The interplay between personality structure and those forces originating in the social field seemed to condition the presence, the absence, and the nature of intolerance.

Thus if the personality is very strong, or if, for particular personal reasons, the individual is strongly committed to tolerance or intolerance, the influence of the social field in respect to tolerance or intolerance is relatively small. The weaker the personality, the stronger becomes the influence of the social field. On the basis of a purely psychological hypothesis, namely that ethnic intolerance is nothing but a cathartic outlet for hostility, it might be assumed that catharsis could be effected by discharging all hostility against a single group and that all other available groups could then go free. This study seems to show (and the combination of anti-Negro, anti-Jewish, and anti-Catholic feeling in certain southern areas seems to corroborate it) that the singling out of one group for hostile discharge seems to be ruled out by the social context.

The difference between anti-Jewish and anti-Negro attitudes, as it emerged in this study, also belies the assumption that ethnic intolerance is purely psychological in origin and hence beyond the reach of social reform. On the other hand, the association of intolerance with subjective rather than objective deprivation speaks against its purely social origin. Nor can the argument be accepted that ethnic intolerance cannot be dispensed with as an outlet for hostility. Hostility is continuously accumulating in the anxious and the insecure, and cannot be discharged in single or infrequent explosions. With rare exceptions it is not possible to discharge the accumulation of years of hostility, particularly if it did not originate in a particular person whose death or removal alone might yield a cathartic relief. Violent outbursts of ethnic

---

be explained by the fact that they had, in their childhood, experienced the relative stability which characterized Germany at the turn of the century; most of their families had in fact improved in economic status during those years.

The sons of these men had been infants when their fathers were away at war. Their early childhood was often characterized by instability; food had been scarce, and their mothers, in addition to worrying about their husbands, had been working in war factories to keep the family going. They were still boys or had grown into early adolescence when their own and their parents' hopes for a better life after the war were terribly shattered by inflation, deflation, and unemployment. As young men in the thirties, they could not believe they would ever be able to secure a decent life for themselves through their own efforts. Therefore they had to rely on a strong "leader," a father figure, to give them the emotional and economic security which their own fathers had been unable to provide. They had also to discharge the frustrations and hostility which had accumulated over a long period of insecurity and suffering, if they wished to retain their tenuous integration. Explosive action against minorities was then a convenient outlet.

intolerance are still so relatively rare, and provide so few of the intolerant men with direct or vicarious outlet, that the rationalization of the need for ethnic discrimination seems untenable. Moreover, it should be realized that while ethnic hostility only rarely provides full outlet for hostility, it frequently adds to already existing frustrations. Compared to the underlying hostility toward Jews and Negroes which some of the subjects revealed, the outlets of verbal animosity and an occasional physical aggression of little consequence seemed quite insufficient. On the other hand, a mental preoccupation with the hated minority together with a felt inability to do anything about it seemed to add more to the frustration of the very intolerant than it gave outlet for hostility.[7] For these reasons it does not seem true that ethnic hostility is incorrigible because it originates in the hostile personality and is needed as an outlet. Less hostility and less continuous frustration would accumulate if the intolerant person were forced to recognize once and for all that this outlet was no longer available. Some intolerant men would have to find other outlets, but many others would learn to integrate those hostile tendencies which they now try forever and in vain to discharge against ethnic minorities.

On the other hand, it seems invalid to argue that intolerant personality structures can no longer be changed and that similar changes in the future could be achieved only through a different form of personality formation.

The German example has certainly shown that radical changes in the social order produced deep-reaching if not necessarily permanent or desirable changes in the personality, although one must admit that it seems easier to disintegrate personality structure than to influence it toward higher integration.[8] Nevertheless, it is untrue to assume that nothing can be done about an existing generation and that all hopes for tolerance must rest with the future. Clinical experience also demonstrates that considerably greater and more permanently effective in producing modifications of personality structure than the extreme methods of National Socialism are those modifications of the environment which make it reassuring, secure, comprehensible, and thus manageable for the young individual. Such environments and their gentle

7. In seeking to understand prejudice, tolerant persons who reject ethnic hostility for valid reasons, as well as ethnic minorities who suffer from discrimination, often fail to realize that intolerant persons labor under an undischarged hostility which accumulates in them precisely because they are prejudiced. They experience constant frustration since they feel unable to do anything about a minority which they experience as a threat.

8. For example, see Bettelheim, B., "Individual and Mass Behavior in Extreme Situations," *Journal of Abnormal and Social Psychology* 38 (1943): 417–52.

but powerful challenge to identify with persons offering gratification and, therefore, to restrain hostility, produce changes in personality which are far-reaching indeed. This they do partly by reducing frustrations which derive from the environment, and partly by providing amply for all needs which can be satisfied. Under such conditions, little additional hostility is created, and existing or developing controls and powers of integration prove sufficient to contain it.[9] As one of many indications, it suggests that environmental changes may well be able to produce changes in personality structure and hence in intolerance.

As long as there are personality structures which remain poorly integrated—first because of upbringing and later because of too much tension created by insecurity and frustration—and as long as the individual's upbringing prevents him from acquiring adequate controls, for so long will society have to offer outlets for the discharge of hostility. On the other hand, as long as society continues to permit or to condone such hostile discharge, the individual will not be forced to integrate his hostilities, or to control them.

9. Even outside of deliberately planned environments, significant changes in personality structure due to changes in environment are constantly being observed. Among the most obvious but dramatic instances are the immigrants to this country who experienced far-reaching changes in personality during the process of adjusting to a socially and culturally different setting.

11

The Psychological Context of Welfare

It is appropriate to speculate about the psychology of the welfare state. The psychological effect of welfare schemes becomes a topic for tough-minded speculation. How can the consequences of welfare institutions be separated from the analysis of the more general influence of industrial and modern institutions? In addition, how does one examine the issue of the impact of modern war—and particularly the threat of nuclear destruction, which supplies the overriding context—a topic that cannot be said to have produced pointed research conclusions?

But the student of the difficulties of the welfare state and its mechanisms of social control can use three bodies of research: (a) the massive body of attitude studies that chart public opinion about politics and the agencies of government; (b) the body of literature that deals with the process of socialization of personality, especially that aspect that has come to stress the centrality of cognitive processes; and (c) the quantitative studies of self-destructive and deviant behavior.

Over the last quarter of a century, social research has made enormous efforts to use the sample survey to examine the structure of social attitudes under advanced industrialism. These efforts have been persistently criticized by writers like Herbert Blumer as using an individualist and mechanistic methodology, which gives their findings little analytic relevance. However, over the years this type of criticism has atrophied, from an intellectual point of view. It is impossible to think of contemporary analysis of social organization and political behavior, as well as collective psychology, without recourse to the massive and continuously collected survey and public opinion data. Sociologists with diverse policy perspectives, such as S. M. Lipset and Richard F. Hamilton, demonstrate their joint commitment to reliance on the sample survey for their analysis of attitudes about political authority and issues.[1]

From *Social Control of the Welfare State* (New York: Elsevier Scientific Publishing Co., 1976), pp. 100–110. Reprinted by permission of Gayle Janowitz.

1. S. M. Lipset and Earl Raab, *The Politics of Unreason: Right-Wing Extremism in America, 1890–1970* (New York: Harper and Row, 1970); Richard F. Hamilton, *Class and Politics in the United States* (New York: Wiley, 1972).

However, a profound paradox is involved in utilizing the sample survey to highlight the psychological context of the welfare state. The central relevance of the sample survey rests on its ability to chart changes in attitudes over time. But university-based sample surveys have essentially been used for ad hoc investigation of specific topics, and only in recent years has there been increased attention to trend data on social attitudes collected by means of sample surveys. Thus, Angus Campbell and Philip Converse's effort to synthesize available findings under the title *Human Consequences of Social Change* could present a comprehensive set of indicators of changes in attitudes about life chances and the expanded institutions of social welfare.[2] The most penetrating analysis of pertinent social attitudes about the effect of the welfare state is contained in W. G. Runciman's cross-sectional study *Social Justice and Relative Deprivation,* which seeks to explore the extent to which existing inequalities are viewed as legitimate by the British population.[3]

However, from the available survey data one can piece together measures about satisfaction with life chances and associated attitudes about the social order. As could have been expected, the emergence of stagflation, since 1970, has contributed to increased levels of personal discontent, less optimism about the welfare of one's children, and a decline in confidence and trust in the institutions of government. However, long-term trend data about intergroup attitudes and levels of prejudice warrant close attention. The tensions of advanced industrialism have been accompanied by continuous decline in prejudice toward minority groups, even during the period of racial disturbance and the subsequent impact of stagflation.[4] It remains to be assessed whether these attitudes reflect tolerance or just studied indifference. But the inference is that the institutions of social welfare serve to inhibit potential negative psychological impacts in this crucial regard.

Likewise, the research literature on socialization presents suggestive but fragmented insights into the patterns of social control under the welfare state. One central stream in this literature has emphasized the

2. Angus Campbell and Philip Converse, eds., *The Human Meaning of Social Change* (New York: Russell Sage Foundation, 1972).

3. W. G. Runciman, *Relative Deprivation and Social Justice: A Study of Attitudes to Social Inequality in Twentieth-Century England* (Berkeley, Calif.: University of California Press, 1966). See also Michael Schiltz, *Public Attitude toward Social Security, 1935–1965* (Washington, D.C.: Social Security Administration, Office of Research and Statistics, 1970).

4. Bruno Bettelheim and Morris Janowitz, *Social Change and Prejudice* (New York: The Free Press, 1975).

cognitive aspects of the socialization process rather than the emotive and unconscious process of human development. This emphasis has involved the formulation of models of human potentials—a shift reflecting the short-term economic productivity and abundance immediately after World War II. The lasting consequence of this form of psychological optimism has hardly been intellectually profound. The psychologist Jerome Bruner has been the leading spokesman for this perspective.[5] He has sought to reject the formulation of Jean Piaget, who focused on the development sequences of maturation. Instead, Bruner has offered this formulation, "We begin with the hypothesis that any subject can be taught effectively in some intellectually honest form to any child at any state of development." Such an assertion is patently not a hypothesis but a moral exhortation, since it rests on the crucial and completely ambiguous, or rather undefined, word "honest." The Bruner model had, for the moment, a strong influence on the American educational system with the proposition that early emphasis on cognitive skills would solve the "tough" questions of the socialization of mature, competent, and self-directed adults. This period, epitomized by the social movement of the new math and the "new curriculum," came quickly to an end under the impact of racial and student unrest.

Instead of a rigid cognitive approach to socialization, a broad and more comprehensive perspective—the institutional orientation—to the issues of socialization appears to have more enduring relevance. James Coleman and his study group have summarized the profound discontinuities associated with the transition from adolescence to adulthood in United States society.[6] They have focused on the narrow pathways mainly associated with academic performance in secondary school and the tensions that result from such overspecialization. The effective process of socialization, from this perspective, was asserted to rest on the combination of the academic with work experiences—in the fashion postulated by John Dewey over fifty years ago. While the ineffective process of youth socialization is concentrated in lower-income groups, the basic disarticulation extends throughout the entire social structure. In *Institution Building in Urban Education,* this author has analyzed the existing organization structure of mass education, which is seen as tending to differentiate the school from the urban

5. Jerome Bruner, *The Process of Education* (Cambridge, Mass.: Harvard University Press, 1960).

6. James S. Coleman, et al., *Youth: Transition to Adulthood: Report of the Panel on Youth of the President's Science Advisory Committee* (Chicago: University of Chicago Press, 1974).

environment and which internally operates on a fragmented basis because of the extreme specialization of its personnel.[7] Thus, the influence of advanced industrialization operates through educational institutions that are limited in their capacity to perform academic functions and to link academic goals to the broader goals of youth socialization.

The research literature on the impact of social welfare institutions is more descriptive and less oriented to the analytical considerations encountered in the study of public education. Nevertheless, the same organization processes appear. Whether one is dealing with the format of public housing or with welfare services associated with family assistance programs and community development, the overall effect on the process of socialization is to separate and in fact isolate the clients from the larger social structure and to seek to treat their needs in a very fragmented fashion. While these programs have eliminated the stark misery of oppressive poverty and the fear of starvation, they contain strong built-in limitations that thwart self-esteem and competence among recipients.

But speculation about the psychological context of the welfare state requires a perspective that goes beyond the social attitudes and even the institutional dimensions of socialization. We are dealing in essence with the most generic aspects of personality and their relations to the welfare state. Social welfare concepts and programs as they have developed in the United States—and even in societies with a strong democratic socialist tradition—emphasize strengthening benefits and welfare rights on an individual basis. The welfare state is a strategy for making use of collective symbols and practices to achieve goals that are cast in an individualist mold. Thus, the welfare state is an extension of the main lines of liberal democracy that are embodied in the political aspirations of the Western nation-state.

Material Conditions and Hedonism

It may well be that Sigmund Freud's argument in *Civilization and Its Discontents* and *Beyond the Pleasure Principle* supplies the underlying assumption for the exploration of these psychological dimensions of the welfare state.[8] The argument rests on the idea that social welfare

7. Morris Janowitz, *Institution Building in Urban Education* (Chicago: University of Chicago Press, 1971).

8. Sigmund Freud, trans. Jean Riviere, *Civilization and Its Discontents* (New York: J. Cape and H. Smith, 1930). Freud, trans. C. J. M. Hubback, *Beyond the Pleasure Principle* (London: The International Psycho-analytical Press, 1922).

has produced the same, or at least converging, psychological responses of frustration as those generated by the material and cultural accumulations of industrial civilization. The impact of civilization renders it more difficult and more complex to pursue "instinctually" grounded pleasure and gratification. One chief characteristic of the affluent society is that it creates a heightened sensitivity or drive for hedonism—it produces, if you will, a concern with raw hedonism. The pursuit of hedonism—and raw hedonism—takes place in the context of ineffective and weak limits on personal control and of self-indulgence. We are dealing not only with the dimension of moral restraints but also with the decline of stylized forms of ritual and ceremony.

The pursuit of hedonism and of impulse gratification under these circumstances becomes difficult to moderate and instead becomes more obsessive. The consequences of the heightened drive for hedonistic gratification in the absence of effective patterns of personal social control are distorted personal response and, fundamentally, an increase in unhappiness. The argument of Sigmund Freud parallels, as has been repeatedly pointed out, that presented by Emile Durkheim in *Le Suicide*.[9]

The admixture of increased material resources and changed normative values sets the context for the institutions of social welfare. The causes of human unhappiness are linked to those elements in the normative structure that emphasize the moral desirability of indulgence and gratification without creating a patterned structure of limits. This argument implies that the psychological distortion is exacerbated by the emphasis placed on the individual as the central judge of his psychic well-being rather than on the development of group standards and norms.

The issue can be stated in alternative terms. In modern society, there is a constant need for institutional efforts to define, redefine, and elaborate moral standards for behavior linked to personal gratification. For example, this is the role of the courts in elaborating the law. But in the drive for hedonism, the experience itself emerges as the central mechanism. The result must of necessity produce unhappiness for the individual person who is not supported by a network of intimate social relations that supply some normative standards about personal gratification.

It is indeed striking that in the 1960s the subject of happiness itself became the topic of empirical research.[10] The direct empirical assault

9. Émile Durkheim, *Le Suicide* (Paris: F. Alcan, 1897).
10. Norman Bradburn and David Caplovitz, *Reports on Happiness: A Pilot Study of Behavior Related to Mental Health* (Chicago: Aldine, 1965).

on the subject has demonstrated that it is elusive. There is no body of trend data to indicate that higher standards of living have produced a discernible increase in measurable "happiness." If anything, the contrary appears to be the case.

Sociologists have also assaulted the issue because of their immense commitment to the study of deviant behavior. Confronted by the increased intensity in the pursuit of hedonistic indulgence, many have sought to explore the sociological and psychological dimensions of pleasure by asserting that the definitions of deviant behavior are arbitrary.[11] One can speak of the spread and diffusion or the "democratization" of hedonism and deviant behavior. The full capacity of the human being for indulgence and gratification requires, from this perspective, an examination of his ability to circumvent the arbitrary barriers of an advanced industrial society and to uncover the real sources of gratification. But highly relativistic sociologists cannot overlook the point at which the behavior involved in the search for gratification becomes a self-destructive response.

As measured by overt behavior and not by psychic states, there have been two long-term trends, revealed by available research, during the emergence of the welfare state since 1945. First, there has been a steady increase in behavior that reflects the intensified drive for hedonistic gratification. This trend rests on increased affluence. The social indicators involve the increased per capita consumption of alcohol, tobacco, and drugs. There has also been a documented "quantitative" increase of sexual behavior. Second, for each of these overt pursuits of pleasure there has been an increase in the forms of behavior—deviant and otherwise—that must be labeled as self-destructive, without recourse to subtle moral, cultural, or political definitions. In addition to the indicators reflecting these particular indulgences, the central indicator of personal and social control remains, as for Durkheim, suicide, with its long-term increase and particularly among youth and minority groups. The joint operation of these trends emphasizes the argument of *Beyond the Pleasure Principle*. While the level of welfare for important segments of recipients leads to no more than a marginal existence, the long-term thrust of the system—actual and potential, with its direct and indirect effects—serves only to integrate the welfare recipient into the ineffective social control system of the larger society.

There are, of course, trends of varying strength and pervasiveness counter to self-centered hedonism. A tiny fraction of persons seek clas-

11. Howard Becker, *Outsiders: Studies in the Sociology of Deviance* (New York: The Free Press of Glencoe, 1963).

sic or modified forms of psychotherapy. The demand for therapy has increased with the spread of mass education and of social welfare institutions, and the welfare state does make some forms of psychotherapy available to submerged groups. The approaches required to adapt psychotherapy to the bureaucratized institutions of welfare remain problematic. Of particular importance has been the rapid emergence of the numerous forms of regressive therapy. (The basic criterion for judging regressive therapy is the likelihood of a damaging impact or a weakening effect on the ego's functions.) Through these forms, this therapy—which is not in reality "therapy"—becomes a further source of distorted and unsatisfactory pursuit "beyond the pleasure principle." [12] Likewise, the drive toward self-indulgence produces a variety of reaction formations in the society at large. Of particular note are the new intense, if fragile, group solidarities, the modern forms of "communalism." In these groups, the individual submerges his self-preoccupation on the basis of opposition to existing mores. The degree of personal commitment that is mobilized is deep and almost fearful. The "rationalistic" advanced industrial society generates its forms of communes—rural and urban—its student groups, its religious movements, and its semisecret formations. It may well be that these are movements of limited viability. There is a point at which they serve neither individual nor social needs, and the individual departs. In a society with great geographical mobility and elaborate role transitions, participation in these forms of "communion" may well be limited in duration for many. But these are psychological constructions of welfare, since these efforts will eventually have their influence on the broader institutions of contemporary society.

12. Kurt W. Back, *Beyond Words: The Story of Sensitivity Training and the Encounter Movement* (New York: Russell Sage Foundation, 1973).

IV

SOCIAL CONTROL: CITIZENSHIP AND DEMOCRATIC POLITY

12

Observations on the Sociology of Citizenship: Obligations and Rights

Equality, rather than citizenship, is a core concern of contemporary sociology. Yet citizenship becomes an indirect interest because it connotes the spread of citizen rights designed to enlarge the realm of equality—political, economic, and social. Sociological writings have therefore dealt with citizenship by and large in terms of the spread of citizen rights and the barriers to the equality of rights.

The result has been a basic distortion or at least pervasive omission in the sociology of citizenship. It is inescapable to me that citizenship involves some sort of balance or interplay between rights and obligations. It is impossible to study a polity, especially a democratic polity, without assessing the significance of citizen obligation. This paper seeks to redress this imbalance in the sociology of citizenship.

The imbalance in the sociological literature clearly reflects the relative priority on rights versus obligation in the political process of Western political democracies. I shall argue it does not require elaborate analysis to conclude that the original meaning of citizenship made reference to a balance of citizen rights and citizen obligations.[1] The long-term trend has been to emphasize and elaborate citizen rights without simultaneously clarifying the issues of citizen obligation. The content of obligation becomes particularly important with the advent of advanced industrialism.

Clearly the notion of citizenship requires continual, conceptual,

From *Social Forces* 59 (September 1980): 1–24. Reprinted by permission of The University of North Carolina Press. © 1980 by The University of North Carolina Press. All rights reserved.

1. If one asserts that citizenship in a political democracy involves a balance or an interplay between rights and obligations, then exchange theory and role theory, and especially the analysis of reciprocity, would be relevant. Such approaches are outside the scope of this paper. We are clearly dealing with exchanges and role relations which involve face to face and small group relations, but the idea of effective civic roles involves complex organizational arrangements. It is for these reasons that this paper focuses on an institutional analysis of citizenship.

philosophical, and value clarification. However, my paper is an institutional analysis of the arrangements of an advanced industrial society which are directly related to the exercise of citizenship. Are the societal institutions organized and articulated so as to make the practice of citizen duties and obligation possible? In particular, do they operate to help or to hinder the exercise of obligation?

I set for myself two tasks. The first is an examination of the formulation of two writers on citizenship. I start with the definitions of Aristotle and juxtapose them to the writings of the twentieth-century sociologist T. H. Marshall, who for the contemporary period is almost unique because he deals explicitly with citizen obligation. Although I clearly recognize the vast oceans of ideas which have been omitted, these men serve my particular purposes. Second, I seek to present my observations on the institutional bases for exercising citizen obligation. This involves updating Marshall's analysis in the light of a quarter of a century of societal change and new bodies of research.

Citizenship is a complex term with various meanings. Its past political success does not imply that its currency has rested on clarity or unity of perception on the part of electorate, political leaders, or intellectuals. Various meanings reflect different usages. First, citizenship is a moral judgment. To be called a good or real citizen is a particular positive judgment about the morality of one's behavior. It implies that the person is concerned with the collective interest and its well-being. Second, it is a concrete, empirical, and descriptive term. In this sense, citizenship refers to a particular set of obligations and rights vested in eligible persons in a specific nation-state. (While there were historical periods in which citizenship meant membership in a city-state, in the contemporary era, citizenship is linked exclusively to the nation-state). Third, citizenship can be thought of as an analytic term. In this sense, citizenship encompasses (a) the protection a state offers to its core members, (b) the opportunities a state creates for its core members for political participation, or (c) a combination of both these elements.

In any case, Aristotle's formulation supplies a symbolic and appropriate point of departure for my analysis. His views were linked to population size since he asserts the crucial importance of small size. Therefore, his perspective requires a fundamental explication to apply to contemporary mass society. But there is a powerful element of continuity between his formulation and that of T. H. Marshall, one of the few contemporary sociologists who has written about citizenship.

For Aristotle, "a citizen is one who permanently shares in the administration of justice and the holding of office" (Barker, 1944, p. 92). I shall make use of his definition of a democratic citizen and recognize that elements of citizenship are to be found in all nation-states, even in the most repressive totalitarian state. However, there is a crucial threshold separating democratic and nondemocratic citizenship, even in the case of a benign nondemocratic state. The difference, of course, is embodied in Aristotle's use of the term "permanent," which in sociological usage becomes an "ideal" term of reference.

Thus, in essence, in contemporary language a democratic citizen is a person who jointly, simultaneously, or in sequence, rules and is ruled. Aristotle himself uses timeless language: "citizens, in the common sense of that term, are all who share in the civic life of ruling and being ruled in turn" (Barker, 1944, p. 134). Only to be permanently ruled is to deny the person's citizenship, and to rule permanently is likewise destructive of citizenship. This means that citizenship is not reduced to residence or confined to rights or private law but involves constitutional rights and obligations under the system of public law. To rule is a form of obligation which a citizen must exercise. By this definition, citizenship rests on a balance, or rather, on an interaction of obligation and rights. Citizenship is a pattern and a rough balance between rights and obligations in order to make possible the shared process of ruling and of being ruled.

This conception is at variance with the popular current usage of the term. One has only to examine the *Oxford English Dictionary* definition as of 1961 to document the contemporary meaning of the term "citizenship" in its mass usage. For the authoritative OED, there is a single meaning of citizenship, "the position or status of being a citizen, with its rights and privileges." The term obligation has been dropped or at least severely attenuated.

T. H. Marshall's influential essay "Citizenship and Social Class," prepared in 1949, examines these trends in the content of citizenship in Western democratic nation-states.[2] He argues that the long-term historical extension of citizenship rights has supplied the basis for overcoming or at least tempering the gross injustices of social inequality. Citizenship is a source of equality. "Citizenship is a status bestowed on those who are full members of a community. All who possess the status are equal with respect to the rights and duties with which the status is endowed" (Marshall, 1977, p. 93). For Marshall, the implication for social stratification and social inequality is clear. "The equality implicit in the concept of citizenship, even though limited in content, undermined the inequality of the class system, which was in principle a total inequality" (Marshall, 1977, p. 93).

2. In this article references to the text of Marshall's essay are from Marshall, 1977.

Marshall's historical overview emphasizes that, in the eighteenth century, civil rights were institutionalized. Then, in the nineteenth century, civil rights supplied the basis for achieving political rights.[3] In turn in the twentieth century, on the basis of the exercise of political rights, social rights were developed. Cumulatively, the extension of these citizenship rights has produced significant economic development and change—both in improving the material standard of living of wide segments of the working strata and in raising the level of well-being of those with the lowest incomes.

For Marshall, civil rights undermined the economic forms of feudalism and made possible the contractual relations essential for the emergence of capitalism with its resulting economic growth. This process of economic growth supplied the material basis for the expansion of the welfare system. The historical process was complex and its course as well as its consequences hardly self-evident. In short, civil and political rights were the precursors of social rights and of the trends toward greater equality. It is an argument which rejects rigid economic determinism. Marshall focuses on the experiences of Great Britain, but his observations supply the basis for comparison among modern Western parliamentary regimes in general.[4]

Marshall presented his analysis in 1949, as the Alfred Marshall Lectures at the University of Cambridge. Three decades later, the full expectations of the welfare state have not been achieved (Janowitz). The standard of living of social groups has risen, but the inherent limitations of the welfare state to contribute to social equality have become the focus of social science debate. Moreover, the prospect of chronic inflation has created new and persistent social inequalities. However, the main outlines of his analysis of the consequences of the rights of citizenship in containing social inequality continue to be highly persuasive.

But the importance of his essay also rests on his effort to deal with the obligations and duties of citizens and of citizenship. Not that he devotes extensive space to the topic; to the contrary, of the more than

3. Marshall uses the following definitions: "The civil element is composed of the rights necessary for individual freedom—liberty of the person, freedom of speech, thought and faith, the right to own property and to conclude valid contracts, and the right to justice." For political rights, he states, "By the political element I mean the right to participate in the exercise of political power, as a member of a body invested with political authority or as an elector of the members of such a body" (1977, p. 78).

4. We are obviously not dealing with a global "theory of history" since that is not T. H. Marshall's style. He is not analyzing representative institutions in ancient Greece and Rome or in the medieval Italian communes.

sixty printed pages in his essay, not more than three or four are devoted to the duties of the citizen. But these references are crucial—both for what is said and for what is left unsaid. There is no doubt that he believes there must be a balance, of some sort, between citizenship rights and obligations. He asserts clearly:

> If citizenship is invoked in the defense of rights, the corresponding duties of citizenship cannot be ignored. Those do not require a man to sacrifice his individual liberty or to submit without question to every demand made by government. But they do require that his acts should be inspired by a lively sense of responsibility towards the welfare of the community (Marshall, 1977, p. 9).

Advanced industrial society involves a high level of governmental intervention in economic enterprises and extensive public institutions to administer the essentials of social rights under the welfare state. In his own particular formulation of the issue, Marshall notes that "duties can derive either from status or from contract" (1977, p. 123). It is striking, but not unexpected, that he argues that the extension of social rights and their defense often involves the subordination of contract to status. Marshall accepts this state of affairs and even the necessity of such subordination with a clear awareness of the implications. "But if the obligations of contract are brushed aside by an appeal to the rights of citizenship, then the duties of citizenship must be accepted as well" (1977, p. 124).

Marshall believes that the balance has moved too far toward rights in contrast to obligations. It was indeed bold for a sociologist oriented toward British socialism to offer such an assessment in 1949 and to imply that a better balance was required for a democratic polity. But British socialist thought, if not practice, has a long tradition of concern with obligation. Therefore, Marshall offers a list of citizen obligations whose appropriateness and consequences he seeks to assess. These obligations conform generally to the conventional actions of civic duties. His list includes, for example, paying taxes, educating one's family, military service, and "promoting the welfare of the community," which he sees as all too general and vague. I shall compare his circumscribed list with a broader list which I will present and which includes a stronger emphasis on participation both in community voluntary associations and in the electoral process.

First, Marshall holds that the citizen has "the duty to pay taxes and insurance contributions." Since he is dealing with the British setting, he is speaking not of private insurance schemes but of obligatory government insurance for unemployment and health, which in the United

States would be called taxes. However, since these are compulsory, "no act of will is involved and no keen sentiment of loyalty." Marshall prefers that obligations of citizenship be voluntary.

Marshall overstates his position on the limited significance of paying compulsory taxes. Often citizen duties and obligations rest on compulsory performance. Because an act is compulsory does not weaken its significance as a citizen duty or obligation. A compulsory act does not have to be performed mechanically and without critical concern for its justice and relevance. In fact, because it is compulsory, the citizen has a special obligation to be concerned about its social and political content and consequence.

Second, Marshall deals with education, not only as a citizen right, but in a bold fashion as a citizen obligation. Throughout the nineteenth and twentieth centuries mass education has grown dramatically. The level of required education has been gradually extended for the population as a whole by raising the age at which youngsters can legally leave secondary school.

Much emphasis has been placed on the explanation for the spread of primary and in turn secondary education in the nineteenth century as a requirement of an industrial society. The more elaborate division of labor of an industrial society, the greater the need for a work force with higher educational qualifications. No doubt, the needs of the workplace stimulated state intervention to extend and, in turn, make compulsory primary education and to raise the school leaving age. But the growth of mass education is also a reflection of the political and moral dimensions of the spread of citizenship.

Thus Reinhard Bendix speaks of the "right to an elementary education" as a "basic social right." "As long as masses of the population are deprived of elementary education, access to educational facilities appears as a precondition without which all other rights under law remain of no avail to the uneducated" (p. 87). In short, education is a crucial, if not *the* crucial, social right of citizenship.[5] But in addition, Marshall emphasizes education as a citizen obligation. He is referring to basic literacy but I would add the rudiments of civic education. Under advanced industrial society, one might well want to acknowl-

5. Bendix, drawing on T. H. Marshall, is cognizant of the obligation dimension of elementary and secondary education when he asserts that "the right to an elementary education is indistinguishable from the duty to attend school." In effect, Bendix sees the duty aspect of basic education as essentially the state power to enforce primary school, and subsequently secondary school, attendance. State power takes the form of law which requires parents to insure that their children attend school.

edge that for a portion of the population, higher education becomes a citizen obligation.

Again as in the case of paying taxes, for Marshall the fact that basic education is compulsory makes it a less meaningful act of obligation. If it were a voluntary act, it would in his view be a more meaningful act of citizenship obligation. But it has its obligatory component and it is a striking sociological thrust to point to basic education as a citizen duty or obligation.

Third, Marshall cites military service as a citizen obligation. It is particularly important that he includes military service as an element in his analysis of citizen obligation, since most sociologists merely avoid or neglect the topic. Marshall does not present in his analysis of citizenship the historical background of military service in Great Britain. In fact, when Marshall wrote his essay in 1949, Great Britain had a system of conscription embodying the idea of citizen obligation for national defense. But he is once more uneasy because military service was compulsory. By 1962, Great Britain had ended conscription and reverted to an all-volunteer force and thereby apparently for Marshall ended this form of citizen obligation (Dietz and Stone).

Fourth, Marshall included in citizen obligation the duty "to promote the welfare of the community" (1977, p. 129). Since the term "community" is often used in an all-embracing fashion, it needs to be given a specific delimitation. We can use it to refer to the social and political relations based on residential community. Marshall has, in effect, separated a person's occupational and professional setting from a person's residential community. Industrial citizenship refers to the workplace setting, while community and community citizenship deal with one's social and political relations based on residence. But Marshall is not impressed with the significance and viability of citizen obligations in community affairs. In effect, he accepts the decline-of-the-local-community perspective, the formulation inherent in Tönnies's classical gemeinschaft-gesellschaft sociology.

If Marshall deemphasizes voluntary association participation, it is even more striking that he does not focus on electoral participation as a core dimension of citizen obligation. He makes two brief observations about elections. First, he speaks of the need for a relative balance of financial resources among the competing political parties. Marshall believes this has been roughly achieved in Great Britain since the advantage of the Conservative party in obtaining money from business groups has become balanced by the contributions which the Labor party has come to obtain from trade unions. Second, Marshall holds that effective basic education would increase the quality of citizenship participation in the electoral process. However, he also seems to assume that in a nation like Great Britain, the election process has been institutionalized and that it works to a relatively significant and essential degree. In essence, he believed that the election system has made it possible for the working class to exercise its civil and political rights, thereby insuring the extension of essential social services required for reduced inequality.

Instead of an emphasis on community and electoral participation, Marshall argues that the extension of citizenship from civil to political to social rights has generated, and in fact requires, a new set of crucial citizen obligations which he labels "industrial citizenship." Trade unions are, of course, the central and crucial institutions in this aspect of citizenship. The process of collective bargaining is of paramount importance. Collective bargaining derives from the accumulation of civil and political rights. The result of these rights is to create a powerful institutional base to press for social equality. Industrial citizenship rests on the right to organize and to bargain collectively rather than individually, for the resulting improvement in the position of those workers who participate directly or indirectly in the bargaining process. Because this process is so important, the rights of collective bargaining must be balanced by its obligations. These obligations must be fulfilled; there is no alternative for Marshall.

Trade unions have in effect created "a secondary system of industrial citizenship parallel with and supplementary to the system of political citizenship" (Marshall, 1977, p. 104). He believes that the system of industrial citizenship should be thought of as less secondary and more parallel with political citizenship. In fact, given his conclusions about civic obligations to be discussed below, that market value and social rights remain at odds, the arena of industrial citizenship has become equal in import from Marshall's perspective, if not actually outweighing the existing system of political citizenship as far as the reduction of social inequality is concerned. In other words, Marshall sees industrial citizenship as a distinct set of rights and obligations, but a set which has crucial political consequences.[6]

In retrospect, Marshall's assessment of citizen obligation in the arena of industrial citizenship appears naive, as it deals with the British scene and increasingly so for the United States. He concludes that, by and large, national trade unions are responsible and meet their obli-

6. Émile Durkheim also emphasizes the centrality of the workplace as the locus for promoting "civic morals."

gations. He fails to present criteria for judging performance. However, there is sufficient evidence for him to point out that there is a lack of industrial citizenship among local trade union leaders.

Marshall's analysis of industrial relations is hardly adequate for Great Britain. The long-term trend in national performance hardly conforms to his assessment, while local trade union citizenship has become dismal. Moreover, he argues mainly as if obligations of industrial citizenship are a matter of good will and good faith. He is oblivious to the consequences of different trade union structures and different patterns of collective bargaining in stimulating or frustrating the expression of industrial citizenship. He fails to highlight the pervasive adversary form of labor-management in Great Britain with its decisive liabilities for industrial productivity and effective conflict resolution. He wrote without reference to the alternative forms of industrial citizenship, as for example the system of co-determination in the Federal Republic of Germany which, allocating elements of industrial decision-making to the trade unions, has produced greater trade union responsibility. Nevertheless, it is essential to keep in mind that for Marshall, collective bargaining was central in the search for social equality. Clearly, for him the search for social democracy hinges on the practice of rights and obligations in the workplace and these aspects of citizenship equal, and at crucial points outstrip, the importance of civic and electoral obligations.

Three decades have passed since Marshall offered his sociology of citizenship. I believe that it is possible to expand his list of obligations in the light of societal trends in social structure and social organization. While a further analysis of citizen obligations hardly modifies the widespread dismal assessment of the dilemmas of democratic polities under advanced industrialism, they do indicate the potential for voluntaristic efforts in institution building as well as the required tasks of the "sociological imagination."

First, as to the citizen's obligation to pay taxes, the fact that this obligation is compulsory does not weaken or restrict its importance or eliminate the need to strengthen meaningful compliance. The citizen's duty is to comply with honesty and good faith and in terms of the spirit and objectives of the law. In an advanced industrial society, especially the United States, there is much latitude for legitimate cheating—taking legal but undue and unwarranted advantage of the complex and even inconsistent or vague portions of the tax code. This is especially the case for upper income groups.

In Marshall's analysis of the citizen's obligation for paying compulsory taxes, what he does not mention is most striking. One would assume that the citizen has an obligation to be concerned with the appropriateness of the tax expenditures. This duty would involve being informed about expenditures and, through the party and electoral system, to exert political influence on governmental expenditures. These obligations (which Marshall neglects) appear crucial for effective citizenship and require electoral participation. There is an additional aspect of the obligation to pay taxes. The trend in the tax code has been toward greater and greater complexity, not only because of political pressures of special interest groups, but paradoxically because of the efforts of responsible legislators to make taxation more fair. This results from their efforts to take into account the particular circumstances of more and more specific groups.

The details of an obligation must be relatively understood by the population at large. However a larger and larger proportion of the citizen population has increasingly less understanding of income tax regulation. This can be measured by the increased proportion of the population who make use of professional assistance, even among those who seek to use the most simplified tax return forms. In essence, the structure of tax codes and even the efforts to reform them have reached the point where they discourage effective citizen obligation.

Second, although Marshall is pointed in his emphasis that education is in part an obligation and not only a right, the sociological analysis of education as an aspect of citizenship needs to be extended. The duty or obligation aspect of elementary or secondary school education does not derive from compulsory attendance. In fact, almost the contrary. The compulsory aspect obscures the real citizen obligation, namely the obligation of a citizen to prepare for citizenship which entails a basic literacy and the rudiments of a civic education.

The duty aspect of education in a democratic polity was and remains the necessity of the citizen to make informed judgments both in private and public life. Education is, of course, required if the citizens are to understand and make use of their rights. But education is an obligation because it is the means to understand and perform all other citizen obligations.[7] It is the hallmark of a citizen. It is insufficient to emphasize that education prepares one for an occupation. We are dealing with the political and moral definition of the good citizen.

A modern democratic society is a society in which all strata have the potential of being democratic citizens (Shils). Under such circum-

7. In the United States the Voting Rights Acts of 1965 and 1970 in effect eliminated literacy requirements and thereby weakened the link between the obligation of education and citizenship.

stances, for the individual person and the members of his or her household to relate themselves politically and morally to the rest of society, it is essential that they be able to read and write, to have basic literacy. To acquire basic literacy requires deliberate efforts by parents and deliberate steps at institution building by the state. It is the duty of parents not merely to insure mechanical compliance with compulsory education—school attendance—but to assist their children in obtaining the elements of a core education.

Moreover, the emergence of basic education as a citizen obligation does not require attendance at a state school. Historically, in Great Britain and Germany there were voluntary efforts to extend basic elementary education to lower-class children. With the development of state schools, such efforts, which were not extensive, declined. State intervention was required to develop mass primary and secondary education. Although compulsory school education became accepted in Western nation-states, it was not attendance in state-run schools which was compulsory. Confessional cleavages remained profound, so that attendance at religious schools financed by the state was an acceptable alternative. In Holland, for example, a threefold school system developed—Catholic, Protestant, and humanistic. In the twentieth-century United States, the courts have repeatedly upheld the rights of parents to select the type of school they wish to use, and acceptable forms of alternative education have been defined broadly.

Clearly, education remains a meaningful citizen obligation, and the sociologist is interested in charting the trends in meeting this obligation. It is equally clear that there is widespread difference among professional educators as to the minimal levels of required literacy for an advanced industrial society. There is also continued pressure to raise the minimum standards, but formal standards are a poor measure of actual achievement. While one can speak of continued progress in the United States, the goal has hardly been achieved and, in important respects, appears more and more elusive and distorted by institutional barriers.

If parental attitudes and expectations are taken into consideration, as for example in the United States, survey data (Gollady and Noell) indicate that the aspiration for their children to graduate from high school was, by 1976, in fact universal (how far would you like your child to go?). Moreover, it was an almost universal expectation (how far your child really would go); only about 5 percent thought that their children would not graduate from high school or did not know. And these expectations were not wildly unrealistic. As of 1977, in the total age group 25 to 29, 89.6 percent has completed four years of high school or more; of course the percentage among the blacks dropped to 67.2 percent (U.S. Department of Commerce).

It is worthwhile to pause for a moment to consider that there is a segment of the population which is incapable of achieving basic literacy because of constitutional, medical, or psychological disabilities. From the extensive social indicators which social statisticians are collecting, it is not readily possible to estimate the size of this category, but clearly the potential for basic literacy is less than universal.

In any case, a real issue emerges from societal efforts to extend citizenship, that is, selected and meaningful rights, to such persons. As the family becomes more and more specialized in its functions, its inability to sustain its offspring who are incapable of basic literacy becomes more obvious. The state has, in fact, assumed the task of dealing with this social category which society finds difficult to define and embarrassing to label. The gradual changes in language from imbecile to mentally defective, to mentally retarded to mentally handicapped reflect the extension of the idea of citizenship. These are persons from whom one cannot reasonably expect the exercise of citizen rights.

No doubt of even greater importance are the built-in limits of the educational system to provide basic components of mass education, especially since mass education has come to include preparing a large proportion of each age cohort to attend college- and university-level institutions. In the light of the ambitious goals of mass education, as for example in the case of the United States, effective institutional limits are only dimly understood.

The decline in the performance on the college entrance examinations supplies a powerful indicator of the dilemma an advanced society must face in meeting the goals of citizenship education. There is no doubt that there has been a decline in test scores; the decline in the period 1963–72 has been carefully documented (Wirtz). Of course, the bulk of the decline has been due to the changed social composition of the students being tested. There has been an increase in the number of students who are less well prepared to score well on these examinations. Careful statistical analysis has indicated that between two-thirds and three-fourths of the decline is due to changes in social background (Wirtz). However, an important element of the decline reflects the limits of the educational system, limits which I judge have increased as compared to earlier periods.

We are dealing with system-wide factors, and I attribute these trends to at least three sets of variables. While these variables have their maximum impact on low-status groups, the effects are felt throughout the whole social structure:

1. Decline in professional competence and commitment among educational administrations and teachers which started in the decade of the 1960s and which by the end of the 1970s has not yet been decisively reversed.

2. Increase in the personal and social disorganization of family life, or perhaps stated alternatively, an increase in the disarticulation between family patterns and the institutions of mass education.

3. Increased disarticulation between school and employment opportunities. The increase in the number of years of required secondary schooling has had, paradoxically, the consequence of thwarting the motivation of a fraction of youngsters to achieve basic literacy and to develop academic skills. The capacity of the public school system to combine education and work experience remains extremely low. In addition, various experts agree that after World War II, the curriculum of the secondary school became excessively oriented toward college preparation at the expense of serving the needs of youngsters who enter the labor market after leaving high school (Trow).

In addition to achieving effective literacy, the citizen's obligation for education includes some rudimentary civic education. By rudimentary civic education, I mean a measure of understanding of national political traditions, and of the organization of contemporary political and governmental institutions, as well as the person's linkage to these institutions. We are dealing with a configuration of cultural values and group identifications. Civic education also involves developing a sense of group membership in the larger society (Marshall, 1977, p. 101). Civic education is relevant for the entire social structure, but has particular relevance for the offspring of low-status and minority groups. The rudiments of civic education at this point are also closely linked, the consequences of the school and even of the college and university in the acculturation (not assimilation) of ethnic, religious, and racial minorities to the larger society. The effectiveness of these institutions to assist the citizen in his pursuit of civic education cannot be judged to be extensive or even adequate. In addition, in the United States we are dealing with the consequences of the sociopolitical movements of the 1960s on mass education.

Before the decade of the 1960s, educational institutions in the United States served as relatively effective bridging institutions for immigrants as minority-group members. (This was, of course, not the case for racial minorities.) In varying degrees, primary and secondary education operated to teach basic English language skills and to present a point of entrance into the larger society by means of access to the labor market and to increased opportunities for post–secondary

school education. The primacy of English language instruction was
not interpreted by immigrants as a barrier to the preservation or even
enhancement of ethnic and linguistic heritage. Civic education was facilitated because the public school system operated as an acculturation
mechanism and was overtly limited to small amounts of nationalist
and patriotic history. It is striking that this low-key process did make
effective but incomplete contributions to a sense of national consciousness required for citizenship.

In the 1960s, these educational processes were strongly attacked
and called into question initially by black ethnic nationalist sociopolitical movements. Other deprived and low-status groups became involved and in these groups an increased ethnic sensitivity emerged.
While the long-term trend toward acculturation has continued, the immediate impact of ethnic nationalism was profound and reinforced by
the mass media. In particular quarters, the school was no longer defined as a bridging institution. Instead, it was an arena for developing
ethnic nationalistic identification and for immediate political mobilization. This is dramatically shown by the slogan, "Teaching English as
a Second Language." English was not thought to be primary. During
this period of turmoil, the capacity of many schools to perform basic
education was strained and their reconstruction is a long and painful
task. (In Great Britain, the growth of immigrant groups after World
War II produced similar trends.)

The period of ultra ethnic nationalism was destined to be short-
lived in the United States, but residues are relatively enduring. (In the
case of the Spanish-speaking groups, such ethnic nationalism appears
to be more persistent because of the proximity of native homelands.)
The result was to disrupt the limited civic education in primary and
secondary schools. The simplistic patriotism and mild nationalism of
public school milieux came to be viewed by educators as naive and
excessively status quo oriented. Professional educators withdrew from
civic education, especially since they were more and more faced with
powerful competition from television.[8] As a result, educators found it
expedient to open their school doors to special interest groups with
particular political programs. Two of the most spirited groups which
entered the public school system were advocates of economic education, that is "free enterprise" advocates, on the one hand, and, on the
other hand, environmental and ecological control spokesmen. Clearly
an ad hoc mixture of pamphlets and film strips and lectures supplied

8. For an analysis of the limited treatment of nationalism and national value in mass
television see Ben Stein.

by these two competing pressure groups hardly supplied an effective basis for civic education, especially the obligatory responsibilities of citizens.

Basic literacy education and the rudiments of civic education are not distinct goals. One cannot in the contemporary period expect to increase basic literacy without concern for effective civic education. I would like to offer the hypothesis that *under industrialism, basic educational achievement requires effective national identification and an operative sense of citizenship.* If in the past we believed that basic education was required for citizenship, in the contemporary setting, a sense of national civic sentiment is required to achieve basic literacy.

This hypothesis implies that community attachments, as well as ethnic and religious attachments, are not sufficient normative and motivational bases for effective educational achievement and performance. These attachments, if not excessively self-contained, can serve positive functions; but under advanced industrialism, a national level of identification is also required. In the simplest terms, the political and economic institutions of contemporary society are obviously national in scope. Educational institutions, while moving gradually to a more national system, have neither for lower socioeconomic strata nor for the middle strata contributed to meaningful national attachments related to citizenship. For the lower strata, this failure creates strategic barriers for the individual's life chances. For the middle strata, we are dealing with important limitations for political participation and political decision-making. Of course, civic education is hardly limited to formal instruction, but encompasses meaningful and realistic participation in community and public affairs. Michael Hanks and Bruce K. Eckland have carefully documented the effect of participation in high school extracurricular activities on membership in adult voluntary associations. A national sample of high school adolescents studied in 1955 were followed up in 1970 at about age thirty. Independent of social origins, ability, and academic performance, participation in extracurricular school activities had a strong, direct effect on participation in adult voluntary associations. In turn, membership in adult voluntary associations increased voting behavior and decreased political alienation, demonstrating the effect of school socialization on citizenship.

The third obligation of the citizen is military service. The important issue of military service requires more elaboration than Marshall offers. Citizen obligation for military service has in particular been linked to conscription. However, it does not depend on any one type of service but involves a variety of forms of "citizen-soldier." Great

Britain is of special importance. It does not have an extensive history of conscription but it has gradually fashioned its own definition and form of the citizen-soldier. The idea of the citizen-soldier is less a particular military type and more a political status. Under the citizen-soldier concept, the person in uniform basically remains a citizen. He may have to forego political rights, but the less the better. He is, as the contemporary Federal Republic of Germany emphasizes, a "citizen in uniform." He is not a marginal person. Instead, with the completion of his military service, his citizenship status is enhanced.

The professional cadres of the armed forces are also citizens although the expression of their citizenship rights needs to take into account their special military status. The forms of citizen participation of professional military personnel in a democratic polity may vary from nation to nation, but the contemporary professional military is a citizen, not a feudal mercenary [force]. Thus in West Germany professional military personnel on active duty may campaign to be elected to the Bundestag. In the United States, the code seeks to prevent partisan party affiliation but encourages civic participation in the local community. In Great Britain, the civic posture of the professional military as citizen is much more circumscribed.

The idea of the citizen-soldier had its origins in ancient Greece and Rome, but it was a political formula which was institutionalized in modern times by the American and French revolutions. However, such a perspective overlooks the particular contribution of the British experience. Great Britain has had a long history of opposition to a standing army. Since its military institutions have special national features, Great Britain has had its own version of the citizen-soldier in the past and its residues penetrate the contemporary British military establishment. The citizen-soldier concept took various forms in Great Britain. It had to compete with other military forms, and existed alongside persistent feudal residues. But the citizen-soldier concept over the long run made decisive contributions to civilian supremacy and a military establishment which has remained compatible with the value structure of the larger society.

In the seventeenth century, opposition to a standing army in Great Britain was mobilized. A standing army meant the centralized military establishment which the absolute monarchs of the European continent were organizing. This was a military subsidized by the central government, officered by men of aristocratic background—mostly from lesser landed gentry—and, in the other ranks, men with long-term service who were in effect mercenaries or merely impressed into service.

Such a military was seen by segments of the political leadership as a repressive institution and one whose values thwarted the growth of free economic endeavor. It was inappropriate for a society searching for internal economic development and struggling for new democratic political institutions. The politics of civil-military relations in Great Britain had a deep influence in fashioning civil supremacy in the United States.

The rudiments of a standing army in Great Britain were subject to elaborate parliamentary control, especially budgetary control, and organized on a highly decentralized basis and with fragmented leadership. Of central importance in civilian control was the use of local militia as a counterweight to the king's standing army. The local militia was considered of crucial importance in handling local civil disturbances. The objective was to avoid whenever possible the intervention of the standing army.

The local militia had its obvious military limitations; they were of limited importance when crucial continental battles had to be fought. But the local militia embodied the idea of the citizen-soldier. Although hardly truly representative, the militia's officers and men were much more socially representative than the personnel of the standing army. Since there was an element of obligation in service in the local militia, the officers had a middle-class element, and the enlisted personnel were not the dispossessed elements of British society. Despite its limited military utility, the militia served as a political device of civilian control and parliamentary rule.

Ernest Barker wrote:

> The local militia was a part and a pillar of local self-government; its control was virtually in the hands of the local gentry; and it could be, and was, regarded as the prop of the Parliamentary State, which was thus able to "balance" the king's contracted mercenaries by a force sympathetic with the knights of the shire and their brother burgesses (Barker, 1946, p. 51).

The militia also had a role to play in domestic disorder which it could play with restraint and relative legitimacy.

The local militia was an institution which was compatible with the political changes brought by the Reform Act of 1832. In fact, British aristocratic officers, whether in the local militia or in the standing army, were more predisposed to accept the civilian parliamentary leadership than their continental counterparts. In general one is struck by the willingness of important segments of the traditional feudal officer corps in Great Britain, and even to a noteworthy extent in France, to

fragmented efforts, and the all too limited civic consequences. If one focuses on community voluntary associations as vehicles of citizen obligation, as opposed to the mobilization of citizen rights, the results confirm Marshall's conclusion that "the obligation appears remote and unreal."

In essence, there is a social ecology of citizenship which has yet to be effectively worked out and institutionalized (see Janowitz and Suttles). Under advanced industrialism, those citizen obligations to one's community which can be expressed and maintained by informal networks and by direct interpersonal influences reveal considerable vitality. But as soon as one examines the network of organized community associations, the opportunity structure for expressing citizen obligation is hardly to be described as impressively vital. This network is not without considerable symbolic significance and it has strong veto power, but veto power is only a partial expression of citizen obligation.

We are dealing with both the horizontal and vertical dimensions of voluntary associations and their defects and deficiencies in each respect. First, horizontally, the networks of voluntary associations are based on constituent units which are highly localistic and narrow in territorial scope. These networks operate without efficient mechanisms of communication and interaction. As a result, they tend to reflect the needs and aspirations of relatively homogeneous social groupings. Such groups supply only a limited institutional base for formulating and implementing citizen obligation. Second, these voluntary associations and their resulting networks are incomplete and inadequate vertically. The tasks which they confront require metropolitan, state, regional, and national policies and solutions. The agencies of government to which these voluntary associations must relate are part of metropolitan, regional, and national hierarchies. Yet the bulk of the voluntary associations which operate at the grassroots level are not only fragmented territorially but are limited in their organizational layers. In the United States, in the aftermath of the experience of the 1960s in community action programs, there has been a limited movement in the decade of the 1970s to link local community organizations into metropolitan aggregations under various forms of roof organizations. There has also been a trend to join local community groups into national federations. Such trends seem indispensable if these enterprises are to express citizen obligation as well as citizen rights.

We must not overlook the experiences of community action programs. In the 1960s in the United States, and correspondingly in Great Britain, the proposal was offered and in fact became a powerful if short-term demand, that the federal government assist in the organization of community groups, especially in fostering communal groupings of low-income minority groups. These were the segments of an advanced industrial society which were not sufficiently integrated into the processes of citizenship. As a result of the efforts of the national government, community action programs became the source of powerful and pervasive controversy. With the passage of time, the original impetus and the initial programs weakened and were transformed or frequently terminated.

But it would be an error to overlook the considerable amount of social learning which took place or the new cadres of local community leaders which were developed (see Janowitz, chap. 12). The original goals were hardly achieved, to a considerable degree because they were utopian and based on unrealistic timetables. Nevertheless, the network of local associations was strengthened and the idea of community participation more effectively institutionalized. But the outcome of these experiences in the United States indicates that more integrated community organizations, both horizontally and vertically, will require and will rest on private initiatives. They can only be assisted indirectly by federal governmental intervention and resources. The image of the government organizing voluntary citizen associations to exercise citizen rights and obligations is difficult if not impossible to incorporate into the contemporary partisan politics in the United States. To be both effective and legitimate, voluntary associations must basically be without governmental sponsorship. In any case, the essential point is that over the last thirty years since Marshall wrote, voluntary associations have increased in their actual and potential importance as mechanisms for expressing citizen obligation.

Likewise, Marshall's analysis does not pay sufficient attention to the organization and consequences of national elections as mechanisms for channeling citizen obligations. As noted above, for him, the importance of partisan politics has receded, and instead the real issue of institution building rests in industrial democracy, in the arena of collective bargaining and the internal management of the productive and service sectors of society. While the enlargement of industrial citizenship is required, it is hardly sufficient. The obligation of responsible collective bargaining cannot resolve the full range of issues linked to economic growth as well as to the management of social services and the welfare state. In addition, crucial issues of international relations and national defense transcend industrial democracy. Contrary to Marshall, citizen obligations must be effectively expressed in the electoral arena. Thus, I remain wedded to the definition of citizenship offered by Aristotle. And in fact, the specific citizen obligations which have been discussed cannot substitute for effective participation in the various facets of the electoral process.

From the point of view of citizenship obligations, at stake is the strategic effectiveness of competitive elections in insuring political democracy and political control of economic relations. Drawing on the writings of Joseph Schumpeter, there has been a body of theoretical and empirical analysis which highlights the limitations of the competitive election system especially in the aggregating of decisive political majorities. Under a competitive election system, the crucial obligation of the citizen in the electoral arena is to calculate and implement his enlightened self-interest and simultaneously, the national interest. In other words, his operative obligation is to be judged by his contribution to the outcome of the electoral process; that is, by the decisions and mandates which elections produce. It is my view that the growth of social services and the welfare state makes it more difficult for people to calculate their enlightened self-interest, and the corresponding national interest. They must calculate the relative advantages and disadvantages of particular policies of economic growth versus the complexities of alternative programs of social welfare. These are calculations which need to be made in terms of relatively enlightened self-interest and broad national interest.

But we are traveling down an extensive circular pathway. The crucial defects of the electoral system are not to be found in the educational level of the electorate or in the mechanics of voting or in the organization and funding of the political campaigns, relevant as these questions are. They are to be found in the imbalance between citizen obligations and citizen rights and the intrusion of this imbalance into the electoral arena. Exhortations and moralizing do not make for more effective citizen pursuit of obligation. Reasoned and purposeful voluntaristic leadership is a core "variable"; but I believe that intellectual clarification of the institutional barriers to implementing citizen obligation is, to some limited degree, a relevant contribution.

If one focuses on the electoral process, there are two interrelated questions. First, the individual's position in the social structure, and his political self-interest, are not a simple derivative of income or occupation. Instead it is a complex matter involving a wide range of factors, such as age, sex, ethnicity, religious identification, as well as primary interpersonal influences, and the impact of the mass media plus community and associational attachments. The task of calculating political self-interest is more than just difficult, it is extremely difficult. As a result a person's electoral decisions can and do become unstable, unduly influenced by single issues or distorted by one's interest in political personalities.

Second, in a competitive national election, the alternatives proposed by the competing parties have become oversimplified, given the complexities of the sociopolitical process. The effort of political leaders to achieve a decisive majority thwarts the posing of meaningful and differentiated political alternatives. In the end, neither is achieved.

To rule and to be ruled, it is necessary to relieve periodic national elections of excessive political burdens—to make them less overburdened and thereby to increase both the legitimacy and effectiveness of electoral outcomes and legislative decisions. The more effective pursuit of citizenship obligations, I would argue, would be a direct contribution to these goals. The implementation of the basic citizen obligations discussed thus far would result in a more enlarged and more continuous process of citizen involvement in decision-advising and decision-making than periodic national elections can provide. To relieve the national election system of excessive burdens means to resolve or at least to reduce specific conflicts by other forms of citizen participation.

Obviously, Western democratic polities make extensive use of such arrangements or otherwise the level of political conflict and political stalemate would indeed be higher. The range of deliberate experiments is enormous, almost bewildering, and the consequences by no means clearcut. One can make reference to the above-mentioned West German system of co-determination in industrial relations as a relatively successful enterprise. The arrangement facilitates trade union participation in selected aspects of industrial management, under terms which obligate the unions to demonstrate and exercise increased collective responsibility in industrial production and in the management of the social welfare system.

In the United States, we have taken very limited steps to place representatives on the boards of directors of large corporations. Of course, the increased use of citizen representation in public education, health, community, and urban planning organizations represents an extensive movement, no doubt with mixed results, but results which cannot be overlooked. Even the regularizing of exchange of information and points of view between competing voluntary associations operates as a contribution to conflict management.

However, the clarification of citizen duties and obligations is not designed only to make a specific if limited contribution to the process of political bargaining which goes on continuously within and outside the electoral arena. To the contrary, it has as its goal a decisive contribution to articulating a moral framework by means of which social democracy can be pursued. It was and remains a basic assumption of this sociological analysis of citizenship that a democratic polity rests as much on the implementation of citizen obligation as it does on the exercise of civil and political rights.

After a century of growth of the welfare state we are witnessing a fierce and intense political debate about the scope of social welfare and in particular about the appropriate balance between the marketplace and the allocation of grants and subsidies. The effort to handle the tension between marketplace value and social rights has led to a massive increase in formalized relations between occupational and economic groups, a kind of modern scientific version of guild regulations. But the formalisms are not adequate since they will always be insufficient and the source of chronic discontent.

In reality, it is not possible to organize a modern industrial society without considerable reliance on market mechanisms. Even with essential government ownership of basic industries or extensive control of such industries there is no alternative to the considerable utilization of market mechanisms to achieve reasonable efficiency in allocation of resources and economic expansion. Reliance on markets is especially [needed] if one wishes to maintain a real measure of separation between economy and polity required for a democratic regime. Or to state the issue alternatively, the search for equality, if it is to be pursued within a democratic framework, requires a striking toleration of the looseness, ambiguity, and tensions between market value and social rights.

The elaboration of rigorous economic analysis cannot supply a fundamental solution to the conflict of social rights and market value. Of course, it can and does supply crucial but partial assistance. The wide range of evaluation studies by sociologists and others of the welfare state and of the related educational institutions supply even more modest assistance, because of the difficulty of relating these findings to concrete policy alternatives.

Both from an intellectual and policy point of view we require continued explication of the normative content of citizenship obligations, and of the institutional barriers which prevent their implementation. Such a sociological perspective has no logical priority over economic analysis, but given the imbalance in concern with rights versus obligation, such a clarification is, at this time, centrally important.

Because there is no logical solution to the fundamental tension between market value and social rights, men and women must be reasonable, especially in their citizen duties and obligations. There is no escape from a pragmatic morality, although the dangers of excessive moralism which incapacitates must be avoided. Thus is it striking, for example, that T. H. Marshall concludes his analysis of industrial citizenship with the assertion that "of paramount importance is the duty to work . . ." (1977, p. 125). This view of citizenship, in my judgment, offers a sounder basis for social democracy than that offered by those who speak of a postindustrial society and who would rely on a technological basis for the "good society." I agree that effective citizenship rests on moral consciousness, and particularly in the redefinition of civic consciousness. But I would add, and hope I have indicated, that in a sociological view, deliberate and purposeful efforts can result in institution building which would promote the development and the exercise of such moral consciousness.

Sociologists have moved beyond T. H. Marshall. We have at hand detailed research which throws light on the contemporary limitations of the ideals of citizenship in the management of the welfare state. But sociologists continue to see the organization of contemporary politics as essentially a derivative of the existing patterns of social stratification and inequality. But I started this paper with the observation that the normative and political definitions and organization of citizenship rights and obligations have had and continue to have an independent effort in fashioning social structure and social institutions. I conclude with the parallel observation that the ideals of citizenship are not yet exhausted, if we keep in mind the unresolved issues of citizen obligation. The task is to clarify those which are relevant and for which an institutional base exists or can be constructed. This remains an essential academic enterprise but one with important social and political consequences. Furthermore, in a highly interdependent world community, the varying definitions of citizenship have special relevance for those persons who seek to extend their obligations beyond the national frontiers, and who believe that there is no inherent incompatibility between national citizenship and the search for a more world-oriented set of obligations.

References

Barker, Ernest. 1944. *The Development of Public Service in Western Europe, 1930–1960.* London: Oxford University Press.
———1946. *The Politics of Aristotle.* Oxford: Clarendon Press.
Bendix, Reinhard. 1964. *Nation-Building and Citizenship: Studies of Our Changing Social Order.* New York: Wiley.
Dietz, P. J., and J. F. Stone. 1975. "The British All-Voluntary Army." *Armed Forces and Society: An Interdisciplinary Journal* 1 (winter): 159–90.

Durkheim, Emile. 1958. *Professional Ethics and Civic Morals*. Glencoe: Free Press.

Gollady, Mary A., and Jay Noell (eds.). 1978. *The Conditions of Education*. Unpublished data, National Survey of Children, Foundation for Child Development. National Center for Education Statistics, U.S. Department of Health, Education and Welfare. Washington: Government Printing Office.

Hanks, M., and B. Eckland. 1978. "Adult Voluntary Associations and Adolescent Socialization." *The Sociological Quarterly* 4 (summer): 481–90.

Janowitz, Morris. 1978. *The Last Half Century: Societal Change and Politics in America*. Chicago: University of Chicago Press.

Janowitz, M., and G. D. Suttles. 1978. "The Social Ecology of Citizenship." In Rosemary C. Sarri and Yeheskel Hasenfeld (eds.), *The Management of Human Services*. New York: Columbia University Press.

Marshall, T. H. 1950. *Citizenship and Social Class*. Cambridge: University Press.

————1977. *Class, Citizenship and Social Development*. Chicago: University of Chicago Press.

Schumpeter, Joseph. 1943. *Capitalism, Socialism and Democracy*. New York: Harper & Bros.

Shils, E. 1962. "The Theory of Mass Society." *Diogenes* 39:45–66.

Stein, Ben. 1979. *The View from Sunset Boulevard: America as Brought to You by the People Who Make Television*. New York: Basic Books.

Tocqueville, Alexis de. 1963. "Of the Use to Which the Americans Make of Public Assistance in Public Life." In *Democracy in America*. Vol. 2. New York: Knopf.

Tönnies, Ferdinand. 1971. *On Sociology: Pure, Applied and Empirical*. Chicago: University of Chicago Press.

Trow, M. 1961. "The Second Transformation of American Secondary Education." *International Journal of Comparative Sociology* 1–2: 144–66.

U.S. Department of Commerce, Bureau of the Census. *Educational Attainment in the United States: March 1977 and 1976*. Series P-20, No. 314. Washington: Government Printing Office.

Wirtz, Willard. 1977. *On Further Examination: Report of the Advisory Panel on the Scholastic Aptitude Test Score Decline*. New York: College Entrance Examination Board.

13

Military Institutions and Citizenship in Western Societies

This paper focuses on those sociopolitical changes in Western Europe and the United States that can be linked to the rise and subsequent decline of mass popular armies from the end of the eighteenth century to the present. The armies of Western Europe and the United States during this era can be called mass "citizen" armies, in varying degrees. They have embodied professional cadres of officers and enlisted personnel, augmented by conscripts and in wartime by mobilized citizen reservists. We are dealing with military institutions in which these conscripts and civilian reservists were defined as citizens rather than "mere" subjects . . . . Citizenship in Western nation-states is not only a result of industrialism and urbanism and the associated sociopolitical movements. In fact, the thrust of my analysis is embodied in the formulation of Friedrich Engels: "Contrary to appearance compulsory military service surpasses general franchise as a democratic agency." In the 1960s, mass military institutions based on citizen conscription began to be transformed into smaller, more "volunteer" forces—with profound implications for social structure, political power, and nationalism.[1]

How can one account for the simultaneous emergence of massive modern military institutions and of multiparty parliamentary institutions in the Western industrialized nations? The experiences of the Western nation-states are relatively distinct from those of other nation-states which underwent industrialization (e.g., Russia and Japan), and much more distinct from those of contemporary developing nations. The analysis offered here seeks to encompass three sets of factors in order to generate hypotheses which may help clarify the complex role of the military in the historical development of Western nation-states:

From *Armed Forces and Society* 2:2 (February 1976): 185–87, 189–204. Reprinted by permission of Seven Locks Press. © 1976 by The Inter-University Seminar on Armed Forces and Society.

1. Morris Janowitz, "The Decline of the Mass Army," *Military Review* (February 1972): 10–17.

(a) technology and organizational format, (b) social stratification and professionalization of the military institutions, and (c) the normative and symbolic content of the social and political movements supplying the ideological foundation of the Western nation and the rationale for its military institutions.

The modern professional mass armies of Western Europe emerged from the postfeudal institutions created in the eighteenth century by the absolute monarchies. The military institutions of the United States were deeply influenced by these developments. It was only in the West that military service, in the mass conscript armies of the nineteenth century, was seen as compatible with the duties and rights of citizenship. In fact, military service was defined as an integral aspect of citizenship, and two general hypotheses emerge. First, the institutionalization of citizen conscription has been an essential component in the emergence of Western parliamentary institutions. The continuing task for research is to account for this variant of conscription as it appeared in the West, since conscription in the nineteenth century was also compatible with, for example, serflike sociopolitical relations in Czarist Russia. The second hypothesis also relates to the transformation from the feudal type of military to the bureaucratic and professional armies of the nineteenth century. It will be argued that the "heroic" model of the Western officer corps, rooted in European feudalism, has been significant in facilitating the acceptance of parliamentary and civilian control. The military elite, or at least a significant portion who were traditionally conservative because of their conception of personal fealty, could readily transfer their allegiance from the reigning monarchy to the leaders of the new political regimes. The failure or the reluctance of the professional military to intervene directly in the political process in the nineteenth-century West more extensively than they did requires explanation. Throughout the nineteenth century, their behavior was markedly contained, compared with the military groups of the developing nations since 1945. The military leaders at various points in the development of Western political institutions monopolized coercive power to at least as great a degree as do the military in contemporary developing societies. Moreover, they often operated in a setting in which political parties were as weak as or even weaker than those in the new nations. . . .

Military Institutions and Citizenship

This paper maintains that military institutions have been of central importance in fashioning the type of nation-states that emerged in

Western Europe and the United States. The role of the military is linked to nationalism; in fact, the armed forces of the nineteenth and twentieth centuries epitomize modern nationalism. But modern nationalism hardly insures the emergence of elements of political democracy.[2] For the purposes at hand political democracy is linked to the normative notion of "citizenship." The essential problematic issue is that of establishing the connections between military service in selected Western nation-states and the political concept of "citizenship." The analytic terrain that requires investigation is complex and the theoretical formulations involved are easily misunderstood. The first hypothesis offered above requires careful examination. To the extent that mass armies defined their recruits in terms of political and normative ideas of citizenship, military service functioned as an essential and necessary contribution to political institutions. Of course, the political meaning of military service is generated and imposed by political elites external to the military. There is another element in the mass conscript army which contributes to the democratic political institution. Revolutionary nationalism, in the United States and especially in France, broke the monopoly of the higher social groups over recruitment into the officer corps. In theory, and to some extent, all social groups were eligible to become officers.

However, it must be emphasized that military conflict and war created social and political tensions which weakened democratic political institutions. Moreover, throughout the nineteenth and early twentieth centuries, civil-military relations were influenced by the pattern of the "military-industrial complex" of that time. Industrial groups aligned themselves with the military (e.g., Krupp under Kaiser Wilhelm, and Schneider during the Third Republic) in such a manner as to strain parliamentary control over it.

Reinhard Bendix, in *Nation-Building and Citizenship*, argues that the extension of the franchise is the key indicator of nation-building in Western Europe in the nineteenth century.[3] Stein Rokkan also has developed this theme in considerable detail.[4] Such analyses are too cir-

2. Alfred Vagts, *A History of Militarism: Civilian and Military* (New York: W. W. Norton, 1937).

3. Reinhard Bendix, *Nation-Building and Citizenship: Studies of Our Changing Social Order* (New York: Wiley, 1964); Bendix has a single sentence in this study on military institutions as part of his analysis of opposition to elementary education and the franchise: "Similar questions were raised with regard to universal conscription, since arms in the hands of the common people were considered a revolutionary threat."

4. Stein Rokkan, "Mass Suffrage, Secret Voting and Political Participation," *European Journal of Sociology* 2 (1961): 132–52. See also "The Comparative Study of Polit-

cumscribed. Alternatively or in amplification, I would argue that, starting with the French and American revolutions, participation in armed conflict has been an integral aspect of the normative definition of citizenship.

Historically, the American Revolution and the French Revolution were crucial points in the origin of the modern mass military formation. In those conflicts, political leaders armed extensive segments of the civil population and thus broke decisively with traditional patterns. That the rank and file could and should be armed and that the armed citizenry would be loyal was a "revolutionary" formulation. In a similar vein, the establishment of the principle that the officer corps was open to recruits from all social groups was also revolutionary. Under feudal and postfeudal arrangements from the Renaissance to the neo-Classical age, 1417–1789, military formations were officered by groups dominated by the nobility and were manned by mercenaries, men impressed into service, and by small delimited groups of volunteers.[5]

The citizen-soldier concept, of course, had its origins in the Greek city-state and in the early Roman military system. The interconnections among military service, control of the armed forces, and political democracy were explicitly formulated and institutionalized to varying degrees. It is significant that some of the central leaders of the French Revolution were explicit in their references to these ideas and practices. Moreover, the citizen-soldier format had its institutional antecedents, before the American and French revolutions, in the militia and national guard units. Variations of these types of units were widespread both in Western Europe and in the North American British and French colonies. The part-time character of their officers and the more representative character of their members anticipated the social format of the mass citizen-conscript armies. Particularly in France, the national guard units played an important role in armed conflicts of the Revolution.

The legitimacy of the revolutionary movements and the political democracies they sought to establish rested on the assertion that citizens had been armed and had demonstrated their loyalty through military service.[6] Military service emerged as a hallmark of citizenship and cit-

ical Participation," in A. Ranney, ed., *Recent Developments in the Behavioral Study of Politics* (Urbana: University of Illinois Press).

5. Theodore Ropp, *War in the Modern World* (New York: Collier-Macmillan, 1962).

6. It is interesting to note that social anthropologists concerned with political institutions have turned their attention to the analogies of the presence or absence of the idea of "citizenship" as a central approach of the politico-jural structure of tribal and peasant

izenship as the hallmark of a political democracy. The citizen army which made use of civilian reservists was not only an instrument of nationalism but a device for political control of the military professionals. To stress the political and normative consequences of mass military service is not to overlook the essential requirement that the military leadership of the mass armed forces which emerged during the nineteenth century had to be depoliticalized or politically contained if any variant of political democracy were to be achieved and institutionalized.

For purposes of comparative macrosociology, the worldwide view which assumes a general process of "modernization" of feudal, traditional, or peasant societies is much too global. In Western Europe, industrialism was well developed by the end of the nineteenth century, the emergence of modern large-scale military institutions was closely intertwined with the growth of industrial institutions, and, furthermore, both were relatively indigenous processes. While it is possible to speak of the emergence of modern armed forces in Western Europe in the nineteenth century, such a general observation cannot obscure the profound differences in the organizational and normative basis of mass participation in the military in different nations.

The linkage between citizen-soldier and the effective extension of the franchise, with its resulting impact on political institutions, reflects different historical patterns in Germany, France, Great Britain, and the United States. France can be taken as the nation where the conception of the citizen-conscript was most clearly enunciated as a principle designed to assist civilian political control of the military. Conscription was institutionalized early and was widely accepted; it has been gradually reformed and expanded, with the result that it has served as an accepted institution in French social structure. In contemporary France, the political commitment to conscription remains the strongest among Western nations, although, with the development of nuclear weapons and the end of the French empire, it has come under increasing attack. The United States is the nation in which the ideological and political basis for the citizen-soldier has been strong and extensive from the period of the American Revolution. However, national and military requirements made it possible to avoid introducing conscription, except in wartime, until the end of World War II. From World War I onward, citizen military service has been seen as a device by which excluded segments of society could achieve political legitimacy

---

societies. See, for example, Meyer Fortes, *Kinship and the Social Order: The Legacy of Lewis Henry Morgan* (Chicago: Aldine, 1969).

and rights. Until Vietnam, for example, blacks pressed to be armed and integrated into the fighting military as a sign that they had effectively attained citizenship and the concomitant privileges. While professional military officers have informally been excluded from elected office, with the exception of a few wartime heroes who became president, service as a citizen-soldier has been a powerful asset for candidates seeking election to the U.S. Senate and House of Representatives.

Germany and Great Britain can be considered as the limiting and alternative examples of the impact of mass military participation on citizenship. Germany's parliamentary institutions until after World War II were weak in comparison to those in France, Great Britain, and the United States. Nevertheless, the linkage between military service and the extension of the franchise was explicit in "nation building" in Germany. For example, in 1871 Bismarck institutionalized male suffrage immediately after the unification of Germany in response to the political realities created by new forms of military service. In contrast, throughout most of the nineteenth century, British military institutions were an admixture of feudal forms intertwined with slowly emerging professional officers. The extension of the franchise was likewise very gradual—indeed, limited. World War I transformed the structure of the British military and witnessed the dramatic extension of the franchise. It is striking that conscription was not instituted in Great Britain until after World War I had caused enormous manpower losses. The political consequences of extensive military mobilization produced legislation in 1918 which extended the franchise and was explicitly linked to the necessity of giving political rights to those who had been conscripted.

Moreover, it is obviously necessary to distinguish between the process of "modernization" in the West—Westernization, if you will—and the equivalent processes of sociopolitical change leading to the emergence of the nation-state in other regions and cultural areas that occurred later. For our purpose, it is well to recall that the traditional Ottoman Empire before the nineteenth century had large-scale military formations which rivaled those of the West. But the "modernization" of the Ottoman military depended on importing Western science and technology. The associated industrial development did not produce its own internal momentum until well into the middle of the twentieth century. Alternatively, Japan in the second half of the nineteenth century introduced both Western technology and military forms and experienced a simultaneous and continuous development of its industrial and military institutions. But it must be pointed out that during this period neither Japan nor the Ottomans developed or assimilated the notion of citizenship—as a political definition or as an aspect of military service.

Intellectual Traditions

Besides the classical writings, the comparative analysis of armed forces and society draws its vigor and associated variables as well as its limitations from three theoretical-empirical intellectual traditions. These focus on (*a*) the technological and organizational dimensions; (*b*) the social stratification and professionalization of the armed forces; and (*c*) the normative aspect of social and political movements, in particular of political nationalism. The transformation of each of these variables is related historically to the rise of the mass military and then to its contemporary decline. While the variables illuminate the emergence of the mass armed force in the Western nation-states and, to varying degrees, the incorporation of the notion of citizenship, they also are sources of the contemporary dissolution of the mass army and the attenuation and, in fact, separation of the notion of citizenship from military service.

Technology and Organizational Format

Technological explanations, if one must select a single or unidimensional explanation, appear to have great expository power but at the same time often seem to have tautological elements. The bulk of historical writing on the emergence of the mass armed force emphasizes the technological dimension. The sociological approach, of course, is to regard technology as a set of factors impinging on organizational format. The technological base of the mass armed force has rested on two elements. One is the increase in firepower effected by the introduction of the rifle and modern artillery. The other is the development of transportation and communication systems, permitting the concentration of large numbers of men and machines. Obviously, these technological innovations could utilize the manpower generated by conscription and thereby contribute to the development of large-scale bureaucratic military organization and the elimination of feudal conceptions of military life. In short, a citizen's army is compatible with such a military format.

However, citizen participation in the military antedated the full impact of the new technology. Modern technology was only at the incipient stage during the French and American revolutions. Likewise, modern technology has been incorporated into military systems where the notion of citizenship and the attendant political implications have been completely absent. At best, technology can be considered a facilitating variable in determining the military's role in the emergence of the modern state.

Modern technology contributed to the development of the strategic conception of total war.[7] Progressively larger and larger proportions of the civilian population have been mobilized into the military or into war-related production. The slaughter of human beings has increased, especially with the introduction of airpower, with less and less regard to the disinction between the military and the civilian. The deployment of nuclear weapons represents the "perfection" of the modern military by vastly increasing its destructiveness. At the same time, the advanced technology carries the "seeds of its own destruction," since the outbreak of total nuclear war can no longer be perceived as in the national interest. After 1946, the military function shifted from making war to deterrence, to the extent that rational considerations could be applied.[8] Peripheral wars prolonged conscription in the United States, but the trend toward eliminating or reducing conscription has been a general development in Western industrialized nations, with a stronger emphasis on all-volunteer professional forces augmented by various types of part-time soldiers, or short-term militias. It is difficult, under these circumstances, to define military service as an integral aspect of citizenship or vice versa.

Social Stratification and Professionalization

The second continuing research tradition focuses on the changing social stratification of the military and the military's development into a bureaucratic institution with its particular format of professionalism. Despite important structural differences from nation-state to nation-state, a generalized pattern of stratification of the military in Western nations—including the United States—has been identified. It stands in marked contrast to the institutional history of other regions of the world. The officer corps of Western Europe before the French Revolution was an elite whose social recruitment was rooted in the feudal-based landed aristocracy, especially the minor gentry. Its social recruitment not only gave it its conservative political outlook but was also an integral aspect of its code of honor, as the armed forces became more and more technical. The system of land tenure enabled a social enclave

7. Hans Speier, *Social Order and the Risks of War* (New York: Stewart, 1952).

8. Morris Janowitz, "Toward a Redefinition of Military Strategy in International Relations," *World Politics* (summer 1974).

to persist in which these traditional values could be maintained and from which "reliable" officers were recruited.

A body of careful scholarship traces the broadening of the social origins of members of the military profession as new technology and mass armies developed. In all the militaries of Western Europe for which studies of historical trends are available, the professionalization of the military in the nineteenth century meant the introduction of middle-class elements into a structure dominated by the upper class with its close connections to the landed elements. Karl Demeter in his study *The German Officer Corps* presents the prototype of this. Comparable trends have been documented in Great Britain, France, Italy, the Netherlands, Belgium, Sweden, and Norway.[9]

Even before the French Revolution, technological necessity and the growth in size of the military establishments in Western Europe required that middle-class officers be introduced to fill the cadres of artillery and engineering and logistical specialists. The French Revolution, of course, speeded up the social transformation of the French military establishment (the absence of a comparative process in England permitted the feudal type of domination to persist through much of the nineteenth century).[10] In France, the transformation represents a balance between the infusion of new non-noble elements and the persistence of important elements of noble personnel. S. F. Scott, in "The French Revolution and the Professionalization of the French Officer Corps, 1789–1793," has traced the extent to which traditional elements persisted in the "revolutionary" armies.[11] At the lower ranks of the officer corps the influx of new personnel was most extensive, including men promoted from noncommissioned status the higher ranks, a carryover in personnel predominated. As of 1793, nobles still constituted 70 percent of the generals.

By the end of the nineteenth century, throughout Western Europe,

9. Karl Demeter, *The German Officer-Corps in Society and State, 1650–1945* (New York: Praeger, 1965); Morris Janowitz, *The Professional Soldier, A Social and Political Portrait* (Glencoe, Ill.: Free Press, 1960, 1971), pp. 79–103; Bengt Abrahamsson, *Military Professionalization and Political Power* (Beverly Hills: Sage Publications, 1972), pp. 22–58.

10. Katherine Chorley has sought to investigate the conditions under which "armed forces" either support or do not oppose revolutionary movements, using the historical materials of Western Europe, Russia, and the United States. Katherine Chorley, *Armies and the Art of Revolution* (London: Faber, 1943).

11. Samuel F. Scott, "The French Revolution and the Professionalization of the French Officer Corps, 1789–1793," in Morris Janowitz and Jacques Van Doorn, eds., *On Military Ideology* (Rotterdam: University of Rotterdam Press, 1971), pp. 5–56.

middle-class social elements were extensive in the military and frequently dominated it in number—except in selected elite infantry and
cavalry units with high personalistic attachments to surviving monarchies. But the concentration of numbers was less important than the
fact that political conservative traditions and the heroic model persisted until the outbreak of World War II. In the United States, although there was no feudal tradition, a comparable social selectivity
in recruitment served to develop a similar set of values. Recruitment
was concentrated among native-born white Protestant families from
rural and hinterland backgrounds, especially in the South.

Social recruitment does not determine political behavior. In particular, with the growth of professionalization, there are more and more
links between political behavior and professional socialization.
Jacques van Doorn has traced the historical development of professionalism in the Western military and has focused the type of professionalism with its heroic element, which developed within a bureaucratic structure.[12] In the nineteenth century, the social role and
professional format of the officer corps of Western industrialized nations were compatible with the variety of political forms, but such
compatibility included acceptance and alliance with struggling democratic institutions. In England, France, and the United States, revolutionary movements left their impact on the officer corps, although
there were strong continuity and only gradual transformation from
feudal types of forms. The heroic model inhibited the officers' direct
intervention in politics.

Thus, the residues of the heroic model, with its emphasis on traditional values plus personal allegiance to the ruler, permitted acceptance of emerging parliamentary forms. This is not to assert that, in the
nineteenth century, the military profession was without political influence or that its political power was only the result of struggles between
competing civilian elite groups. Rather, social origins, and the social
mold of the military with its upper-class sense of guardianship of the
state, worked in the United States and Great Britain, on balance, to
serve the processes of internal parliamentary government. In France,
the balance was more unstable and disruptive, but the military did not
fundamentally undermine the parliamentary system—although they
challenged its existence. One outcome of the Napoleonic period was a
constitutional monarchy and a legislative arena. On the other hand,

12. Jacques Van Doorn, "Political Change and the Control of the Military: Some
General Remarks," in Jacques Van Doorn, ed., *Military Profession and Military Regimes: Commitments and Conflicts* (The Hague: Mouton, 1969), pp. 11–35.

the officer corps that emerged in Germany was compatible with and served to support the monarchial–civil service regime.

In sharp contrast, for example, the Ottoman military did not rest on a feudal social structure as the term had meaning in Western Europe. The system of land tenure and sultan's position ruled out an independent nobility either as a source of officer recruitment or as a political base for a check on the sultan's power. Instead, for centuries, the armed forces were recruited by the Ottoman Empire on a broad and diverse base, including a slave type of component, in order to strengthen the sultan's power. The military was a form of government service under the authority of the sultan.[13] It had no specific conservative orientation reflecting attachment to a landed upper class.

The significance of the Western military officer corps as a social type during the nineteenth century is highlighted in comparison with the posture of the Ottoman military—and the military of many new nations. In the absence of a feudal and heroic tradition, the Ottoman military leaders, as they have developed modern armed forces, have been more committed to their own notions of revolutionary political change and more accessible to and involved in direct domestic political action.

During the first half of the twentieth century in Western industrialized nations, the growth of the military establishment, more than the social origins or professionalization of its officers, contributed to its markedly increased political weight. With the decline of the mass armed force and the movement to an all-volunteer system, social recruitment reemerges as a more relevant variable, since recruitment becomes less representative. In the post–World War II period, the trend in many Western industrialized nations has been toward a heavier concentration in the officer-corps of self-recruitment, especially among sons of noncommissioned officers. There is evidence of disproportionate reliance on particularistic sources, such as special preparatory schools catering to old established families with regional affiliations. The existence of highly unrepresentative officer corps during the emergence of the all-volunteer force does not necessarily present a "putschist" threat to parliamentary institutions, but it does weaken the legitimacy of military institutions. Moreover, selective factors in recruitment are already tending to increase the conservative political bias of the officer corps and to produce more rigid attitudes toward international affairs.

13. Morris Janowitz, "The Comparative Analysis of Middle Eastern Military Institutions," in Morris Janowitz and Jacques Van Doorn, eds., *On Military Intervention.*

Natural History of Revolutionary Nationalism

The third set of variables focuses on the normative and symbolic content of the social and political movements which have supplied the ideology of the nation-state. A wide range of economic and social structural variables have been offered to explain the transformation of European feudalism. Each of these theories must also be judged in terms of its ability to account for the variation in degree of political democracy that emerged in a particular nation-state. The tradition of such intellectual endeavors is rich and unending: for example, de Tocqueville's *French Revolution and the Ancient Regime,* Thorstein Veblen's *Imperial Germany,* and Barrington Moore, Jr.'s *Social Origins of Dictatorship and Democracy.*[14] However, the common concern of these analyses is with underlying economic and social structures. The explanations or at least prerequisites for the process of "modernization" and the emergence of political democracy versus totalitarianism are recognizably incomplete or partial.

The alternative or supplementary perspective in comparative macrosociology seeks to conceptualize the process in terms of social and political movements—purposive and collective agitation, if you will. Such theorizing is hardly so systematic and comprehensive, but it does highlight the voluntaristic elements in historical processes. Of course, the writers who use social and economic structural explanations are fully aware of the limitations on their perspectives and the need to assign a degree of "independence" or causality of organized collective political agitations and institution building. One has only to examine the prerequisites for the development and growth of political democracy offered by Barrington Moore, Jr. In effect, they reduce to two elements: (*a*) an elaboration of de Tocqueville's stress on an effective balance between central monarchial authority and local centers of power and initiative; and (*b*) Moore's social anthropology of peasant life and the importance of the commercialization of agriculture. He then adds a third: (*c*) the necessity of a "revolutionary break with the past"— which, in effect, is an undifferentiated awareness of the social and political movement perspective.

In short, it is necessary to join to the social structural analysis of nation building a systemic concern with "nation-building" as a social

14. Alexis de Tocqueville, *The Ancien Regime and the French Revolution* (Paris, 1856); T. B. Veblen, *Imperial Germany and the Industrial Revolution* (New York, 1939); Barrington Moore, Jr., *Social Origins of Dictatorship and Democracy: Lord and Peasant in the Making of the Modern World* (Boston: Beacon, 1966).

and political movement, that is with the organizational and leadership aspects of mass agitation as elements of sociopolitical change.

One can point to the origins of contemporary theoretical-empirical research in this vein in the seminal and incisive monograph *The Natural History of Revolution,* by Lyford P. Edwards, published in 1927. It served as the prototype for the much more widely recognized but derivative volume by Crane Brinton, *The Anatomy of Revolution.*[15] Edwards was strongly influenced by Robert E. Park of the University of Chicago, whose doctoral thesis on "Massen und Publikum" was an early effort to study, systematically, social and political movements in their own right.[16] Edwards's analysis included the sociology of the intellectual, and mass agitation as a central element in fashioning nationalistic movements. It anticipated contemporary studies of liberation movements in developing nations.

The American and French revolutions were social and political movements whose ideological and normative content and leadership styles had independent effects on the sequence of "nation" building. These were revolutionary movements whose ideological content fashioned the social cohesion of the central leadership and contributed to the mobilization of activist cadres, both military and civilian. These movements led to extensive armed conflict against existing standing armies, in which the revolutionary forces were victorious because they could mobilize new rank-and-file cadres and could use professional officer elements. Moreover, the effective consequences of these revolutionary movements were not military dictatorships or oligarchies, but parliamentary institutions with varying degrees of stability and effectiveness. The Cromwellian Revolution, which contributed to making England the first modern nation-state, had these elements as well. In England and in the United States, and to a lesser extent in France, military leaders did not succeed in establishing their legitimacy for political leadership.

15. Lyford P. Edwards, *The Natural History of Revolution* (Chicago: University of Chicago Press, 1970); Crane Brinton, *The Anatomy of Revolution* (New York: Random, 1957).

16. Robert E. Park, *Massen und Publikum* (*The Crowd and the Public and Other Essays*), Henry Elsner, ed., Charlotte Elsner, trans., in Heritage of Sociology Series (Chicago: University of Chicago Press, 1972). Park was strongly influenced by W. I. Thomas, who presented a penetrating sociological analysis of the nationalist movements in subjugated Poland at the end of the nineteenth century. William I. Thomas and Florian Znaniecki, *The Polish Peasant in Europe and America,* 5 vols. (Boston: Richard G. Badger, 1918–1920); vols. 1 and 2 were originally published by the University of Chicago Press in 1918.

For the purposes at hand, three elements in the ideological content of the American and French revolutions (and again, on an equivalent basis, of the Cromwellian Revolution) were significant in influencing their character and consequences. First, their ideology and political propaganda were explicitly nationalist. That is, they created a nationalist symbolism of identification within which to press for sociopolitical change and demand social and political justice. National symbols were offered in contrast to existing localistic and traditional boundaries of the polity. The idea and appeal of nationalism, as a basis for collective action, were extremely powerful and enduring. Nationalist symbolism supplied a basis for the political legitimacy of revolutionary leadership and a particularly effective basis for organizing the armed forces. The interpenetration of ideological nationalism and military organization persisted until the middle of the twentieth century. Nationalist ideology operated as a convenient vehicle by which feudal elements could find their social, professional, and political positions in the emerging polity and in the postrevolutionary mass armed forces.

Second, the ideological and normative definition of citizenship and the notion of civic participation in the revolutionary armed forces were equally pervasive and powerful. The legitimacy of these armed forces was based on an appeal to defend individual freedom and achieve social and political justice. To arm the ordinary person and to declare his right to bear arms constituted a revolutionary appeal, serving the immediate requirements of raising military cadres and drawing elements from a wide variety of social strata. But this ideological and propaganda call was not only a military formula. It was a political definition which served to enlarge the concept of who were effective members of the polity. Like nationalism, it supplied a key ingredient in the expansion of the electorate. The duties and obligations of the armed citizen set the framework for the concept of the electorate in civil society, although actual enfranchisement came in subsequent steps.

From the Cromwellian Revolution onward, the actual competence of military leaders to rule as a leadership group in Western nation-states has, indeed, been limited. Philip Abrams's study of the Cromwell military government by generals and colonels has shown it had dilemmas and fatal shortcomings comparable to the difficulties of the contemporary military oligarchies of new nations.[17] The generals and colonels could not convert their ability to seize power into a legitimate

17. Philip Abrams, "Restoring Order: Some Early European Cases," in Morris Janowitz and Jacques Van Doorn, eds., *On Military Intervention*, vol. 2, pp. 37–61.

base for a stable government. In the case of the United States, historians emphasize George Washington's political commitment to civilian rule, but this in turn represented the pervasive ideological and normative definitions of the American Revolution.

The intertwined notions of nationalism and citizenship participation had continuing impact until World War I, when the immense slaughter of alliance warfare weakened their viability. World War II only undermined their organizing effectiveness further. Nevertheless, for 150 years they supplied a basis for transforming the military from a distinct status group into more and more of a civil service organ of the state. In Germany, where the concept of citizenship was indeed weak, the military continued to operate as a detached status group, as a state within a state, even after World War I. It remained for the National Socialist regime, with its ruthless and distorted forms of "democratization," to end the Prussian military assumptions. But the reconstructed armed forces, after the Allied victory, have assumed a conventional modern Western format. In most Western European nations where modern industrial systems have emerged, the standing armies could exist alongside parliamentary systems—a special historical development of limited frequency. This has been so not only because of the patterns of civilian social structure but because of the basis of legitimacy which the military has come to accept.

The weakening of the power and attraction of nationalism and the contraction of mass armed forces do not automatically strengthen parliamentary institutions. The attenuation of nationalist sentiments and ideology is not caused only by the increased destructiveness—actual and potential—of war. It is also a popular expression of an advanced industrial society with a high level of income and education that produces strong and powerful hedonistic concerns. Resistance to military service becomes widespread as the logic of nationalism is questioned and the rationale for the military is obscured by the reality of nuclear weapons. Social and political movements become intensified. A tiny minority of college-educated youth are prepared to engage in confrontation politics designed to "undermine" contemporary military institutions. However, their conspicuousness should not obscure the fact that there is a broader suspicion of existing authority, which has especially strong antimilitary overtones.

There is a convergence of consequences which derives from the new dimensions of technology, social stratification, and the normative content of social and political movements in Western advanced industrial nations. All these dimensions threaten to separate the military from the larger society and render it an internal but more isolated body with selective linkages to that society. The consequence is a greater ideological differentiation between those who offer themselves for a military career and the wide segments of the population who accept the necessity of a military but accord it little moral legitimacy. S. M. Lipset and others have asserted that an advanced industrial society would not be racked by social and occupational cleavages.[18] This assertion has come to be rejected. Age, sex, ethnic-religious, and racial differences and new forms of occupational stratification do not supply the basis for "revolutionary" social conflict but do create social divisions which are persistent and deeply disruptive.[19] Issues of civil-military relations, such as the internal position of the military and the military's role in foreign affairs, also become another basis for profound cleavage which burdens the parliamentary system of an advanced industrial society.

18. Seymour M. Lipset, "The Changing Class Structure and Contemporary European Politics," Daedalus 93 (winter 1964): 271–303; Robert E. Lane, "The Politics of Consensus in an Age of Affluence," American Political Science Review 59 (December 1965): 874–95.

19. Morris Janowitz, Political Conflict (Chicago: Quadrangle Books, 1970), pp. 5–35.

14

Mass Media and Popular Distrust

In analytic terms, the capacity of the mass media to mold attitudes and behavior is the result of both immediate or short-term effects and of long-term consequences. We are dealing with the accumulation of specific consequences which are manifestly discernible and long-term consequences which at any given moment are barely perceptible. The mass media have both an indirect effect through opinion leaders—national, metropolitan, and local—and a more direct effect on the person.

On the first issue, the research of Hadley Cantril on the Columbia Broadcasting Corporation's dramatic presentation on radio in 1939 of Orson Welles's "Invasion from Mars" documented the extreme behavior which specific mass media messages can produce under conditions of short-term panic.[1] Persons uable to check the authenticity of the Orson Welles program fled from their homes in the New York City area to the outlying areas of northern New Jersey in considerable numbers. By contrast, only from fifty individual studies, to be described below, could the gradual impact of televised violence on children and youngsters be discerned, and in this case mainly by inference. From the point of view of social control, it is these long-term consequences which are central.

Our underlying hypothesis is that the major trends in the mass media have not contributed to the growth of those personal controls required for more effective social control in advanced industrial society. More specifically, rather than strengthening those ego controls which contribute to realistic self-interest and stable group attachments required for effective political participation, the long-term effect has been to heighten projective (and accordingly suspicious) personality predispositions and defensive group affiliations. The most adequate research data center on the second content trend, of sustained concern with violent themes, rather than on the first theme, of mass consumption and interpersonal management, or the third one, the rise of advo-

From *The Last Half-Century*, pp. 347–59, 362–63. © 1978 by The University of Chicago. All rights reserved.

1. Hadley Cantril, *Invasion from Mars: A Study in the Psychology of Panic* (Princeton: Princeton University Press, 1940).

239

cacy in the presentation of public affairs. But it is the confluence of the
three elements that is the essential component in accounting for the
mass media contribution to the attenuation of social control.

First, popular culture content, the content dealing with both interpersonal relations and with mass consumption, is augmented by extensive time and space devoted to mass advertising. By and large the
audience views the mass advertisements as blending in with the popular culture portion. Raymond A. Bauer and Stephen S. Greyser have
summarized the available survey research on attitudes toward advertisements.[2] The audience take advertisements for granted—indeed,
they are a positive attraction. The overwhelming, uniform finding is
the favorable attitude toward mass advertisements dating from the
1920s when such studies were first executed. Over time there has been
no discernible trend. In 1964–1965 considerable debate began about
truth in advertising, which led to various legislative and administrative
steps. But there is no evidence of any basic change in attitudes toward
institutionalized advertising. In fact, the interest of better educated
persons in "artistic" advertisements in the "better" magazine has increased and reflects the strong appetite for the symbolic content of
consumerism.

As indicated above, the notion of "consumerism" involves the increased use and reliance on material goods without a corresponding
increase in sense of satisfaction; consumerism implies a growth of dissatisfaction. In the absence of effective personal and social control, increased material consumption creates only demands for more indulgence. Consumerism implies that the pursuit of material goods in the
absence of appropriate moral standards is a destructive act, one with
implicit and explicit aggressive overtones. This characteristic is manifested by the compulsive rather than satisfying overtones in the acquiring and utilizing and consumption of material objects. . . .

In terms of social control, the response to mass advertisements—as
well as the consumption content of popular culture—is not to be
judged by the sales effectiveness of particular advertisements or campaigns but by the long-term consequences on attitudes and social personality. The most suggestive evidence is contained in the endless series
of commercially sponsored research called "motivation research." Social scientists cannot dismiss these findings, although very few of them
enter the published literature and most fail to meet minimum research

2. Raymond A. Bauer and Stephen S. Greyser, *Advertising in America: The Consumer View* (Cambridge: Harvard University Press, 1968), passim; see also Leo Bogart,
Strategy in Advertising (New York: Harcourt, Brace and World, 1967).

standards. In addition, some of the intensive probing in this type of research may border on violation of privacy.

Such advertising research underlines that an important component of consumer decisions is based on the gratification of primitive impulses—on irrational motivation, if you will—rather than on rational economic choice.[3] Moreover, such research supplies guidelines for mass advertising designed to appeal to the nonrational aspects of social personality, and to give these aspects greater prominence. Of course, the results do not permit quantitative measures of the relative importance of these variables. But the advertising strategy which has been developed can well be described in terms of dynamic personality psychology. The "operational code" of the mass advertiser is, in the simplest language, to reduce conscience (superego) resistance, to appeal directly to primitive pleasure impulses (id), and either to avoid rational objections (ego) or at least to fuse the rational and the pleasure appeals.[4] The evidence of the success of appropriate advertising in specifics is interesting but not very persuasive. Competitive use of motivation appeals can well reduce the advantage one advertiser has but not the cumulative impact mass advertising has on social personality. One can make the analogy with the effect of the cumulative exposure to televised violence to be described. The long-term results have been to increase impulse buying, as it is called by the experts, which reduces rational considerations and contains personal controls.[5] The availability of credit cards reinforces such consumer behavior. . . .

What can be said about the social implications of the popular culture content of the new style "sophisticated" "soap opera"—the serials concerned with "modern" interpersonal relations and tensions? The soap operas of the 1940s had explicit, simple moral messages. The

3. Ernest Dichter, *Handbook of Consumer Motivation: The Psychology of the World of Objects* (New York: McGraw-Hill, 1964).

4. For the analytic background of this type of analysis, see Harold D. Lasswell, "The Triple-Appeal Principle," *American Journal of Sociology* (May 1932): 523–38.

5. A typical case is the change in advertising ice cream. Before motivation research, old-fashioned advertisement for ice cream cones was simple and realistic about size; the information content was that it was made of good ingredients (ego appeals), good for you (superego), and tasted good (id). The new format avoids any discussion that it is good for you, since to raise the conscience question might well raise psychic resistances; even ego appeals have been reduced. Instead, the approach is toward emphasis on primitive gratification. The cone is twice life size; the cone is packed to overflowing. Often it is presented as dripping slightly down one side, since the "mess" is thought to present a primitive appeal. Children are added in media with adult audiences, since the symbol of the child is a positive appeal of childlike gratification. The major social psychological issue the advertisers face is not to overemphasize the primitive appeals, but their scope has been greatly enlarged.

analysis of housewife reaction to the "traditional" and moralistic "radio daytime serial" prepared by W. Lloyd Warner and William E. Henry showed the symbolic influence of this type of popular culture.[6] They describe these radio—and later television—presentations as "contemporary morality" plays which allowed the housewife vicarious indulgence in other people's adventures and wayward behaviors, but "in the end" her own day-to-day morality was validated. Drawing on the content analysis presented above, we cannot describe the new sophisticated soap opera as functioning in such a fashion. The comic interludes, even comic definitions of interpersonal strain and trauma, offer considerable catharsis and tension reduction, which no doubt account for the audiences. But the emphasis on the hostile and destructive impulses of the "outsider" and the reliance on humor to deal with hostility is likely to generate suspicious responses. There is little reason to assume that the viewer gains insight into his own motivations or is supplied with enriched understanding of social and psychological reality so as to reinforce or modify moral judgments and enhance self- and personal controls.

The growth in mass audience for popular culture raises the question of the discontinuity between popular culture and high culture.[7] Unfortunately, very little can be said on this topic which is not polemic and self-serving. The well-known argument is that the growth of popular culture has weakened the creation and in turn the influence of high culture. There are writers and artists who may have made a contribution to high culture who began producing popular culture for career and economic reasons. However, there is no evidence that there has been a decline in interest and exposure to high culture under advanced industrialism; if anything, the audiences for it appear to have increased.[8] This is not to pass judgment on the lasting quality of the newly produced high culture under advanced industrialism—either on its intrinsic and lasting humanistic quality or on its effect on society, and especially on elite groups.

The long-term consequence of the strong concentration of violence

6. W. Lloyd Warner and William E. Henry, "The Radio Day-Time Serial: A Symbolic Analysis," *Genetic Psychology Monographs* 37 (1948): 3–73.

7. Edward Shils, "Mass Society and Its Culture," in *Culture for the Millions: Mass Media in Modern Society*, ed. Normal Jacobs (New York: Van Nostrand, 1959), pp. 1–27; see also Herbert Gans, *Popular Culture and High Culture* (New York: Basic Books, 1975).

8. Edwards Shils, "Daydreams and Nightmares: Reflections of the Criticism of Mass Culture," *Sewanee Review* 65 (1957): 586–608.

content on personal and social controls has its crucial test in the impact of television on children and youngsters. Television is the major carrier of violent content. The new generation grow up in a setting of increased access to violent content and they continue to be exposed to varying degrees for a lifetime.

It was not academic interest which produced a comprehensive synthesis of the available analytic thinking and empirical research on televised violence. Rather, congressional concern with public morality, crime, and aggressive behavior stimulated a cooperative and interdisciplinary review. . . .

Aggressive behavior was the focus—the dependent variable. The results of over fifty separate studies, experimental endeavors and sample surveys, indicated that exposure to televised violence increased aggressive behavior as a result of imitation or instigation. The more clear-cut experimental findings were confirmed by sample surveys, although in general surveys produce, for the reason set forth above, less definitive results. The observed relations were low but repeatedly encountered. Given the multiple bases of aggressive behavior, if the encountered influence of televised violence on children and youngsters had been more extensive, the results would have had to be judged as truly devastating. Moreover, if one makes the effort to read the descriptive details of the experimental studies one is struck by the scope and impact of instigated aggressiveness.

Of course, individual studies are only indicators; the essential inferences must be drawn from these findings. If the research methods which sampled social reality at particular moments in time had produced discernible results of increased aggressive behavior, then the long-term cumulative effects on the audience would most likely be stronger and clearer. Moreover, the correct question about televised violence involves a much sharper focus on societal socialization. In the frame of reference of social control, the increased complexity of the occupational sector and the disarticulation of work and communal residence require a higher level of personal controls. Thus, the task of the mass media is to develop a more adequate relation to authority— that is, greater capacity to store and manage aggression. In short, the findings of these researches indicate a tendency toward weaker personal controls, that is, just the opposite. In fact if the mass media exposure to violence had had no effect, the consequences could still be viewed as disruptive, since the societal requirements are for more effective personal control in order for there to be more adequate societal control. In part, this question was argued in 1937 by Mortimer Adler, when he was evaluating the effect of movies on the criminal behavior of youth.[9] As discussed previously, the content of the media sets the limits for their contribution to socialization. Adler's humanistic analysis and the findings of social research converge; if the proportion which has been allocated to violence had been used for civic education, the social personality of the U.S. citizenry would have been discernibly less accepting of illegitimate violence.

In assessing the consequences of the third indicator of mass media content, namely, the shift toward a stronger emphasis on advocacy, our focus must be less on specific subject themes, and more on style and format. Nevertheless, it must be remembered that less than 5 percent of all of the contents of the mass media, it is estimated, deals with public affairs. This limited amount is given prominent exposure and, because of its political importance and drama, it commands widespread attention. Media competition in the presentation of public affairs makes possible a competitive electoral system with all its inherent and accumulated defects.

Media competition has the objective of ensuring relative accuracy in reporting the events of the day and in producing a measure of balance in opinion and commentary. There is competition among channels of the same medium, among different media, and especially among the generalized and specialized media. However, media competition does not guarantee that the relevant content will be disseminated; nor does it guarantee that in a particular medium an overall representation—a holistic picture—of public affairs will be offered.

The strongest limitations on the competition of the mass media are the constraints which ensue from their profit-oriented management, producing widespread interlocks and a "community" of interests among the owners. However, there is no simple relation between type and patterns of ownership, including degree of concentration, and content. My reading of the scattered research on this issue is that the outlook of particular owners and managers, and the level of professionalism of the staff, are more decisive in determining journalistic performance.

Nor is it simple to assess the consequences of government-imposed regulation—legislative, judicial, and executive. Such regulations are designed to enforce competition and maximize standards of performance. There is reason to believe that the degree of competition, although not necessarily the level of performance, has been enhanced by governmental intervention on behalf of competition. Government

9. Mortimer Adler, *Art and Prudence* (New York: Longmans, Green, 1937).

standards of performance—for example, amount of public service programming—strengthen minimum performance but do not ensure adequate achievement. The sheer administrative burden of the existing government regulations indicates that the point of diminishing returns has been reached. But on balance, it is reasonable to conclude that, without these regulations, as in the case of economic enterprise, the amount of media competition would probably be lower. However, the important conclusion to be drawn for the analysis of the structure of the mass media in the United States is that, under advanced industrialism, private ownership has not been a barrier to the growth in the movement toward advocacy journalism. In fact, the owners and managers appear to have stimulated and supported this trend, while the main incentive comes from the operating journalistic personnel themselves.

It is now necessary to spell out the requirements laid down for the mass media by democratic political theory. Political theorists and sociologists have elaborated these requirements in different language, but there is considerable agreement about the essentials. The mass media must (a) contribute to a high level of participation by all ordered segments of society; (b) stimulate effective political deliberation on the issues and candidates and contribute a meaningful basis on which citizens make their voting decisions; and (c) operate to preclude either side from monopolizing or even exercising pervasive influence by means of them. The mass media must also contribute to a sense of political self-confidence and enlightened self-interest on the part of each citizen. To the extent that these criteria are not met, the election process is not one of consent but degenerates into an exercise in mass pressure. In specific terms, the danger of an advanced industrial society with an elaborate system of mass communication is that the presentation of public affairs will contribute to suspicion and projective distrust and weaken the relevance and legitimacy of the electoral process. How far has this actually taken place in the United States? Does the extensive body of research on political participation make possible an estimate of the magnitude of influence of the mass media on voting behavior and the quality and character of this influence?

It has been argued by some critics that the mass media inherently contribute to suspicion and projective distrust. In this view, political democracy rests on face-to-face communications and in the real world there is an inherent element of remoteness between the mass communicator and his audience. In addition, there is an imbalance of influence and in "feedback" which undermines the process of building consent. Such a line of reason is extreme and self-defeating. The interpersonal basis of political democracy is essential, but one can still reject the assertion that the mass media inherently or uniformly undermine the process of political persuasion. In realistic and pragmatic terms, it is sufficient to offer the criterion that democratic debate and elections depend on the extent to which interpersonal influences operate substantially independent of the influence of the mass media. Thus the question is the strategy and tactics in the handling of public affairs content by the mass media. What is the character of the political struggle between the political elites? Is the approach one in which the emphasis is on building realism and insight (appeals to ego), or is it highly personalistic in format, combative with irrational overtones and appeals to defensive group solidarities (distorted superego appeals)?

Human personality has a great capacity to simplify social reality and to select congenial elements from the mass media. In fact, the immense extent of self-selection is one of the most persistent findings of social psychological research on exposure to the mass media. But the political process of necessity involves simplification of complex issues. The human capacity to simplify the external world makes possible social relations and political decisions. From the point of view of social personality and social control, the basic question is whether these simplifications—stereotypes, in the sense used by Walter Lippmann—are being influenced by a component of personal control and by an appeal to insight, realism, and enlightened self-interest, or by the reverse, including accumulative distrust.

Our hypothesis is that the growing dominance of television, with its stress on a personalistic presentation of public affairs, and the increased emphasis on advocacy journalism make a discernible contribution to the distrustful and projective audience response to public affairs. In essence, the effects of the mass media on public affairs, particularly during election campaigns, conform more to the Lasswell model of systemic significance than to the Lazarsfeld tangential model.

When we offer the hypothesis of the increased influence of the mass media on political behavior after the 1952 election, of course, we are not certain that was the actual reality or whether we are relying on an improved mode of research and analysis. However, we do have more adequate bodies of data for 1952 to 1976, and we are dealing with the shift from radio to television. No one could overlook the significance of radio in the political strategy of Franklin D. Roosevelt. However, the weak political regimes have emerged and political party affiliation has declined during the growth of television, which has highlighted the salience of personality in the political campaigns. The electorate's assessment of the candidate's personality is an essential aspect of public affairs and political campaigns. But what are the consequences of an overwhelming reliance on television as the principal medium of news and commentary during a period of increased complexity of political decisions? The available evidence, I argue, is at least compatible with the observation that while, in 1952–1976, the electoral process operated as a system of generating consent, in varying and fluctuating degree, the mass media have contributed a discernible component of mass distrust and thereby to a weakening of personal and social controls.

The basis for the "disruptive" contribution of the mass media to the electoral process is the convergence of the dominance of television as the major public affairs medium with its very personalized style plus the growth of the advocacy format. National samples demonstrate the long-term increased reliance on television as the source for "most of your news." The relative standing can be seen in table 1, where citizen answers are presented. In 1959, 51 percent reported television, 57 newspapers, and 34 radio; by 1974 television had reached 65 percent, newspapers had dropped slightly to 47 percent, and radio had declined to 21 percent. Perhaps a clearer picture of the dominance of television is obtained when responses are grouped. By 1974, the largest single group comprised those who relied only on television, 36 percent; the second, those who relied on television and newspaper, 23 percent; and the third, those who relied on newspapers only, 19 percent. By 1972 the reliance on television among the college educated almost equaled

TABLE 1 Trends in Mass Media Sources for News, 1959–1974
(Based on National Sample Surveys)

"First, I'd like to ask you where you usually get most of your news about what's going on in the world today—from the newspapers or radio or television or magazines or talking to people or where? "

Source of most news:	1959	1961	1963	1964	1967	1968	1971	1972	1974
Television	51%	52%	55%	58%	64%	59%	60%	64%	65%
Newspapers	57	57	53	56	55	49	48	50	47
Radio	34	34	29	26	28	25	23	21	21
Magazines	8	9	6	8	7	7	5	6	4
People	4	5	4	5	4	5	4	4	4
Don't know no answer (DK/NA)	1	3	3	3	2	3	1	1	●

SOURCE: Adapted for the Roper Organization, "Trends in Public Attitudes toward Television and Other Mass Media, 1959–1974" (New York: Television Information Office, 1975), p. 3.

TABLE 2   Trends in Credibility of Mass Media: 1959–1974
(Based on National Sample Surveys)

"If you got conflicting or different reports of the same news story from radio, television, the magazines and the newspapers, which of the four versions would you be most inclined to believe—the one on radio or television or magazines or newspapers?"

Most believable:	1959	1961	1963	1964	1967	1968	1970	1972	1974
Television	29%	39%	36%	41%	41%	44%	49%	48%	51%
Newspapers	32	24	24	23	24	21	20	21	20
Radio	12	12	12	8	7	8	10	8	8
Magazines	10	10	10	10	8	11	9	10	8
DK/NA	17	17	18	18	20	16	12	13	13

SOURCE: Adapted from the Roper Organization, "Trends in Public Attitudes toward Television and Other Mass Media, 1959–1974" (New York: Television Information Office, 1975), p. 4

that of the less than college educated group. Moreover, television had emerged as the dominant source of news for national, state, and local elections.[10]

But the most striking aspect is the mass audience's trust and approval of television. The text of the specific question is relevant: "If you get conflicting or different reports of the same news story from radio, television, the magazines and the newspapers, which of the four versions would you be most inclined to believe—the one on radio or television or magazines or newspapers?" (See table 2.) From 1959 onward television credibility has grown from 29 percent to 51 percent, while newspapers have declined from 32 percent to 20 percent.

These surveys also probed the performance of local television stations and compared "the job" they were doing with other local institutions. Again, on the basis of national samples, television stations were rated very high; and there has been a long-term increase in the view that they are "doing an excellent or good" job, from 59 percent in 1959 to 71 percent in 1974. The newspapers were rated somewhat lower and experienced a slight decline from 64 percent in the excellent and good category to 58 percent in 1974. The performance of television stations and newspapers was rated higher than that of schools and especially local government.

These findings are noteworthy, in the context of the marked decline in expressed trust in other institutions of U.S. society. The increase in trust in television has been gradual and therefore not linked to partic-

10. A lower level of reliance on television for news is reported in a survey sponsored by the Newsprint Committee. See H. Bagdikian, *The Information Machines: Their Impact on Men and the Media* (New York: Harper and Row, 1971).

ular events. But coverage of the war in Vietnam and of the proceedings of the Watergate investigation has contributed to popular trust in television as a public affairs medium. However, I argue that television and its news commentators are trusted in part because of their consistently suspicious view of public affairs. The commentators help define public affairs as suspect; in effect, they direct suspicion away from themselves to other persons and institutions. They have assisted the audience to project their mistrust and to select targets for their mistrust, almost as if television were a counter "phobic device." The individual must have a focus for his trust, and to trust mainly the devices of the mass media with their exposé orientation is a weak basis for rational appeals and for strengthening ego control. The result is more and more a form of mass media dependency.

The style of the television commentator is to mix news and commentary, to emphasize advocacy posture—often less content and more style.[11] One can point to particular commentators who adhere to a "neutral" style, but the interpretative advocate posture is pronounced. The limitations of time requires more oversimplification than in printed media. If there is to be coverage in depth, one issue is selected—such as the war in Vietnam or Watergate—to the exclusion of others. Television, with its advocacy overtones, is concerned mainly with crises, tensions, and problem formation, not with performance and achievement.[12] Finally, the dissemination of public affairs by personalistic commentators heightens the definition of politics as a struggle between persons, and deemphasizes concern with and debate about underlying issues.[13]

. . . Our analysis converges with the results of the reanalysis of survey data by Michael J. Robinson for 1960–1968 which emphasized

11. Reuven Frank, "An Anatomy of Television News," *Television Quarterly* 9 (1970): 1–23.

12. M. Robinson, "American Political Legitimacy in an Era of Electronic Journalism: Reflections on the Evening News," in *Television as a Social Force: New Approaches to T.V. Criticism,* ed. D. Cates and R. Adler (New York: Praeger, 1975), pp. 97–140. This argument was in the past made about "sensational" newspapers. See H. L. Mencken, "Newspaper Morals," *Atlantic Monthly* 113 (March 1914): 289–97.

13. This analysis of the role of the mass media in creating projective distrust versus insight was stimulated by an essay entitled "Trends in Twentieth Century Propaganda," by Ernest Kris and Nathan Leites, first published in *Psychoanalysis and the Social Sciences* 1 (1947): 393–409. The authors of this essay emphasize the range of potentialities of the mass media in an advanced industrial society. They point out that democratic leaders such as Winston Churchill did make effective use of the mass media by skillful ego-oriented appeals, the contributions of the mass media—in particular television—are not inherent or predetermined.

the "counter phobic" or politically suspicious element in the response to television content.[14] He employs the term "political malaise" to describe the loss of political confidence which extensive exposure produces. Of course, an interactive effect is at work. Great reliance on television rather than on the other media for news is found among persons with a low sense of political efficacy. Some self-selection is at work, but this relationship holds for persons with low and high educational backgrounds. Self-selection then is not an adequate explanation of these and other correlates of high exposure to television news. For example, persons who rely more on television news believed more often that congressmen quickly lose touch with people; and this relationship cuts across education and income groups as well.[15] These results underline the projective influence of television content as it is actually organized and disseminated. Paralleling the consequence of violent content, the effect of television news is cumulative, so that its long-term contribution to political suspicion, which weakens political legitimacy, cannot be denied or overlooked.

In summary, the trends in mass media content and popular response highlight the vulnerabilities of the citizenry to appeals and content which weaken personal control. An advanced industrial society is dependent on the mass media to generate consensus and coordination, but the essential conclusion is that the vast apparatus of the mass media fails to contribute adequately to the articulation of the institutional sectors of society and to contribute to the socialization required for effective social controls. However, it is our assumption that the consent—cultural and political—which is generated by the mass media is conditioned by the extent of popular legitimacy according to the mechanisms and agencies of legal coercion and by the effect of coercive sanction of societal socialization.

14. Robinson, "Public Affairs," See also Jarol B. Mannheim, "Can Democracy Survive Television?" *Journal of Communication* 26 (1976): 84–90.

15. As in the election of 1952, the 1968 election, which Robinson analyzes in some detail, television assisted Nixon, the Republican candidate, and Wallace as well, if both income and educational differences are considered.

15

The Social Ecology of Citizenship

The expansion and intensification of industrialization in Western Europe and the United States have been accompanied by repeated forecasts of the disappearance of the local community and most forms of primary association. From Durkheim to the prophets of mass society, the most available image of the emerging present has been that of an atomized society in which the most durable units of solidarity are social classes linked by economic interests.[1] Most sociologists have been especially inclined to accept this perspective along with its central proposition that new social forms arise by replacing older ones.[2] Gesellschaft replaces gemeinschaft, organic solidarity replaces folk society, rationalism replaces traditionalism, and universalistic associations replace particularistic ones. In their subsequent elaboration, these ideas have become so embedded in the vocabulary of sociological analysis that it is necessary to make a special intellectual effort if one is not to assume that new social forms invariably replace old ones.

There is, of course, a lesser but persistent counterstream of sociological writings that offers a more differentiated "philosophy of history," one that is more cumulative and more closely attuned to con-

Coauthored with Gerald D. Suttles. From *The Management of Human Services*, ed. Rosemary C. Sarri and Yeshebel Hasenfeld, pp. 80–100, 104–4. Reprinted by permission of The Columbia University Press. © 1977 by The Columbia University Press.

1. Kornhauser (1959) and Arendt (1951) have both used the concept of "mass society" to indicate an atomized society in which the individual is uprooted from primordial and primary associations and prone to involvement in popular enthusiasms. Shils (1975) has seriously and effectively questioned this conception of modern society and pointed to the broadening participation provided by modern societies. Nonetheless, the concept of mass society has continued to have a negative connotation and, for most readers, to imply a fragmented or atomized society. For analyses which run in somewhat the same direction, see Nisbet (1953), Stein (1960), and Webber (1961).

2. Some recent enthusiasts have drawn upon the work of Thomas Kuhn (1962) and see in his analyses of scientific revolutions a paradigm for all social change. Such a proposition seems not only premature, but embraces the implausible proposition that all forms of social change are shaped by cognitive considerations parallel to those which have developed in academic physics. The limits to this approach to even academic disciplines are only beginning to be worked out in an empirical fashion; see Stephan Cole (1975).

temporary, empirical findings. Certainly the growing scale of territorial units, especially the nation-state, modifies and refashions groups
like the local community, the family, and the peer group. Yet, despite
competing loyalties and the emergence of more inclusive intermediary
social groupings, the smaller and older social forms seem to have sur-
vived in Western Europe and the United States.[3] The process of social
change appears to have been less one of replacement than one in which
older, local, and provincial social forms become more specialized and
more delimited in their social claims. At new levels of sociocultural
integration (Steward, 1955), such groups usually develop specific links
which relate them to the wider society in a mutually supportive manner. Thus, while the family has lost many of its economic functions, it
has become the central institution providing support for economic activity (Schumpeter, 1942, p. 160), educational attainment (Coleman et
al., 1966), and a generalized form of patriotism to the nation-state
(Coser, 1951). Similarly, the widely hailed militancy of local control
groups and ethnic groups probably represents less an outright effort at
separation than a visceral urge to create some reciprocal avenues of
influence between themselves and the centralized bureaucracies of the
wider society.

The popular idea that new social forms replace old ones has not
only confused the intellectual work of social scientists, but it has also
had negative consequences in the management of public affairs, particularly in our ideology guiding the organization of partisan politics. Of
course, the nation-state has become the dominant social form in the
contemporary societies of Western Europe and the United States. But
this has not meant the loss of their local communities, their families,
their religious congregations, and the like. Nor has it meant the clear
formation of the population into contending social classes with a
stable identity and a persistent recognition of their unitary interests.
Confrontation and outright efforts at secession are present, but in general the contest between subnational and national groups has been resolved by clarifying and narrowing the respective responsibilities of

3. This is so much the case that some sociologists are regularly required to hail the
"reemergence' of pre-modern social forms. Thus, in the last decade and a half we have
had the "resurgence of ethnicity," an "emergent" local control movement, a "back to
Jesus movement," and a "withdrawal" to communitarian social life. There is little doubt
that some of these social movements involve a genuine increase in public interest, but by
and large they are continuations of past forms of social affiliation and activity. Much of
the surprise registered by some authors is due to a premature belief that such groups
were moribund. Studies documenting the continuity of primary and primordial relations
have regularly provided an available counterbalance (Janowitz, 1967; Shils, 1957).

local communities and those of more widely based institutions. Indeed, the general pattern seems to be one where the older, more localized social forms retrench their holistic claims on the loyalty of members and maintain their vitality both by specializing and by forging new reciprocal links to the wider society.[4] The local community remains a primary catchment area within which many national organizations attempt to recruit and mobilize their memberships. The church congregation may retain only delimited liturgical forms, but it has become a major institution in shaping the delivery of social-work services. While most ethnic groups retain some distinctive celebrations and consumptory practices, they also find occasion to honor national values and symbols (Thomas et al. 1921; Warner, 1959; Herberg, 1955; Glazer and Moynihan, 1963).

Current political debate tends to pass over these persistent accommodations between national and local forms and to beguile us into a "crisis of legitimacy" in which the Local Control Movement and the resurgence of primordial groups is seen as a profound and possibly terminal confrontation with the nation-state. This is particularly the case with the Local Control Movement, whose demands are usually juxtaposed to the powers of the central government and most other nationwide organizations, including those representing broad social classes (Lowi, 1971). In the case of the local community this preconception seems especially misleading to us and in this article we will attempt to recast this issue in different terms. In our own view the major issue is not a final solution to the competing claims of the local community and the nation-state, but a profound disarticulation between the "natural" territorial groupings of the local community and the more contrived ones of political and administrative hierarchies. There is strong evidence that the natural community survives in the continuing effort of residents to conceive of themselves as belonging to small neighborhoods, or what we will call the *social bloc*. These social blocs, however, are frequently embedded in at least two other levels of geographic mobilization: an *organizational community*, which adopts explicit goals and strategies on behalf of local interests, and the *aggregated metropolitan community*, which is an attempt to aggregate diverse organizational communities on behalf of the political economy

---

4. Some of the followers of Mills and Hunter have chosen to work with such an undifferentiated notion of "power" that the qualitative dominance of the nation-state is seen as totally one-sided (Domhoff, 1971). Such an undifferentiated and qualitative conception of power is useful only if one wishes to slide over the distinction between totalitarianism and social democracy. Lasswell (1958) pointed out the difficulties inherent in his approach as early as 1958.

of the metropolis. In the contemporary metropolis, then, community is a diffuse form of social organization, and in fact the citizen finds himself involved in multiple communities. Properly conceived, the local community is a staging area in which diverse interests are mobilized and joined in an aggregative political process that can shape, strengthen, and legitimize the actions of political and administrative hierarchies. The failure to see this is attributable in part to the "decline in community" approach but is also due to an overly simple and reified conception of local communities.

The Local Community and Citizenship

According to democratic theory the most rudimentary social responsibility of local communities is to transform the ideals of citizenship into effective and self-governing action. The idea of citizenship centers on political rights in the first instance but has gradually come to include economic and social rights as essential to a competitive parliamentary democracy. Political rights, such as free speech or enfranchisement, have become the basis for arguing for economic and social rights. In turn, the latter (that is, the right to essential economic security) have come to be seen as requisites to the exercise of political rights. Each affirmation of citizenship leads to a general claim for the extension of rights—political, economic, and social. . . .

We accept this line of argument, but it is partial and far from complete. The extension of rights—political, social, or economic—presupposes an effective extension of obligations or voluntary stewardship. Rights or "freedom" can be extended only when and where there is some assurance that citizens and the smaller groups to which they belong will accept their newly won liberties with circumspection and self-imposed responsibility.[5] Parliamentary democracies, then, are workable only when they maintain a delicate balance between the extension of individual freedoms and the willingness of subgroups to become contributors to the maintenance of social order. By themselves, bureaucratic norms, universalistic standards, and the civic ideals of democracy seem uncompelling unless they are endorsed and given exemplary weight in the smaller confines in which individuals can feel the consequences of their action by "taking the role of the other." Except in rare instances, it simply seems impossible for individuals to

5. See Shils (1957) for his observations on how the failure of subnational groups to accept such responsibilities retards the development of social democracies and favors authoritarian governments in the developing nations.

internalize directly the impersonal aims and rules of administrative hierarchies. To the extent that such norms are incorporated into the personality, they must be experienced as consequential for others who are sufficiently close to arouse "empathy." [6] Necessarily, then, it is primordial and primary relations such as those in the family or the local community that translate to the individual the reciprocities which go with nationally declared freedoms and make people more or less willing and responsible citizens whose self-regulation replaces the need for repression by the central state (Janowitz, 1975).

The survival of parliamentary democracies, then, depends heavily upon how nearly its separate, local parts—its more intimate circles— relate to and interpret the larger movements of the wider society. Here, the local community seems to have a central, if not unique, role. Where the family, the peer group, and the church congregation tend to be very homogeneous and to have very narrow interests, the local community creates a potential interface between diverse interests and the opportunity to debate, sort, sift, and balance each against the other. This potential is of extraordinary importance, for while it is the habit of sociologists and most contrived groups to speak of narrowly defined interests, real individuals are the repository of an aggregate of interests, most of them poorly represented by the formal groups that currently have an acknowledged role in the political process. It is in the local community that individuals have the opportunity—by no means always realized—both to internalize and aggregate the diverse gains and costs of public policy.

Understandably, macrosociology has been predominantly concerned with the impact of the global processes of urbanization, industrialization, and bureaucratization. As a result it has given only sporadic attention to the infrastructure of lesser groups which can play either a supporting or corrosive part in the maintenance of total societies. Our intent is to examine the local community—the neighborhood as it is commonly understood—in terms of its continued role in modern parliamentary democracies, including both its existing limitations and its potentialities. In our view modern societies suffer especially from an "irresponsible" citizenry, a citizenry which is able to represent its interests primarily through narrow and mutually exclusive interest groups. Thus, despite widespread evidence of public feeling, people find themselves impotent at conserving national resources, enforcing frugality in public expenditures, or accepting responsibility

---

6. Our statement on this matter is necessarily brief, but it follows the durable analyses of Cooley (1902), Mead (1934), and Dewey (1922).

for the excesses of the past. The fault lies not so much with the citizenry itself, however, as the lack of any systematic structure for articulating grass-roots sentiments with policies of national leadership.

The Moral and Political Functions of Local Communities

We do not insist that the local community is an especially vigorous or simply indestructible social unit in contemporary society. Journalistic and sociological writers have overburdened it with a sentimental obituary. Local leadership is frustrated and prone to accuse all national organizations as the cause of their weakness. Some local spokesmen have retreated into utopianism, demanding complete local control in a nation heavily dependent on the central management of national accounts (Janowitz, 1975). Other spokesmen have deliberately followed a "beggar your neighbor" strategy, trying to shift unattractive installations (power plants, public housing) to other areas while they benefit from the benign placement of clean industries,[7] golf courses, luxury housing, and homes for the elderly. It is easy to dismiss these demands for local control as a fatal weakness of the local community or to conceive of them as only segregationist efforts to obtain the best for oneself to the disadvantage of others. But the outcry for local control is not just a sign of community disorganization, nor is it individualism writ large.

The Local Control Movement reflects a real concern with territorially based or locational decisions made by regulatory, administrative, and public service agencies that affect both public finances and the quality of life in the broadest sense. On the financial level, the movement reveals a chronic discontent with access to employment and the disparate pattern of local taxation and municipal finances. Despite expanding employment and welfare services during the 1960s, financial advantages continued to shift to suburban communities, and even this pattern was highly selective and partial (Kain, 1975). At the public service level, the failure of the mass urban educational system to respond to changing occupational requirements was a core issue but the

7. Universities continue to be popular although medical centers with their detoxification centers and emergency wards are encountering resistance. Even parks, which tend to attract unruly youngsters, seem to be running into some opposition. There seems to be a heightened awareness of the costs associated with public installations and a growing pattern of segregation in which facilities low- and high-income communities are willing to accept. This seems to be particularly true in the suburbs (Logan, 1976). But in general, the lack of any systematic review process vastly prolongs the development of such installations and increases their costs as well.

debate over public management was easily extended to include health services, transportation, and access to cultural institutions.[8] The demand for community control was not merely an expression of a dying social group, but a public judgment on the shortcomings of centralized and bureaucratic arrangements which were thought to be a rational means of serving local populations.

One group of sociologists, economists, and political scientists [has] responded by arguing for another increase in the scale of urban organization, essentially some kind of metropolitan government which would extend to include, in effect, entire SMSA's (Hawley and Rock, 1975; Committee for Economic Development, 1970).[9] Undoubtedly, this strategy would balance some of the inequities so apparent in the local tax structure and the quality of public services. However, metropolitanization has not been a popular or effective success in the United States (Campbell and Dollenmayer, 1975). The few urban areas which have implemented it seem to have experienced only modest gains in improving the equity of their delivery of services or the imbalance in their collection of revenues. Metropolitanization is a defensible organizational effort. It is not a panacea and, in our view, it must be accompanied by an articulate structure for aggregating grass-roots opinions so that local and provincial views are included in the council of government and responded to in such a manner that local groups rightfully feel that they are a party to municipal decisions.

Similarly, the hope of restoring local control by fragmenting existing jurisdictions into small, sometimes overlapping units seems fraught with difficulties. This counterproposal to metropolitanization takes its most explicit form in the public choice literature (Ostrom, 1974; Bish, 1971; Bish and Ostrom, 1973) which argues that government services are most responsive when residents can vote with their feet among many relatively independent territorial units. The central problem, of course, is that family income is a heavy determinant in who can vote in this scheme by changing their residence. Such a pattern of jurisdictional fragmentation may only worsen the discrepancy

8. This diffusion of discontent, as every minority increased its demands, seems to have confused public leaders who seemed unable to distinguish between issues that were of widespread concern and those urged upon them by a tiny number of partisans.

9. We do not disagree with these supporters of metropolitan government, but we do recognize that one of the main sources of resistance to metropolitan government is the absence of any rational and systematic structure within which the residents of local communities can separately manage their own affairs or have a say in the management of metropolitan governance. In this instance as well as many others the drive for centralization does not exclude that for decentralization (Suttles, 1975).

between have and have-not residential groups, since agencies would be responsible primarily to those with a great deal of discretion in where they choose to live. More important, perhaps, a further fragmentation of metropolitan jurisdictions—turning the central city into something like the suburbs—seems likely to only reinforce provincialism and reduce the necessity for trade-offs between groups competing for social services. The "toy governments" of suburbia not only trivialize civic life (Gottdiener, 1977), but fail to attach leaders and citizens to broad-based conceptions of social welfare. Clearly there is a need for including the demands of small-scale local groups, but they must be aggregated in some larger system that permits debates, trade-offs, and transfer payments among diverse groups.

During the later 1960s and early 1970s there has been some recognition of the need for local participation in an increasingly metropolitanized society.[10] Both those advocating metropolitanization and those advocating local control have refined and sharpened their objectives and their rhetorics. Participants in community organizations have become more oriented toward metropolitan organization, while reform politicians have come to realize the advantages of appealing to local community organizations—not only to capture office but also to reshape the distribution of public services and urban policies. Some community groups have shifted away from lobbying exclusively for "their share" to a demand for more direct and continuous participation in the operation of administrative and service agencies. There has also emerged a number of national groups, such as the National Association of Neighborhoods, National Peoples Action, and National Neighbors, which have begun to link groups from different metropolitan areas. A much larger number of metropolitan-wide citizen groups have developed as some specialized public services have achieved metropolitan scale (environmental, sanitation, water) and attracted the attention of citizens hoping to exercise influence in limited areas (pollution, transportation, consumer protection).

Despite these realignments, it would be a grave error to say that broadened community participation or a heightened awareness of localism have been substantial steps toward an effective representative

10. Considerable metropolitanization has already taken place in the form of port authorities, transportation authorities, regional water and sewer districts, and a variety of federal agencies (health, welfare, and pollution) which have regional jurisdictions. As A. Hawley (1971, p. 262) has pointed out, these authorities actually reduce potential political participation since their administrators are not subject to direct election, review, or recall. An example of how the administrators of such authorities may avoid popular consideration is contained in Robert Caro's (1974) biography of Robert Moses.

structure for making both leaders and citizens more responsive to some shared conception of public welfare. The politicization of submerged and marginal groups has broadened participation, but their increasing demands for participation have not been matched by institutional guarantees to insure that new rights would be weighted by assured duties. Indeed, the general tendency of local community organizations has been to heighten fears of irresponsibility and lend additional credibility to the image that all cities are "rip-off cities"—localized, limited liability corporations in which each gets without giving, or the more frequent complaint, gives without getting.[11]

The mechanisms by which the local community can aggregate both public demands and social accountability are varied. Residential areas are above all the social site within which the family life cycle is given moral and symbolic content. It is the locus within which each generation is called upon to invest in the next generation, to transcend generational and territorial existence and expend resources—material and psychic—on the fate of another person. The local school is its most obvious and natural repository of sacred involvement, the core institution by which one generation gives without immediate expectation of repayment. It is both the long-run hope for familial advancement and of one's hope to cross into *la vie serieuse* (Shils, 1975). The neighborhood school, then, is a precious institution and we should not be too surprised that it is so ardently defended as in South Boston and other locales.

The local community also has a caretaker function, and one that is not easily transferred to other groups. Much, if not all, of the physical plant of human society is sessile; that is, most of our public possessions must be located where they can be guarded, cared for, kept clean, or at least left unharmed.[12] Those who live around these sessile resources are necessarily public custodians; people who look out for school windows, the disposal of wastes, and the informal surveillance

11. The recent recession and financial crisis in the urban heartland has also made many city dwellers conscious of the balance between what they contribute in taxes and what is returned to them. This was especially evident during the efforts to get the federal government to help finance deficit spending for New York City.

12. As Anthony Downs (1970) comments, home ownership is the main way in which Americans experience and involve themselves in capitalism. The value of a home is so dependent upon the maintenance of surrounding property that we need not expand on the importance of local caretaking in this respect. Among some Americans, for instance low-income blacks and youths, the automobile seems to be their only secure investment. Such a mobile stake in the society has little consequence in promoting a sense of collective responsibility and a care for long-term aspirations.

of street life. In the diurnal cycle of the citizen, a set of norms emerges—or does not emerge—for disposing of discarded cigarette butts, mowing one's lawn, helping a neighbor in distress, or in the governance of local policy.

The local community, then, is a catchment area in which accountability is identified and made collective; a bounded group in which responsibility is joint, yet so narrowly circumscribed that its members can realistically contribute to the task of self-regulation. Collective investments in the future of children and the caretaking of the nearby physical environment dramatize its moral and political functions. Its more general function, however, is to allow people to internalize the costs and benefits of collective life through face-to-face relations that extend beyond narrowly defined primary groups. If responsibility (and correspondingly guilt) are extensively diffused and circulated throughout a total society, they tend to cancel themselves out, making no one in particular responsible. Diffusion of responsibility relies upon ineffective self-judgment and leaves everyone able to point the finger of blame at everyone else. Put simply, there must be someone innocent enough to accord blame; conversely blame must be so segregated or delimited as to shame the culprit before an audience that is yet a part of his larger social world.

One can summarize these functions by asserting that the local community aggregates and internalizes both public demands and their costs; that its primary functions inevitably involve it in the management of total societies. Its capacity to promote primary relations across diverse groups is its outstanding and distinctive feature. Most other subnational groups are either very homogeneous or unable to capture more than a narrow aspect of the individual's identity. Labor unions and professional groups have come to be seen as bargainers for higher wages and little else, as if their members were not taxpayers, mortgage holders, welfare recipients, or investors.[13] The heads of industrial enterprise and corporate executives are viewed in the same way and cannot act in a credible manner on behalf of the wider community. Through continual reform or bureaucratization, even the big city political parties have lost their direct and intimate contacts with

13. This is evident not only in the very limited participation in most labor unions, but also in the frequent dissatisfaction of their rank and file over working conditions while their leadership continues to lobby for higher wages alone. The failure of American labor unions to grow much over the last two decades also indicates their inability to enlarge their popular appeal. In turn the growth of municipal employee unions has resulted in an escalation of their wages with no apparent increase in their morale or productivity.

precinct-level demands (Lowi, 1971). Despite their recent prominence, ethnic and racial groups have been especially narrow in their demands upon the wider society, arguing for their share of benefits rather than pressing for a general reconsideration of the relationship between the political economy of public and private services and the balance between expenses and social benefits.

Because members of different households share a single territory, each of their special interests—those of housewives, taxpayers, union leaders, public employees, activists, parents, and the like—are brought together so that their relative merit can be debated and transformed into some effective image of "the public interest." Thus, the local community is one mechanism—maybe the only one—in which the diseconomies of a highly differentiated society come into a single social account which weighs both gains and losses. Parliamentary democracy rests on those institutions that reconcile diverse interests and provide a voluntary rather than a coercive social order. Our political parties have the same tasks, but they presuppose a prior sifting and sorting of public opinion—a sifting and sorting that will give political leaders a clear sense of the drift of grass-roots feeling.

It is clear from recent examination of the political parties that they are inadequate as the sole mechanism for discovering the collective demands of the American people. The decline in party loyalty and the rise in voter distrust (Janowitz, 1975) document the weakness of the party system as a sufficient means for finding a shared set of objectives within the "regular political process" (Broder, 1972). Correspondingly the rise of community groups, which explicitly aim to replace the political party or which claim a special legitimacy for their representational powers, is evidence of the limitation of the party system. Not only are our political parties weak, but they are being challenged in their own strongholds—the local community, the ward, the precinct, or the election district. Neither the local community nor the political parties seem to be fully able to accept their responsibility to reach or develop centers of power that are regarded as effective or legitimate. Neither seems to be sufficiently self-conscious to recognize the need for a social reconstruction of the local community or the political parties. Our analysis suggests a mindful attempt to do both.

Sociological and Political Conceptions of the Local Neighborhood

There has been a long-term effort in sociology to define the "local community." The first was an attempt to designate "natural communities"; self-designated and self-generated communities which were thought to be a subsocial construction rather than an intended product. This model was promoted most effectively by Ernest W. Burgess (1929) and his followers, who sought to identify communities which were the product of ecological processes such as proximity, frequent interaction, and the spatially determined traffic patterns which brought local residents into a shared life around common facilities like the school, local shopping facilities, play lots, and local centers for the delivery of social services. In this view, the patterns of socio-economic, ethnic, and racial segregation were an unintended, crescive way of distributing people so that they could form communities—impersonal, subsocial forces which made population aggregates into communities whether or not they liked it.

Following the work of Burgess (1929), the concept of the natural community became progressively less persuasive, and to a considerable extent it was replaced by the concept of the community of limited liability (Janowitz, 1967). The community of limited liability emphasized the voluntary character of personal ties to the local community. On the one hand, residents were seen as having a choice about where they could live and how much they would participate in the local community and in designing the nature of their own schools, convenience shopping centers, play lots, or local services. On the other hand, the community of limited liability emphasized the instrumental momentum of local community relations, the purposeful creation of a community which provided a common way of life to people living in close proximity.

Still again, the community has been viewed as a contiguous clientele for a constellation of public services. In this conception the community is mainly an area of service delivery, some locale large or small, but separated out by the fact that its residents are common consumers in a school district, sanitation district, police district, or the like. Not only do the heads of these public service agencies persistently refer to their district as a "community," but the resident consumers have often mobilized themselves around the same imagery in an effort to control or shape the services they receive (Barsky, 1974).

Each of these conceptions of the local community should not be considered as if it captured, or at least approximated, the full reality of the community. Much debate has gone into the decision as to which is the "true" basis for the local community formation; whether it is a subsocial product, whether it is a construction of individual or group decisions, or whether it is merely a collective consumer. In effect, however, urban residents have drawn upon all three lines of community formation in their efforts to achieve accountability and to aggregate competing self-interests into stable political preferences.

To insure accountability, citizens in the United States, with the aid of the housing market, have tended to segregate themselves into small, homogeneous groups who are relatively well acquainted with one another and can presume mutual trust. These local units range from ethnic enclaves to the well-fenced suburban estate. The social processes which give rise to these territorial units is similar to that which Ernest Burgess (1929) attributed to the natural area segregation, invasion, and succession. However, the social bloc is probably a more appropriate descriptive term for these population concentrations.

Such small residential groups, however, have found it impossible to avoid encroaching on one another's social space; shared schools, shopping areas, parks, local traffic arteries, and the like. Thus, while people have tended to withdraw into provincial enclaves, they have been drawn simultaneously into more encompassing voluntary associations to achieve broader, more integrative goals. Their commitment to such associational forms was always limited and frequently rather instrumental, even downright selfish. However, as de Tocqueville first documented, the vitality in American communities rested not on the coercion of the residents into a single territorial unit, but on the flexibility of developing and settling upon rather pragmatic boundaries and organizational forms. The community of limited liability, then, was founded largely on secondary and voluntary associations aimed to aggregate public opinion across many social boundaries for the purpose of self-help, self-regulation, and negotiation with the wider community. Necessarily, such communities often had shifting boundaries and changing organizational forms. With the increasing scale of most public agencies, community organizations tended to shift the scale of their own organizations as well, creating in many instances yet another tier of organizational life through federations and metropolitan-wide social movements (Hunter, 1974). These organizations are often the most visible forms of community in contemporary America, and they are among the most militant in the demand for decentralization or local control. Typically, however, they represent a loosely coordinated federation whose cohesion rests upon some degree of territorial unity and local leaders concerned to influence specific administrative centers. Such federations, then, tend to move toward a more professional staff and a more self-conscious effort to contrive communities and to enlist support.

It is our contention that each tier to this hierarchy of community organization is an authentic form of the local community and that they represent elaborations of the concept of community rather than the replacement of one concept of community or the replacement of one social type by another. . . .

The fundamental division between the very localized neighborhood or social bloc and the institutional linkages which draw the citizen into the metropolis represents a persistent and enlarged pattern. Under appropriate leadership and conditions, this division might become the dynamic by which competing interests are aggregated and brought to legitimate resolution while also preserving the accountability which is integral to the social bloc. Local demands are the launching platform for demands to intervene—to meddle, if you wish—in the affairs of other communities. In an articulated debate of this variety, it is always a two-way process, one in which narrowly based, often rather homogeneous, residential groups get and give. This is so whether the issue is pollution, school finances, gun control, or public housing. However slowly, the popular debate pushes forward a broader geographic perspective on civic responsibility.

Yet, the contemporary popular debate about community participation has become unusually tardy and unproductive.[14] Much effort is wasted on what is the true community, and social policies are distorted by efforts to arbitrate among competing claims as if one or another community level were more genuine than another. Both local leaders and political aspirants are relieved of responsibility when public officials insist that their administrative districts take precedence over the territorial boundaries promoted by local residents or when the opposite occurs. Even more destructive is the shifting of political decisions from one level of the tier to another, so as to work a persistent bias against one faction or to avoid the aggregation of diverse interests in reaching a resolution that might be defended on the grounds that it is instrumental to the long-term welfare of the larger community. Stalemate and counteraccusations of "conspiracy" are a common product. An "ecology of games" without any moral claim for the need for restraint or compromise in the interests of a larger collectivity is one way of portraying this outcome (Long, 1958).

Thus different proponents of the local community, as well as those who openly discount it, tend to embrace a common outlook, attributing both responsibility and power to a vaguely defined "they" who are

14. Such a debate also tends to discredit the proponents of local community control and lead to Lowi's (1971, 65–80) conclusion that the local control movement is only an opportunistic effort to press narrowly based social interests.

outside the practical management of local affairs. As a result highly centralized authorities such as the Supreme Court or federal regulatory agencies are frequently called upon to adjudicate local disputes. The frequency of federal cases has grown rapidly and it has become a common practice to initiate community controversies with the hope that they will reach the higher courts or federal regulatory agencies.

But the federal courts and federal regulatory agencies have had only a most limited impact on disputes which continue to unsettle local communities. Federal directives on school busing, on public housing, on group living quarters, as well as local taxation, are examples of federal intervention which have resulted in continuing controversy and tension. Federal origination or intervention does not insure public acceptance. But it is also clear that we have not made adequate provision for the effective development of local consultation and debate which might contribute to new solutions or at least give those proposed by the federal authorities the necessary legitimacy.[15]

Both community leaders and those attempting to respond to them generally operate with overly primitive notions about the nature of the local community. Typically they are locked into an inarticulate test of strength with the local community proclaiming its popular mandate, while central, governmental agencies issue formal directives and elaborate plans based on constitutional and legal authority. Neither demonstrates sufficient enlightenment about the potentials of parliamentary democracy, but they do demonstrate the need for a more differentiated conception of the local community and its potential capacity for assuming the burdens of a society that aims at high levels of participation and low levels of coercion. The initial step toward rational change is to identify the levels of the local community and to link each part of this tier to the functions and responsibilities of the public hierarchy which parallel it.

The social bloc or natural community is a persistent and ongoing structure in American life. The social bloc itself is frequently represented or embedded in formal associations which link it to other social blocs and municipal agencies. These formal associations themselves are frequently combined into a web of inter-organizational relations whose natural boundary seems to be the metropolis itself. The first of these levels—the social bloc—arises primarily from the indigenous

15. Although the resolution shown by the federal government is clearly important in reconciling some communities, notably those in the South, to school desegregation, it is also clear that school desegregation has been accompanied by less friction where local community groups have been active in developing community acceptance as in Detroit and Charlotte.

processes usually associated with the local community—propinquity, homogeneity, natural boundaries, and a diffuse pattern of interaction. The other two levels, however, are much more obviously instrumental efforts to link up local residential groups with the bureaucratic order of urban government and they are often initiated by government agencies specifically for this purpose (Taub, 1976). While each of these forms is relatively distinct and only partially coincides in the persons who participate in each, they seem to represent a growing division of labor in which there is considerable potential for coordination.

The social bloc is basic to the structure because it provides people with a sense of joint responsibility and some measure of mutual control and access. Relations within it tend to be intimate and diffuse in character. The reciprocities which are expected within this territorial unit, however, tend to be limited and relatively uncontroversial—the informal supervision of one another's children or pets, taking in another's mail, driving someone to the hospital, or lending a cup of brandy—all the little emergencies that allow us to appeal to proximity as the cause for available kindness. The social bloc tends to be very homogeneous, or it is unstable. People simply move out once differences in ethnic, religious, or other primordial guarantees of trust become imperiled. It is also the level of community within which strong differences of opinion are difficult to broach lest they endanger the limited and diffuse consensus of the co-residents. Typically small and homogeneous, its demands on government tend to be fairly narrow and unmindful of the counterclaims of other social blocs and groups.[16]

For all these reasons the *social bloc* is not the appropriate unit for direct political debate or for formal negotiations with administrative hierarchies. Above all it needs to be given recognition as a natural unit with its own informal processes of developing leadership. One of the great shortcomings of the U.S. Census Bureau and other data-gathering agencies is that they have failed in their original responsibility to report reliably to such small areas on their social health, composition, and the impact of social programs. The failure to report on such areas diminishes the stability of their identity and reduces the likelihood that their leadership will be able to play a role in higher

16. Obviously there are exceptions to this, particularly where the homogeneity of the social block remains uncontested and such areas grow to the point that they include an entire complement of social services—a school district, a political ward, or a historic enclave that is widely recognized, such as our "Chinatowns," "Little Italys," "Bohemias." It is our impression that such enlarged social blocs tend to be remnants of the old ethnic colonies, high-income inner-city areas, or satellite communities which have retained their identities despite suburbanization.

levels of community organization. For this reason the social bloc is most often left out in community-wide decisions and this leads to both a sense of estrangement on the part of its residents and an inability to call upon the natural leaders it produces. The leadership of the social bloc, however, is one of its most valued assets since it may have the ability to open up the channels of communication between it and other levels of community organizations. Indeed the distinctive feature of all the community levels we are proposing here is not their self-contained unity, but their tendency to enlarge their ambitions and their membership.

It is the organizational community that typically makes a much more explicit bid to involve itself in controversies and to shape the delivery of municipal services. The organizational community may range from a very formal association which has an elected body of officers and staff and publicized procedures for participation to little more than a persistent group of "concerned citizens" who meet at the local school, church, or wherever they can find space. Although much of its leadership is voluntary and informally selected, the organizational community usually aspires to a name and to some limited presence in the form of a list of officers, mailing list, and flyers for publicity. The organizational community arises in part from the persistent effort of residents in the social bloc to involve themselves in a larger territorial framework and to enlist allies to shape or redirect the policies of local service agencies in their districts. But the organizational community is also often a response to external demands for "community representation" and its formation usually draws in additional leaders, especially advocates from welfare organizations, the church, and the school (Taub, 1976). Its natural tendency is to form around the district-level delivery of services and to focus on episodic, "crisis" issues that afflict more than one social bloc. It is a purposeful organization, but its ability to mobilize concerted action still depends heavily upon broad support from its constituent social blocs and an informal consensus among its leaders.

The organizational community, however, is continually frustrated by the expanding scale of urban organization and the fragmentation of most municipal delivery systems. If the school district, local ward, police district, and other delivery units roughly coincide, efforts to influence the day-to-day operation of municipal agencies can be effective. But in most cities these delivery districts are badly fragmented (Hunter and Suttles, 1972) and this fragmentation has been accompanied by the growth of super districts—federal, state, and local—which makes decision-making very remote from the organizational community. Thus, despite the ability of the organizational community to enjoin controversial issues and to develop a more instrumental leadership, its aims are frequently frustrated by an inability to reach the metropolitan-wide administration that increasingly makes policy for district-level agencies.

It is to this changing scale of urban organization that Hunter (1974) attributes the growth in confederations of community organizations. This *aggregated metropolitan community* is obviously incompletely formed in our major cities; however, many of its distinctive features are apparent. It tends to have at least some full-time professional staff, to be able to publicize its own efforts and organization, and to acquire sufficient visibility to bring some municipal officials to the bargaining table. So far, such federations have tended to have a rather narrow focus on community-wide services like transportation, housing, or sewage disposal, which are organized on a regional basis. But the ability of these federations to catch the attention of the press and to dramatize gross malfunctions [has] given them considerable political leverage and they have been able to put together razor-thin majorities to authorize mass transportation in Chicago and to help elect the mayor of Gary, Indiana.

Nonetheless these federations seem to be weakened by their narrow focus on services which have a regional base. They are also weakened by the clash-exacerbated by different racial concentrations—between the interests of the inner city and those of the suburbs. Yet even here there are attempts, weak and fragile as they may be, to create some overarching level of community participation. The central issues which have promoted this suburban-city level of cooperation [are] the management of the transportation system because of the energy crisis and the rapidly growing costs of services in the suburbs. Obviously a metropolitan level of government would facilitate the expansion of effort by the aggregated metropolitan community.

It is our argument that these three levels represent the natural or functional division of labor in the search for community in parliamentary societies. Their importance lies not so much in their self-announced presence—although that element should be given due weight—but in their capacity to address the problems of accountability and the management of the new urban *oikonomus*. The issue is more than merely a matter of resolving competing interests, although that is essential. Rather the basis for this selective tier lies in its internal dynamic, the persistent efforts of the social bloc to reach outward through voluntary organizations to meet the administrative levels of the central city and the metropolis. In turn, the sense of participation and the more systematic debate permitted by this tier of community levels provides a responsible role for community groups. This role, then, not only makes them party to municipal decision-making, but reinforces their obligation to bear its costs as well as its benefits.

Certainly we do not mean in these comments to elaborate a structure through which the local community can be co-opted as a passive partner to existing administrative hierarchies. Taken together each of these community levels has real influence under even present circumstances and their aspirations seem to be well justified. Undoubtedly, each level is weakened by the complexity and haphazard contrivances of municipal agencies. The *social bloc* usually lacks any explicit form of recognition and is seldom systematically included in collective efforts to provide an account of its collective welfare. The organizational community is continually frustrated by the fragmentation of district-level delivery systems and the rigidity of bureaucratized and unionized city services agencies. The *aggregated metropolitan community* faces the serious barrier of suburb-city separation and some of the same types of rigid bureaucratization. All of these community levels are overshadowed by the widespread tendency either to dismiss the community as a viable collectivity or to juxtapose its continued existence to that of centralized government. The missing element in the analysis of the local community remains the clarification of the scope and hierarchy of the territorial units appropriate in a differentiated conception of community responsibilities. If the local community is to contribute to citizen accountability and to citizen participation, however, it is obvious that two or more levels are necessary. Localism, in this view, is not provincialism, but potentially an incentive to cosmopolitanism—or, at least, metropolitanism. . . .

References

Arendt, Hannah. 1951. *The Origins of Totalitarianism*. New York: Harcourt, Brace.

Barsky, Stephen. 1974. "Representations of Community." Ph.D. diss., University of Chicago.

Bish, Robert L. 1971. *The Public Economy of Metropolitan Areas*. Chicago: Markham.

Bish, Robert L., and Vincent Ostrum. 1973. *Understanding Urban Government: Metropolitan Reform Reconsidered*. Washington, D.C.: American Enterprise Institute for Public Policy Research.

Broder, David S. 1972. *The Party's Over*. New York: Harper.

Burgess, Ernest W. 1929. *Urban Areas of Chicago: An Experiment in Social Science Research*. Chicago: University of Chicago Press.

Campbell, Alan K., and Judith A. Dollenmayer. 1975. "Governance in a Metropolitan Society." In A. Hawley and V. Rock, eds., *Metropolitan America in Contemporary Perspective,* pp. 335–96. New York: Halsted.

Caro, Robert A. 1974. *The Power Broker.* New York: Knopf.

Cole, Stephan. 1975. "The Growth of Scientific Knowledge." In L. Coser, ed., *The Idea of Social Structure,* pp. 175–220. New York: Harcourt, Brace, Jovanovich.

Coleman, J., et al. 1966. *Equality of Educational Opportunity.* Washington, D.C.: U.S. Government Printing Office.

Committee for Economic Development. 1970. *Reshaping Government in Metropolitan Areas.* New York: Committee for Economic Development.

Cooley, Charles H. 1902. *Human Nature and the Social Order.* New York: Scribners.

Coser, Lewis A. 1951. "Some Aspects of Societal Family Policy," *American Journal of Sociology,* 56:424–37.

Dewey, John. 1922. *Human Nature and Conduct.* New York: Holt.

Domhoff, G. William. 1971. *The Higher Circles.* New York: Random House.

Downs, Anthony. 1970. *Urban Problems and Prospects.* Chicago: Markham.

Glazer, Nathan, and Daniel Moynihan. 1963. *Beyond the Melting Pot.* Cambridge: Harvard-M.I.T. Press.

Gottdeiner, Mark. 1977. *Planned Sprawl.* Beverly Hills, Calif: Sage Publications.

Greer, Scott. 1962. *The Emerging City: Myth and Reality.* New York: Free Press.

Hawley, Amos H. 1971. *Urban Society.* New York: Ronald Press.

Hawley, Amos H., and Vincent P. Rock, eds. 1975. *Metropolitan American in Contemporary Perspective.* New York: Halsted.

Herberg, Will. 1955. *Protestant, Catholic, Jew.* Garden City, N.Y.: Doubleday.

Hunter, Albert. 1974. *Symbolic Communities: The Persistence of Change of Chicago's Local Communities.* Chicago: University of Chicago Press.

Hunter, Albert, and Gerald D. Suttles. 1972. "The Expanding Community of Limited Liability," pp. 44–81, in *The Social Construction of Communities.* Chicago: University of Chicago Press.

Janowitz, Morris. 1967. *The Community Press in an Urban Setting.* Second Edition. Chicago: University of Chicago Press.

———1975. "Sociological Theory and Social Control," *American Journal of Sociology,* 81:82–108.

———1976. *Social Control of the Welfare State.* New York: Elsevier.

Kain, John F. 1975. *Essays on Urban Spatial Structure.* Cambridge, Mass.: Ballinger.

Kornhauser, W. 1959. *The Politics of Mass Society.* New York: Free Press.

Kuhn, Thomas S. 1962. *The Structure of Scientific Revolutions.* Chicago: University of Chicago Press.

Lasswell, Harold. 1958. *Who Gets What, When, and How.* New York: Meridian.

Logan, John. 1976. "Suburban Industrialization and Stratification," *American Journal of Sociology,* 82:333–48.

Long, Norton. 1958. "The Local Community as an Ecology of Games," *American Journal of Sociology.* 64:251–61.

Lowi, Theodore J. 1971. *The Politics of Disorder.* New York: Basic Books.

Marshall, Thomas H. 1964. *Class, Citizenship, and Social Development.* Garden City, N.Y.: Doubleday.

Mead, George Herbert. 1934. *Mind, Self, and Society.* Chicago: University of Chicago Press.

Molotch, Harvey Luskin. 1972. *Managed Integration.* Berkeley: University of California Press.

Nisbet, Robert A. 1953. *The Quest for Community: A Study in the Ethics of Order and Freedom.* New York: Oxford University Press.

————1962. *Community and Power.* London: Oxford University Press.

Ostrom, Vincent. 1974. *The Intellectual Crisis in American Public Administration.* Tuscaloosa, Ala.: University of Alabama Press.

Schumpeter, Joseph A. 1942. *Capitalism, Socialism and Democracy.* New York: Harper.

Shils, Edward. 1957. "Primordial, Personal, Sacred, and Civil Ties," *British Journal of Sociology,* 8:130–45.

————1975 *Center and Periphery.* Chicago: University of Chicago Press.

Stein, Maurice. 1960. *The Eclipse of Community.* Princeton: Princeton University Press.

Steward, Julian H. 1955. *Theory of Culture Change.* Urbana: University of Illinois Press.

Suttles, Gerald D. 1968. *The Social Order of the Slum.* Chicago: University of Chicago Press.

————1975. "Community Design: The Search for Participation in a Metropolitan Society." In A. Hawley and V. Rock, eds., *Metropolitan American in Contemporary Perspective,* pp. 235–97. New York: Halsted.

Taub, Richard, George P. Surgeon, Sara Lindholm, Phyllis Betts Otti, and Amy Bridges. 1977. "Urban Voluntary Association, Locality Based and Externally Induced," *American Journal of Sociology,* 82:425–42.

Thomas, W. I., Robert E. Park, and Herbert A. Miller. 1921. *Old World Traits Transplanted.* New York: Knopf.

Warner, W. Lloyd. 1959. *The Living and the Dead.* New Haven: Yale University Press.

Webber, Melvin M. 1961. "Order in Diversity: Community Without Propinquity." In R. Gutman and D. Popenoe, eds., *Neighborhood, City and Metropolis,* pp. 792–811. New York: Random.

V

INSTITUTION BUILDING AND SOCIAL CHANGE

16

The Ideology of Professional Psychologists

Since the close of World War II, interest has continuously grown among professional psychologists in the question whether or not social values are influencing scientific research and professional practice. This preoccupation, of course, centers among psychologists who define their discipline as a social science; these remarks, therefore, deal with psychology as it relates to the social sciences.

In the rediscovery of the "value question," psychologists are demonstrating the same intense energy, individual honesty, and optimism that have characterized the recent rapid growth of their professional ranks. They are also demonstrating their characteristic intellectual freshness which may, in fact, be the source of a brand new approach to the age-old "philosopher-king" problem. Perhaps it is best that contemporary psychologists have not searched the literature or concerned themselves with the vast amount of previous philosophizing on this topic. Nothing in the existing literature solves the central problems. The efforts of previous crucial thinkers from Plato to J. S. Mill do at least serve to remind the behavioral scientist that others have thought about similar problems. Their statements seem to formulate problems which have the perennial tendency to reemerge.

In any case, what accounts for the recent interest of psychologists in the value question? Some explanation of this renewed interest seems to be a prerequisite to examining psychology as a special case in the general problem of the social limitations of scientific knowledge.

Reexamination of the value question in the social sciences is often linked to crucial theoretical advances. These are the advances or reformulations necessitated by the discovery that explicit or hidden value premises have resulted in defective conceptualization. Such was the process by which John Maynard Keynes reformulated classical economic theories on the basis of his socialist critique of free enterprise values. The value position of the social scientist thus became a positive contribution to scientific development. Current interest in the value

From *The American Psychologist* 9:9 (September 1954): 528–32. © 1954 by The American Psychological Association.

question among psychologists does not seem to be of this origin or variety.

In the simplest terms, the recent political and international crises appear to have forced the psychologists into a revision of their former oblivion of the value question, and perhaps it is only the newer and younger generation of psychologists who express this concern. An explanation on another level can be offered; it relates to the ideology of psychologists. It is, of course, frankly speculative. For social groups, sudden preoccupation with the value question and with social responsibility implies either one of two conditions, or a combination of both: (a) a concern about past group behavior and the possibility of past positive sins; (b) a desire to achieve greater group influence coupled with a concern about the viability of group ethics and social responsibility under such conditions of increased influence.

As to past positive sins, psychologists as a professional group, with the possible exception of certain specialties whose performance is difficult to evaluate, can be said to have achieved a relatively clean bill of health. Foremost among the positive sins of which psychologists have been accused are the sins of manipulation of human beings on behalf of advertisers, employers, personnel managers, and the like. Undoubtedly, there have been cases of antisocial behavior, for psychologists as a group cannot be expected to represent the collective conscience of the human species. Liberal journalists and the "hardheaded" school of social scientists, seeking to uncover plots and to understand the "realities of power," have made the most of these cases. However, the important point is that psychology is neither so well developed nor so effective as to supply such powerful aids to advertisers, employers, or managers. One has only to read a handful of the so-called "confidential" psychological reports. Most of what manipulation exists seems to be limited to the game of charging fees merely for repeating in technical language, and imprecisely, the commonsense basis of operating procedures. There still remains a lack of sufficient evidence that in these areas professionally trained psychologists are any more efficient than practical operating personnel. On the basis of personal experience, I would state flatly that in the area of psychological warfare— which is neither psychological nor warfare—psychologists are by and large much less effective and influential than the practical specialist.

Current preoccupation of psychologists with the value question is mainly related, in my opinion, to the second source of concern—the problems that would be generated should psychology develop a body of systematic knowledge that had decisive capacity to influence human behavior. Whether motivated by a desire for such increased influence or a fear of the consequences, psychologists, like other social scientists, are becoming less and less reluctant to avoid this issue. Psychologists, like typical intellectuals in the United States, are deeply ambivalent in their predispositions toward the exercise of power. They are openly critical of those who exercise influence without the use of scientific knowledge; they entertain elaborate notions of their own potentials, but they seldom seek to enter directly into the struggle for power. The concern about the potentialities of psychology may explain in part why some first-rate psychologists returned to their laboratories after a brief liaison with government or industry during World War II. But now the value implications of psychology must be seen in the light of the tremendous expansion of the facilities for training professional psychologists who are explicitly seeking new social roles in the community.

Analysis of the value position of psychologists starts with an examination of certain of the intellectual postulates and biases of modern psychology. These contribute to what I call the ideology of professional psychologists. They also assist in understanding the actual and potential influence of psychologists. Modern psychology derives its particular orientations in good measure from the social context of American life. The ideology of professional psychology, I shall argue, is linked to the antiphilosophical, antihistorical, narrowly means-oriented and optimistic character of much American thought and culture.

a. Modern psychologists tend to be antiphilosophical and rather unconcerned with the foundation problems of their discipline. The philosophical character of a discipline as opposed to its theoretical character involves both the assumptions that make possible the development of a body of knowledge and the limitations that must be imposed on that body of knowledge. Psychologists seem, in general, to be creating a body of knowledge on the basis of a rather naive empiricism, which in certain respects parallels the formal characteristics of crude logical positivism. Popular semantics might be a more apt designation of the philosophical assumptions of much of contemporary psychology.

As a result two important distortions tend to develop. First, this popular semantics approach is a most simplified affirmation of the arbitrary nature of science. Once the acknowledgment is made, it is in fact quickly forgotten, and the psychologist all too often becomes so involved in his verbal creations that he is not able to delimit scientific knowledge from reality. Scientific knowledge then becomes the same as reality and, indeed, a form of super-reality. Second, psychology has little to say explicitly about the relations between scientific knowledge and other types of social knowledge which have not attained scientific validity. There are not only the intuitive and creative insights which suddenly develop and crucially assist human understanding; there are also the operational bodies of understanding which guide practical men and which have powerful validity. It is naive and misleading to deal with this type of knowledge by merely asserting that ultimately formal scientific knowledge will encompass all of it.

Thus, failure to be concerned with the inherent limitations on psychological knowledge leads to a fantastic exaggeration of the potentialities of social science and to a caricature of the human being as an all-powerful social scientist.

It is difficult to understand the strong reluctance of psychologists to set limitations on scientific knowledge. Undoubtedly the high prestige of science in our society has emboldened them in their claims. This aspect of the social sciences reflects the anti-intraceptive character of contemporary American life. I feel that psychology assumes its pose of rampant positivism in part because it has not come to terms with the specific question of religious knowledge versus scientific knowledge, which is but another specific form of the same general question. The troubled emergence of psychological analysis from religious contexts and the large number of new psychologists still in active revolt against religion might well explain this orthodoxy toward science and the absence of concern with other dimensions of knowledge except to deny their relevance for social action. As a result, psychology appears to be both a scientific discipline and a social gospel, and it is difficult to know where one stops and the other starts.

  b. Modern psychologists fail to achieve adequate comparative analysis because of their antihistorical orientation. But how does the historical dimension apply to psychology? Is it not the case that the genetic phases of individual development must suffice? To speak of history in connection with psychology, it might be argued, would not only present impossible problems of validation, but would completely pervert the scope and method of psychology.

To the contrary, the issue is simply that the generalizations which the social scientist is able to develop are related directly to the types of comparative observation he is able to perform. Value judgments are revealed by the selection of populations on which comparative analyses are made. Hopefully, psychologists have become restive of the limitations under which they have operated in this respect. Therefore, in order to enrich the powers of comparative analysis, they have sought to extend the horizontal range of their research by rushing headlong into the cross-cultural analysis offered by the anthropologists. These developments are undoubtedly meritorious, but they have happened because of a lack of historical perspective and do not substitute for a vertical perspective through time. The results have not only been a distortion of scientific knowledge, but also a degeneration of the value question into the ethical relativism of cultural anthropology.

Cross-cultural anthropological data have many superficial attractions to the behavioral scientist. In particular, there is the security that arises from fifty or so tribes drawn at random, which permits the application of the chi-square test. But random sampling has given way in other areas of research to area probability sampling. For historical comparative purposes the cross-cultural samples must of necessity include the major industrialized areas of Western Europe out of which our society developed. Relative similarities in social structure would highlight and give greater meaning to the differences encountered in psychological research, for all psychological observations postulate some view of social structure.

Comparisons with the other industrialized societies which have been crucial in our historical development and which have interacted with our development supply a sounder basis for generalization and prediction. This is the first step in the development of a historical perspective for psychological research. Secondly, even the crudest time dimensions help to overcome distortions from an ideological preoccupation with the immediate present. Goldhamer and Marshall's data, for example, claim a stability of mental illness rates during the last one hundred years in areas of the United States, and thereby present a fundamental challenge to all who work in the area of psychopathology.

c. Modern psychologists tend to be narrowly means oriented. They have, consequently, an optimistic bias about the psychological potentialities for rapid change in human relations. This narrow means orientation has led to a wasteful preoccupation with bits of problems rather than with meaningful problems. Moreover, often, as in the case of personnel selection, it has led to concern with the wrong problem. For example, military selection procedures are only slowly moving toward the selection of soldiers rather than veterans.

American psychology bears the strong imprint of an intellectual reaction to Freudian theory, in which the foreign matter has been dealt with by partial incorporation. The view of mankind presented by Freud is indeed a gloomy picture, and the reaction to it has produced a markedly different end product. It is the psychology of the here and the now, of three-session psychotherapy, sentence completion tests, and the rapid attitude-change experiments. Such a psychology is a reflection of our engineering culture, of a rapidly changing social context where the laying on of more hands is believed to be able to solve all problems. I fear that many of our researches have been designed to reflect and to conform to these culture imperatives. Indeed, if human nature were as psychologically changeable as might be inferred from certain schools of contemporary psychology, then the social consequences of modern psychology would be most frightening and utterly dangerous.

The intellectual strength and limitations of modern psychology are manifested through the particular way in which psychology is organized as a profession. It is possible to analyze the drive toward professionalization in psychology; it is possible to note the source of funds for psychological research; to speak of the kinds of individuals who become psychologists, and to analyze the image the public holds of them. These factors and a host of others are important. But of all these factors, it is precisely the narrow means orientation of psychology—the concern with specific and immediate means—that is decisive in evaluating the social consequences of psychology. It is this fact which helps explain why, despite the vigor, intellectual achievement, and resources of the profession, psychology has relatively low direct social influence. As a result, psychologists tend to have only rather indirect access to policymakers and public leaders; they are seldom involved in the formulation of policy and goals, but are merely employed as consultants, technicians, or custodians. In this respect, psychologists have suffered a retrogression from their earlier counterparts in the priesthood and ministry.

The ideology of psychologists has resulted in a failure of psychology to produce its own intellectual spokesmen. I am not speaking of popularizers, but of intellectual spokesmen oriented toward the other social scientific and humanistic disciplines, since discussion of the value question must of necessity proceed on an interdisciplinary basis. These are the spokesmen who are required to create a unity of learned discourse out of which the broader social dissemination of knowledge is possible. The major intellectual spokesmen for recent American psychology have not been professional psychologists: Veblen was an economist, Dewey a philosopher, and, more recently, Kinsey a zoologist. To be concerned with the unity of learned discourse requires a broader definition of social means than scientific psychologists seem to employ.

The value question for psychologists ultimately implies concern for the misuse of psychological data by individuals other than professional psychologists. Here I am referring to popular psychology, particularly in the mass media, which seems to cause more confusion than positive harm. Psychologists cannot, of course, wash their hands of this problem although a purely engineering mentality would hinder the acceptance of such responsibility. Likewise, they need not feel that they have complete responsibility for this burden. The psychological profession ought to develop to the point where its members feel that they have exercised reasonable initiative. There are many organizational devices which this lively profession is developing and could develop.

Probably as fundamental is the intellectual task of overcoming the antiphilosophical, antihistorical, narrow means orientation inherent in psychology. This would help the psychologist to be more realistic about his role as a scientist and a citizen. The scientific method, contrary to some traditions of psychology, remains unspoiled and in fact becomes more effective when the social scientist realizes that the value assumptions that guide his technical research and the value assumptions that guide him as a public citizen ought to be part of the same whole.

All the evidence from history, and in particular from modern totalitarianism, shows clearly that in the absence of the study of human relations by the scientific method, human exploitation and manipulation run rampant. The charges that the social scientists per se are the new manipulators seem to be utter nonsense when we observe the fate of social science under the Nazis and Marxists. I am convinced that the efforts of social scientists, if they are constantly mindful of the inherent limitations and biases in scientific knowledge, will serve to enhance the dignity of mankind by clarifying the fundamental nature of human nature.

17

Models for Urban Education

In contrast to the mental health and early education approaches, the strategy of this analysis is to present two alternative models of organizational change in educational institutions: the *specialization model* and the *aggregation model*. Both of these models see the school as a social institution. These models supply criteria for judging and evaluating specific research findings and particular innovations. They are offered as a basis for describing many current practices and for assessing efforts at strategic innovation. It is not enough to point out that they are both hypothetical constructs. The specialization model is in effect an expression of the major trends over the last decade [1960s] of innovation programs. It encompasses a variety of the current segmental and administrative changes. There are very few examples of meaningful or persistent innovation that conform to the aggregation model but they do exist. It is much more than an ideal model; it is a notion of potentialities. The aggregation model is the expression of administrators and staff members who are concerned primarily with a basic format within which change and effective teaching can take place. Specific programs and specific techniques are of secondary concern, as compared with organizational climate, institutional milieu, or operational doctrine. My preference is clearly for the aggregation model, and this needs to be explicitly acknowledged. . . .

Both the specialization model and the aggregation model focus on the classroom teacher. The capacity of the public school system to achieve its goals, both academic and social, involves a central concern with increasing the authority and professional competence of the teacher. The dilemmas that the teaching profession faces are characteristic of every other professional group, resulting from increased available knowledge, the increased complexity of the professional tasks that need to be performed, and societal demands for higher levels of performance.

From *Institution Building in Urban Education*, pp. 41–43, 46–50, 54–58. Reprinted by permission of The Russell Sage Foundation. © 1969 by The Russell Sage Foundation.

Fundamentally, the specialization model appears to be an ad hoc adaptation by introducing, on a piecemeal basis, new techniques, new programs, new specialists, and even new specific administrative procedures, each of which may appear valid. On the other hand, the aggregation model focuses on the totality of the situation in which the teacher finds herself.[1]

Under the specialization model, the traditional activity of the teacher is modified as the teaching process is broken up into more and more specialized roles. The increased level of substantive knowledge and the importance of specific teaching techniques are offered as the rationale for the teachers' subordination to curriculum specialists. The complexities of deviant behavior are given as the reason for their subordination to experts in the management of interpersonal relations. In contrast, the aggregation model emphasizes the necessity for maintaining and strengthening the teacher's role as the central manager of the classroom in which he creates the conditions for teaching and learning. In this model, teaching is seen as a diffuse relationship to the pupil and leadership skills are as important as technical proficiency in the subject. The teacher makes use of specialists and resource personnel, but manages their introduction into the classroom. The term "aggregation" is designed to draw attention to the adding up of the parts of the social system in which the teacher must operate. The aggregation model recognizes that teacher-pupil relations involve direct and immediate response. This model is deeply influenced with the notion of teacher-counselor but it is not the same. The teacher-counselor is a single person who personally seeks, as much as possible, to serve the needs of a classroom of youngsters.

The aggregation model also places the teacher, or more accurately the teacher-administrator, in charge of a group of youngsters. He is responsible for the well-being and educational progress of these youngsters. But the teacher can involve a variety of persons, both within and outside the school, to see that the youngster has access to the basic needs and values. In fact, the aggregation model fundamentally is concerned with expanding the pool of such human resources for the individual youngster. There is no way of knowing in advance to whom a student will relate appropriately and who will in effect offer satisfactory and stable interpersonal contacts. It is the function of the teacher-manager to see that such relationships are facilitated.

1. See David A. Goslin, "The School in a Changing Society: Notes on the Development of Strategies for Solving Educational Problems," *American Journal of Orthopsychiatry* 37:5 (October 1967): 843.

The specialization and aggregation models rest on differing assumptions about human nature and the strategy of learning. The specialization model is actively buttressed by an elaborate intellectualized psychology of learning which is rooted in individual and cognitive psychology. The specialization model has as its goal the elaboration of cognitive processes and the enhancement of academic achievement mainly brought about by reconstructing the contents of the curriculum according to the principles of cognitive development.

Educational psychologists supply a partial rationale for the specialization model, although they would criticize many of the actual applications of their principles into practice. Basically, these educational psychologists have sought to broaden the definition of the maximum amount of the student's ability to learn. Led by the recommendations of Jerome S. Bruner, the dominant intellectual posture of educational psychologists has been to question traditional conceptions of readiness for learning.[2] Their conclusion is that educators have vastly underemphasized the capacities of children to learn. The key to the learning process, from this point of view, is to restructure the subject matter—the curriculum content—so that it articulates with fundamental principles of intellectual and cognitive development of the child. The consequence of this perspective—even though it may be an unanticipated consequence—is to create a group of specialists whose impact is felt through a restructuring of the curriculum, without adequate regard for the full institutional milieu. In this sense it is part of the specialization model.

But the existence of a body of general principles, grounded in research, is still a problematic issue. Therefore, the central notion of the new curriculum development movement is stated in the following terms by Bruner: "We begin with the hypothesis that any subject can be taught effectively in some intellectually honest form to any child at any state of development."[3] Such an assertion is patently not a hypothesis but a moral exhortation since it rests on the crucial and completely ambiguous term "honest."

Suppose it were the case that the process of the child's intellectual development offered by Jean Piaget and adapted by Bruner supported the claim that any subject can effectively be taught at any stage of human development. But then the issue would still exist as to what should be taught at what age to serve the individual's and society's needs. Piaget himself has questioned the American adaptation and ap-

2. Jerome S. Bruner, *The Process of Education* (New York: Vintage Books, 1960).
3. Ibid., p. 33.

plication of his thinking to curriculum reform.[4] He emphasizes developmental stages to a much greater extent than Bruner would and questions the American emphasis on speeding up the learning process. Moreover, a gap between Piaget's concept and the realities of classroom teaching must exist, for Piaget never thought of his work as the basis of specific instructions to teachers. His work and the efforts that it has stimulated have meaning for the classroom teacher not because they supply engineering-type guides for curriculum development, but because, directly or indirectly, they increase the interpersonal capacity of the classroom teacher. In the specialization model, the psychologist makes his impact felt through his general principles of learning, which in turn influence the specialist on curriculum construction teams. In the aggregation model, the psychologist has the same relation to the teacher as the teacher has to her pupil—a direct and diffuse one in which there is a continuous process of interaction.

The end result of the curriculum development movement, based on the theory of cognition, has been an additional pressure toward educational rigidity with a commitment to a spiral curriculum and its mechanical emphasis on earlier and earlier exposure to more intellectually complicated materials.[5] Its grossest form is present in a quotation from David Page, who has been characterized as one of the most experienced teachers of elementary mathematics: "In teaching from kindergarten to graduate school, I have been amazed at the intellectual similarity of human beings at all ages, although children are perhaps more spontaneous, creative and more energetic than adults." [6]

Instead of such a perspective, under the aggregation model the principles of curriculum construction depend not only on cognitive (rational) processes but, equally, on affective (emotional) considerations. Thus, for example, there is a considerable body of experience which indicates that the limitation in reading achievement among these youngsters is based on the fact that they are weaker in comprehension than they are in vocabulary or speed. The experiences of skilled teachers and volunteers lead to the hypothesis that breaking up the curriculum into component parts according to some principles of developmental learning and repeated instruction does not necessarily serve these youngsters. To the contrary, these youngsters require a more con-

4. Frank G. Jennings, "Jean Piaget: Notes on Learning," *Saturday Review* 50 (May 20, 1967): 81–83.
5. In fact, curriculum reform has many elements of a social movement with strong overtones of romantic ideology in which the children have the role of saviors of mankind by their classroom exploits.
6. Bruner, op. cit., p. 39.

figurational approach in which the interrelations of component elements are stressed and the students presented with an opportunity to respond to the elements in a variety of settings.

Concern with the structuring of materials is of less importance than the sheer question of mobilizing interest in the subject matter. A central question is a set of rewards and pattern of motivation which lead youngsters to undertake the necessary "intellectual" struggle and effort. These rewards are most effective if they are immediate, mediated through personal relations, and are strengthened if they are unconditional. Frustration and instability of interpersonal relations are all at work. Academic exploration outside of one's immediate life space can become difficult and even at times painful. Human beings and human referents are the most effective carriers of meaning, not abstractions. The case of a twelve-year-old girl who could not comprehend the notion of the United States or "our country" is illustrative. Efforts to develop an understanding of these words failed when maps and charts were used. The tutor succeeded when, by accident, she presented the girl with a picture of President Kennedy standing next to an American flag. The girl was able to identify the flag as the "Kennedy flag," and from that it was possible to introduce the notion of her own flag and in turn to develop an association to our own country and the concept of the United States.

In short, compensatory education must confront elements of a powerful egocentrism. The teachers and the materials they use need to be able to convince the youngster that they are concerned with his basic needs. It is no accident that the after-school study centers, as part of their procedures, feed youngsters, and there is no effort to withhold food as part of the incentive system. In developing the details of the aggregation model, strong emphasis is placed on making available to the youngster tutorial assistance offered by one person. The youngster who is falling behind wants to command the attention of a single person; even assistance in a small group, valuable as it may be, hardly suffices to reach the core of his internal pressures. This in turn leads to those recommendations that stress intensive human effort rather than elaborate but impersonal technology.

The effective teacher is one who is able to personalize the curriculum and present it as projecting her own personality and presence. The effective teacher, on the basis of her own efforts, must be able to implement this notion regardless of the official content of the curriculum. This involves a fundamental professional perspective, not a set of specific techniques, although it can be manifested by means as diverse as calling the child by his proper name and not a nickname, the preparation of materials about the youngsters in the classroom, and the creative use of ethnic and racial pride and heritage.

The reservation implied in the aggregation model about a cognitive theory of curriculum reform can be stated in alternative terms. Cognitive psychology is an insufficient basis for institution building, relevant though it may be. Basically, the theory fails to take into consideration the social class and cultural elements that condition learning and supply the context in which the school as an institution must operate. This is implied in the notion of organizational climate. Thus, by contrast, the aggregation model is grounded in a set of assumptions about the slum school as a normative or moral order in which there are group solidarities and the need for legitimate authority.

The moral order of the slum school cannot be characterized by simple generalizations if only because of the variation from school to school and from classroom to classroom. But more fundamentally there is no necessity to assume that the moral order of any low-income school is by its very nature incompatible with the requirements of a civil society. There are older and relatively stable low-income communities where the school functions on the basis of mutual consent and a relative sense of legitimacy even though its educational effectiveness may be limited, or serve to limit the aspirations of the youngsters it serves.[7] But the slum school in most Negro ghettos has lost much of its legitimacy. . . .

In contemporary society, there is considerable concern that the school system prepare youngsters for the "competition" they are to encounter in the "real" world, and therefore, the aggregation model must anticipate a curious argument. This argument runs as follows: If the suburban school system continues as currently organized and the inner-city school succeeds in moving toward the aggregation model with its emphasis on self-respect, and on an educational strategy that emphasizes continuous as opposed to age-graded education, would not "the result be a further separation of inner city youngsters and suburban ones in terms of life chances after grammar school." This is a point of view that sees competition—rather than group solidarity— as the basis of educational motivation.

First, this point of view fails to recognize that emphasis on socialization and self-respect is not at the immediate or long-term expense of academic achievement, wherever and whenever it can be effectively achieved. At the risk of repetition the assumption of the aggregation

7. See Gerald Suttles, *The Social Order of the Slum* (Chicago: University of Chicago Press, 1968).

model is that present arrangements do not operate effectively and more intensive and extensive exposure to existing programs will not [produce] and have not produced higher levels of academic achievement. Second, and more pointedly, the aggregation model does not rule out or overlook the role of competition in the school or in the "real" world although it recognizes the limits of competition. The aggregation model emphasizes that the inner-city youngster first compete with himself and second with his immediate peers, before he is thrown into competition with all of his age group. It holds that merely to emphasize competition is to perpetuate an unequal race that is certain to maintain current privileges and inequalities. Finally, on this point, it needs to be stated that the aggregation model is designed to increase equality of education and to improve individual and group mobility. But equality of educational opportunity and improved education do not alone and directly solve the issues of social change in our society. It is dangerous to have a person's position in society determined exclusively by his performance in school, and it is equally dangerous when school performance guarantees great and persistent degrees of social inequality. In a democratic society, persons must be able to achieve their goals to some measure on the basis of a display of their skills, which can continue to grow throughout adult life.

The new "crisis" in public education has meant that educational administrators, especially those in the inner city, must develop a new hierarchy of educational goals. The superintendents of the major big city school systems and their top assistants have been forced to accept the position that academic and vocational achievement is not possible unless the school becomes more directly and explicitly involved in the socialization of its youngsters. This has meant a reformulation of the logic with which they have operated during the formative years of their own administrative careers. Many view the shifting and broadening of goals with considerable skepticism.

The most common response to the expansion of educational perspectives is contained in the repeatedly encountered phrase, "the school cannot do the whole job." From this point of view, which is the dominant view of school administrators, socialization goals are adjunctive or secondary objectives that the school must undertake in order to fill its primary function—the transmission of skill. Special personnel, special functions, and special programs are added to achieve these adjunct goals. Such a broadening of goals of the public school system, especially in the inner city, conforms to the specialization model. The specialization model is an expression of an incremental philosophy of change in which delimited and specific steps are taken, although it may be questioned whether the particular steps are powerful enough to produce the desired objectives.

By contrast, the aggregation model, in theory, emphasizes not an incremental conception of organizational change, but rather a concern with minimum standards of performance. Thus, the aggregation model is influenced by the holistic strategy of change of the mental health movement. What type of organizational structure and what amount of resources are required in order to create an educational environment and a moral order that would meet the minimum requirement of effectiveness? With the establishment of basic requirements, step by step, programs become justified. In short, academic or vocational goals are fused with those of socialization. This is not to say that socialization goals are made equal to those of academic achievement. They are seen as interdependent. Interdependent means a flexible balance including the circumstances in which socialization goals, for a particular time period and for a particular group of students, might well outweigh academic or vocational objectives.

The aggregation model does not assert that the addition of specialists in either curriculum development or in the management of interpersonal relations will insure an adequate social climate in the public school system. To achieve this goal, the aggregation model is not limited to an increased emphasis on socialization processes. To the contrary, the school is seen as the central coordinating mechanism in the personal and social development of the youngster. The school not only seeks to organize itself to a system based on mutual self-esteem and dignity; it is also concerned with the entire existence of the youngster outside of the school.

To state that the school becomes the coordinating institution in the lives of its youngsters does not imply that it manages their total life space. It does not mean that the school directs the local health agency, the social agency, or the police in the immediate environment. It means that the requirements of the school serve as the stimulus for insuring relevant policy and practices by all these agencies. In particular, the school and the teacher become the central locus for all information about its students. The school is the only institution, except perhaps for the police, which touches the lives of all the residents. Therefore, this conception means that the school is the point at which the various directed efforts at social change, both public and private, can be meaningfully related.

The school is the essential institution, but the aggregation model does not imply that it becomes the controlling institution in the slum. If the school sought to be a substitute for the family or welfare institutions, it would be destined to fail. But the school, because of its unique characteristics, can operate as a coordinating mechanism for formal and informal programs of intervention. Moreover, this approach is predicated on the notion that a minority of youngsters will not succeed in school. For them the experience of work, military, or other forms of vocational service will supply for them, as for earlier generations, essential socialization experience. It is hoped that this minority can be minimized. It is outside the scope of this analysis to deal with the artificial barriers and institutional defects that such youngsters must face.

An additional dimension for exploring the operational elements of the specialization and the aggregation models is derived from reference to the economic distinction between capital- versus labor-intensive approaches. The specialization model stresses capital-intensive measures while the aggregation model stresses . . . labor-intensive ones. Of course, both approaches are present in each model and the basic issue is the most appropriate combination. Capital-intensive methods imply high investment costs which can be used for the training and professionalization of personnel, and the extensive use of complex technological devices. Effectiveness and efficiency result from the high output which each costly input of effort is designed to produce. Labor-intensive methods center on the notion that in the educational process there is need for significant amounts of inexpensive effort and simple human resources. This is dictated by the diffuse nature of the teaching function and by the increased emphasis on the fusion of academic and socialization goals. Socialization goals cannot be achieved on a mass basis by capital-intensive techniques alone.

It should be noted that the aggregation model asserts that although it emphasizes the incorporation of labor-intensive techniques, the coordination and utilization of these resources requires very high levels of managerial expertise. The teacher and principal who can make effective use of volunteers, teacher aides, homework helpers, and adjunct specialists must have additional training, higher levels of professionalization, and higher rewards. In fact, this is the element of professionalization that the aggregation model stresses; the restructuring of work so that teachers can become master teachers and principals become principal-teachers. The capital-intensive elements in the aggregation model are therefore to be found in the higher level of professionalization required to utilize effective labor-intensive resources . . . .

18

Institution Building for
Military Stabilization

The fusion of new concepts with the day-to-day realities of military organization has presented, and continues to present, deep problems in institution building. The behavior and perspectives of the military are influenced by the immediate realities of manning particular weapons systems as much as they are by the formulation of doctrine. These day-to-day realities maintain traditional combat philosophies. It is true that, in the parliamentary nations of the West, the terminology of deterrence has been incorporated into the language of the professional officer. There is much discussion of the phrase, "peacekeeping through a military presence." The phraseology of the deterrent force in the format of a constabulary or various alternatives is extensively debated in military circles. The formulation presented in *The Professional Soldier* continues to require clarification and explication. "The military establishment becomes a constabulary force when it is continuously prepared to act, committed to the minimum use of force and seeks viable international relations rather than victory, because it has incorporated a protective military posture." [1] However, verbal pronouncements are not reliable indicators of institutional change.

It is difficult to assess the actual and potential capacity of a military organization to transform itself and to meet its changed function. To move beyond the strategy of deterrence and consider issues of stabilization versus destabilization will be even more difficult. In the Soviet Union, the existence of a capacity to fight a conventional war in Europe, the possibility of intervention in socialist countries of Eastern Europe, and the confrontation on the Sino-Soviet border help to maintain traditional perspectives. However, the specter of nuclear weapons and their relation to conventional military operations has produced an

From *World Politics* 26:4 (July 1974): 499–508. Reprinted by permission of The Princeton University Press. © 1974 by The Princeton University Press.
    1. Morris Janowitz, *The Professional Soldier* (New York, 1971), p. 418.

equivalent but highly muted debate in Soviet professional circles about the nature of the military profession under nuclear arms.[2]

Comparison with the medical profession may be appropriate. In order to develop preventive medicine, a separate structure and, in effect, a separate profession—the specialist in public health, with different training, career, and perspective—had to be brought into being. Clearly, it is not feasible to think in such terms in the case of the military. The transformation in professional capacities must take place within existing operational units. For the military profession, the overriding consideration is whether a force effectively committed to a deterrent philosophy and to peacekeeping and the concept of military presence can maintain its essential combat readiness.

To the detached outside observer, this problem hardly appears insoluble, but to the professional officer it is a central and overriding preoccupation. Does deterrence carry with it the seeds of its own destruction? Will such a strategy, especially under a parliamentary system, undermine the credibility of the military? Can a military force maintain combat readiness without any combat experience or an equivalent? Does not an inherent advantage accrue to nations under single-party political systems which accord the military a different social position and a broader range of functions—functions that presumably make it more viable?

Institution building in the military, creating and maintaining a stabilized military force for deterrence, must be seen as an aspect of the long-term decline of the mass armed force based on conscription. The expansion of the military organization to fight a total war had the paradoxical consequence of "civilianizing" the military. The line between the military and the larger society weakened because of military dependence on civilian industry and science, and because of the impact of the mobilization of large numbers of civilians for wartime service. "Total war" made both soldier and civilian objects of attack and served further to attenuate the distinction between the military and civilian sectors of society. Notions such as Lasswell's "garrison state," Mills's "power elite," and Eisenhower's "industrial-military complex" served to highlight the political problems associated with the expansion of the military and the blurring of the distinction between the military and the civilian sectors.[3]

2. John Erickson, "Soviet Military Power," *Strategic Review* (spring 1973).

3. Harold D. Lasswell, "The Garrison State," *American Journal of Sociology* 46 (January 1941); C. Wright Mills, *The Power Elite* (New York, 1956).

The emergence of an all-volunteer military slows the trend toward civilianization. While there is no return to a highly self-contained military establishment, the "new military" displays a strong preoccupation with maintaining its organizational boundaries and corporate identity. Top military leaders in particular struggle to maintain the distinctive features, qualities, and mystiques of military life as they see them. Although they are dependent on technical expertise, they press to select for the highest command posts those who have had combat experience; as the opportunities for combat decline, the emphasis is at least on operational experience. The military continues to recruit top leaders from those who have attended the prestigious military academies. It seeks to build housing on military bases and to maintain the separate structure of the community and its own style of life. The issues of civilian control are changed under the volunteer-force structure, and focus more and more on maintaining the social integration of the military into the larger society.

In Great Britain and in the United States, conscription has been terminated. In France and in NATO nations, the trend is toward reduction in the length of service and toward exploration of new forms of military service (the Netherlands, Belgium, Denmark). Even in West Germany, questions of conscription and its form have come under continual administrative and political scrutiny. In the Western parliamentary democracies, the moral and political legitimacy of military service is thereby being transformed. The military profession and military occupations are seen as one set of "jobs" with special characteristics and qualifications, but the profession is weakened in its special mystique and special status.

Comparable trends are under way in the Soviet Union and the Warsaw Pact nations. The research of John Erickson has demonstrated that, although conscription remains intact and will continue to persist, forms of modern professionalism and an emphasis on "voluntarism" are increasing.[4] The military is becoming more and more concerned with recruiting and retaining volunteers who will man the highly complex weapons. In the navy and the air and rocket forces, manpower is volunteer—no doubt assisted by the volunteers' desire to avoid conscripted ground-force service. In the ground force, a double system—a fused organization of long-term professionals and conscripts—has been emerging. Military service for the conscript is less and less a pos-

---

4. John Erickson, *Soviet Military Power* (London, 1972).

itive experience, as the Russian equivalent of affluence creates its own youth culture. The military must reluctantly accept its role as an ideological indoctrinator while its main concern is with military effectiveness.

In any military organization, there is a gap between the "big ideas" of military function and the immediate tasks which military personnel must continually perform. Military leaders hope that day-to-day routine will create, or at least contribute to, a sense of military readiness and essential social solidarity. In essence, the more a unit during its normal routine is a military force in being, the more able it is to maintain the sense of military distinctiveness. There are, of course, limits to this observation—for example, when the task becomes excessively tedious or irksome.

Thus, the air force is the service most able to recruit personnel and maintain morale under voluntary manpower systems, because the routines of flying aircraft create military units in being. Even missile crews and radar units, because of the deadly character of the weapons which they handle, feel a sense of urgency which helps them to overcome boredom. Naval units have traditionally represented a force in being and maintained a group solidarity derived from the vitality of seamanship. However, the tedium and pressure of the new naval life—for example, of the submarine at sea for months and months—has transformed some of these conditions and increased the problems of recruitment and self-conception.

The crisis of the military style of life is sharpest in the ground forces. Here the gap between preparation and training and presumed combat is the greatest. Training is only periodic and often lacks the sense of urgency, reality, or risk that routine operations in the air force and navy entail. Airborne and parachute units are closest to units in being, because of the risk and danger in training. As a result, parachute training, ranger training, and wilderness activities are emphasized, not only because of their functional importance but to maintain the professional ideology of combat readiness and military distinctiveness.

The actual disposition of forces conditions military perspectives. The military man maintains his traditional conception of combat readiness more easily if he is stationed abroad or close to a strategic border. The Canadian military thinks of its NATO commitment as an essential ingredient in the military profession. Loss of its overseas assignment would reduce its self-esteem; it would become simply a super-gendarmerie. With the end of a commitment east of Suez, the British military establishment fears a loss of morale in the ground forces, which only operations in North Ireland have staved off temporarily.[5]

Such manifestations of organizational traditionalism raise grave questions about the capacity of the military to operate as a deterrent force in the context of changing military utility. Theoretically, the deterrent force must be prepared for combat regardless of previous combat experience or strategic disposition. Moreover, the more effective concepts of deterrence are, the fewer are the opportunities for traditional ways of maintaining combat readiness. There can be no doubt that the military seeks out opportunities to maintain and to perfect its combat readiness in training. Training exercises and the analysis of previous campaigns often leave the professional unsatisfied, although they are pursued relentlessly. Military observers are sent to wherever military confrontation occurs; peripheral warfare is still seen as a device for the experimental testing of new weapons and tactics. The military seeks to become involved in those operations which it defines as directly relevant for maintaining the combat mystique: intelligence operations, military assistance programs, and training foreign military personnel.

In parliamentary democracies, the preparation for and intervention in domestic disorders have become a highly divisive issue, one which has divided the military itself. Most officers see such involvements as weakening the legitimacy of the armed forces, and a task which must be assumed only under the gravest circumstances. A minority conceptualizes this domestic role of the military both as an essential aspect of the military operation and as a device for maintaining combat readiness. In the United States, the ground forces have, since their intervention in the race riots of 1968, pressed hard to have their role in domestic disorders curtailed. For example, in the events surrounding Wounded Knee, representatives of the ground forces counseled, and succeeded in implementing, a policy of restraint. Increased use of local and state police forces plus the expanded activities of federal marshals have been a resulting trend—but they have left many crucial legal and administrative issues unsolved.

The concern with combat readiness cannot be judged merely as irrational traditionalism, a desire to maintain special privilege, or a fetishistic involvement with the rituals of violence, although all these elements are involved. Combat readiness is a genuine problem, for

5. John Erickson and J. N. Wolfe, eds., *The Armed Services and Society* (Edinburgh, 1970).

there is insufficient experience to satisfy operational military officers.[6] The pressure of this uncertainty carries the danger that the military will develop an inflexible posture likely to stand in the way of prag- matic adjustment to emerging realities. One possible response is the acceptance of doctrines which distort the utility of military force in international relations and which are excessively ideological, absolut- ist, and assault-oriented.

The essential issue is to restructure the organizational milieu of the military so that combat readiness is not an expression of personal ag- gressiveness or rigid ideological perspectives, but rather a meaningful element of organizational effectiveness. To the outsider, a military or- ganization appears to be a highly routinized institution—an agency governed by rules and regulations and concerned with the precision of its daily life.

However, such an image belies the essential character of military organization, whether a mass armed force based on conscription or an all-volunteer system. The routines of military organization obscure the sense of emergency and crisis to be found in the military. In the mass armed force, emergency and crisis were expected in time of mobiliza- tion and combat; for the volunteer force, it is an ever-present immedi- ate potentiality. Emergencies and crises derive from both anticipated and unanticipated technological, economic, and political events; from accidents, miscalculations, or unforeseen contingencies. The military commander is the man who, in his own image, is able to respond to emergencies and crises. The expectation of risk and uncertainty, al- though narrowed under deterrence, pervades the military from lowest rifleman to operational leader to ranking commander. The capacity to restore balance effectively or to create a new balance is the contempo- rary dimension of the heroic.

As an element of continuity with the past, the capacity to respond to the unexpected is indeed a core military value, but one only dimly perceived and appreciated. That is the relevance of the "combat spirit"

---

6. The concern to maintain combat readiness also pervades the Russian forces. Their leaders are deeply concerned that they have had no combat experience for a quarter of a century; in their own terms, the occupation of allied socialist nations is not considered war. Their response has been to conduct frequent large-scale maneuvers, with which they are obsessed. The threat of a Sino-Soviet confrontation supplies a realistic stimu- lant. Russian military leaders cannot engage in candid discussion of these issues, and very little is known of the scope and quality of their thinking on these points. They must accept the insistence of political leaders that ideological training is a device for maintain- ing combat readiness—although, of course, they are fundamentally aware of its limita- tions.

in the context of deterrence. Military men need to be able to act decisively to insure that accidents are avoided, resources mobilized, appropriate responses implemented, and information not distorted under pressure. Physical prowess is involved, but motor responses have always required mental precision; under deterrence, an element of rational steadfastness is paramount.

The notion of deterrence in a military organization is not merely a routine capacity; it requires ability to pursue existing, detailed operating procedures and to apply them with intelligence in new situations. When military men speak of problematic issues involved in maintaining combat readiness, they are in effect seeking to maintain this ability. Thus, for example, it is understandable that in 1973 the Royal Air Force seized the opportunity to mount a quick emergency food airlift to remote regions of Nepal. It thereby demonstrated its emergency capacity, since its pilots had to fly over unfamiliar and dangerous terrain. It was an acceptable exercise in the heroic impulse and a legitimate exposure to danger.

A military force is a complex organization, and the motives and interests of its professional perspective can certainly not be expected to be uniform. In the past, social background was believed to be an essential criterion for selecting military personnel. At present, professional socialization—that is, education and training—is considered essential to fashion and refashion the military man.

However, available data on education and socialization in the military supply no assurance that the process of transformation in the profession will be automatic or certain. In reality, the dominant impact of socialization is negative. Military socialization does not fundamentally alter the attitudes of recruits; it merely rejects those who do not conform to central norms and values. Moreover, the longer the time men spend in a military career, the more homogeneous their orientation becomes; and, all too often, the more pessimistic are their views about international relations.[7]

Tough training is necessary and may make for group loyalty, but it does not necessarily guarantee the professional perspectives required for a deterrent force. Moreover, as Marine Corps experience documents, there appears to be a modest supply of human beings, even in

---

7. Bengt Abrahamsson, *Military Professionalization and Political Power* (Beverly Hills, 1972); John P. Lovell, "The Professional Socialization of the West Point Cadet," in Janowitz, ed., *The New Military: Changing Patterns of Organization* (New York, 1964), pp. 119–59; David E. Lebby, "Professional Socialization of the Naval Officer: The Effect of the Plebe Year at the U.S. Naval Academy," unpub. Ph.D. diss. (University of Pennsylvania, 1970).

an advanced industrial society, who are prepared to expose themselves to the extreme rigors of Marine Corps training. But the responsibilities given to such men are limited to initial military assaults.

To adapt to the new realities of international relations, the military profession must first have a conceptual clarity about its strategic purpose. The new element is that such understanding is not reserved to the top leadership. In appropriate degrees, all professional levels must be aware of the redefined aspects of the military function. In fact, professionalism is not to be delimited in terms of skill, but includes the dimension of awareness of the goals and purposes of deterrence. An educational system which assumes that an officer is trained for a tactical mission and subsequently educated for strategic goals as he advances through the military hierarchy has become irrelevant and outmoded.

Second, since men are not guided by strategic concepts alone, group cohesion and collective motives are essential. In the United States, particularly in the aftermath of the war in Vietnam, core elements in the military are deeply concerned with keeping alive their concept of the "fighter spirit." In Western Europe, the military forces acknowledge this problem but are less concerned, since they accept the validity of their training and operational format. One cannot separate self-conceptions from public reputations. In comparison with the military in Western Europe, and especially in Great Britain, it does appear that the lower prestige and social standing of the United States military contributes to its concern with "tough" military virtues.

In reality, most men in the military profession perform routine organizational tasks which need not attract any particular types of personality. However, military men think of themselves as specialists in violence. The deterrent force cannot have its organizational climate fashioned by men acting out aggressive impulses; rather, it must be the expression of effectively internalized professional norms and values.

The vast apparatus which the military has erected for personnel selection hardly solves the underlying issues.[8] Of course, it does serve to eliminate a tiny minority of unstable and undesirable personalities. The social personality of the military profession is the result of a complex series of training and operational assignments and an elaborate process of self-selection. In the past as well as the present, the military profession has placed great emphasis on rotation of assignment as a

8. Paul D. Nelson, "Personnel Performance Prediction," in Roger W. Little, ed., *Handbook of Military Institutions* (Beverly Hills, 1971), pp. 91–122.

means of developing and testing for the kind of social personality desired. Although such a system is costly and disrupts family life, these procedures are stubbornly justified and maintained by the military. The content of military education and diversity of recruitment are key mechanisms of refashioning the military perspective. Another central step is the careful selection of innovative personnel for the role of chief of staff, a task which legitimately falls to civilian political leadership. It should also be possible to develop the military career so that it can be the first step in a lifetime of public service.

Predictably, sons of military personnel enter active duty already socialized to a considerable extent into the profession. It is doubtful whether the military could operate without a strong element of occupational inheritance from father to son. In addition, the military life appeals to men seeking an active athletic existence (although the image of engineer-technologist has been strong in recent years).[9] These men are initially prepared to learn to pilot a fighter aircraft, make repeated military parachute jumps, or navigate a fast destroyer escort. Although such experiences serve as rites of passage and create organizational solidarities, there is no reason to believe that they improve a person's capacities for the detachment and administration required for higher command. But in any career there are multiple requirements and contradictory pressures, and the military is no exception.

Standards of personal behavior are a central issue. If it is to be seen as legitimate and reliable, a force which handles nuclear weapons cannot engage in the deviant practices found in civilian life. The constant screening of "human factors" becomes part of military medicine, and the personal and social controls required to deal with the difficult and tedious tasks of the "new military" will have to be different and more constrained than those in the civilian society.

In a parliamentary democracy, it has been assumed that an officer corps which is not excessively self-recruited and which is reasonably representative of the larger society would have a political orientation compatible with the larger society and would have internalized the advantages of civil control.[10] There can be no explicit political criteria of recruitment into the officer corps. The professional soldier—officer or enlisted man—has the right to personal privacy and to civic involvements, provided he does not engage in partisan behavior. Moreover, it is assumed that he will remain integrated into the larger society. (In the

9. Janowitz (n. 1), pp. 21–37.
10. Samuel P. Huntington, *Soldier and State* (Cambridge, Mass., 1957).

Soviet Union, political reliability is required and enforced by police controls, and the military is isolated from the larger society in order to insure continuing loyalty to the Party.)

However, in an all-volunteer force, especially in states with a long tradition of citizen-soldiers, all of these assumptions are being tested.[11] The strategic conceptions of deterrence and of stabilized military systems which do not produce tangible "victories" create high levels of professional tension and frustration, especially in a period of strong antimilitary sentiment. Recruitment becomes more difficult and the recruits tend to be less representative of the larger society. The potential danger is not simply that the military will become ingrown and socially isolated, although there is clearly a trend in this direction. The real danger is that the military will become both ideologically rigid and more specialized in its contacts with civilian society, and that these contacts may move it toward a more explicitly conservative and rightist orientation.

The result is hardly to produce a potential cadre for counterrevolution. Rather, the military emerges as one additional element of political controversy in a society already racked with extensive political conflict and dissensus. Unless this alternative can be avoided, the military is likely to operate as a pressure group against the realistic military policies required in the search for a new pattern of stabilization in international relations.[12]

. . . The emergence of nuclear weapons and the decline of colonial rule have combined to decrease the relevance of traditional conceptions of military intervention that are concerned with the "defeat" of national adversaries or the drastic restructuring of the balance of power. In a very crude way, the term "deterrence" represented a partial, incomplete, and ultimately unsatisfactory advance that sought to recognize realities and to reformulate international political analysis. The intellectual limitations of the notion of deterrence are varied; basically, the term denotes the military objectives without adequately encompassing the political, social, and moral ends.

11. Janowitz, "The U.S. Forces and the Zero Draft," *Adelphi Papers* 94 (London, 1973).

12. For one of the earliest sociological explications of the norms required for an international order, see Charles Horton Cooley, *Social Process* (New York, 1918), p. 256: "A ripe nationality is favorable to international order for the same reason that a ripe individuality is favorable to order in a small group. It means that we have coherent, self-conscious, and more or less self-controlled elements out of which to build our system. To destroy nationality because it causes wars would be like killing people to get rid of their selfishness. . . ."

In a period of search for military détente, the increased obsolescence of the notion of deterrence rests not merely on the changed character of the threat of national adversaries, although this is a relevant dimension. The concept of stabilizing versus destabilizing military systems is an attempt to move beyond the notion of deterrence. In particular, it is an attempt to explicate more specifically the political and moral objectives of military systems. It is an intellectual orientation concerned with the potentialities and limitations of military systems in creating new rules and new norms which are designed to reduce the threat of nuclear and limited war and at the same time to enhance the process of orderly change at the international level.

In each historical period, it is essential to avoid the extrapolation of trends that characterize much of international relations analysis. Therefore, my formulation of stabilizing versus destabilizing military systems should highlight the built-in limitations in the contemporary trend toward détente. It does not de-emphasize the centrality of force in international relations. I am hopeful, however, that it does offer a sharper set of categories for estimating changes in the utility and the legitimacy of the military function.

19

Toward the Reconstruction of Patriotism

Civic Consciousness and Citizenship

During the last two hundred years, the apparatus for civic education
in the United States has grown into a complicated enterprise. But it has
not become more effective or sensitive. To the contrary, the machinery
of civic education as it expanded has produced less real consequences
than earlier efforts.

From the American Revolution to the outbreak of World War II, the
relative success of civic education in the United States resulted from
two central efforts. First, a simple and rudimentary civic education
was pursued in the schools. Second, the American armed forces followed to a considerable extent the pattern of the "citizen-soldier"
which came into being during the American Revolution. The United
States is one of the very few nation-states where a revolution ultimately strengthened, rather than weakened, internal democracy. The
citizen-soldier concept helped both to win wars and to institutionalize
democratic practices.

Until the outbreak of World War II, primary and secondary schools
served as agencies of acculturation for immigrants. Although the con-
stitution guaranteed separation of church and state, the impact of civic
education rested in part on an uncomplicated religious ritual in the
schools. The decline in religious orientation weakened the school system as a device for spreading a sense of nationalism. Civic education
did not develop a model of the new American but, rather, generated
cultural pluralism, which until the years of the Great Depression can
be considered relatively successful. The growth of the media, especially
television, became a powerful factor after 1945 in shaping images of
citizenship.

After World War II, there was considerable discussion of the need
for new forms of civic education. It was claimed that "real" life train-

From *The Reconstruction of Patriotism*, pp. 192–203. © 1983 by The University of
Chicago. All rights reserved.

ing in the form of political obligation was needed. To what extent and in what form could national service, or aspects of national service, assist the struggle for more effective civic education?

The school system and forms of military service contributed to a balance between individual rights and civic obligations. Civic education in the past implied that each ablebodied male had a series of military and nonmilitary tasks to perform on behalf of the nation-state. It is for that reason that I stress the American Revolution as a form of civic education. In the conduct of that war, officers and enlisted personnel learned that sheer destruction of the "enemy" was less important than winning them over politically to the goals of the Revolution. They developed a strategy which stressed the need for restraining the use of military force. (Unfortunately, such a strategy did not dominate the Vietnam intervention.) The principle of civilian supremacy was established, together with a locally based national guard.

The relative balance between federal forces and local militia was beneficial to democratic forms of control of the military. Political pluralism was strengthened by the interplay of federal forces, which represented aspirations for a national state; on the other hand, pluralism was strengthened by the vitality of national guard units which represented local aspirations.

It is my observation that this dual system, even as it began to decline, continued to contribute to patriotism. Cross-national surveys show Americans very much more likely than citizens of other Western industrialized countries to report patriotic sentiments. Surveys conducted in the middle and later 1970s contain the question "What nation in the world do you have the most respect for?" ("None" was a possible response.) The percentages naming their own countries were: United States, 59; Canada, 35; United Kingdom, 33; France, 26; Italy, 15; and West Germany, 12 (*Public Opinion* 4[June–July 1981]:27).

Yet Americans are suspicious of institutional programs of civic education, especially those with overtones of manipulation. Wide segments of the American people would like to see stronger patriotic sentiment and greater emphasis on civic obligation. But Americans are skeptical about the ability of present-day public schools and agencies to mold civic consciousness.

Military service still contributes to a sense of patriotism, but the meaning of patriotism has become less and less clear. The public is resistant to any form of civic education that gives the impression of partisanship. Nevertheless, in the period after 1945, the need for more civic education became apparent, although there is little agreement about the form, content, and locus of efforts to strengthen patriotic attachment. The Korean war increased demands by public leaders for increased efforts in civic education to strengthen patriotism. The Vietnam war produced renewed debate about the strengths and weaknesses of patriotism in the United States.

The result of my research effort has been to reinforce my belief that a simple-minded program of increasing civic education to reinforce patriotism is of little import. Old-fashioned, uncritical patriotism is not effective in the current interdependent world. The more relevant term *civic consciousness* implies the persistence of love or attachment to a country—a territorially based political system. Civic education becomes a pressing issue when we realize that immigration into the United States is and will continue to be immense. Most immigrants are non-English-speakers. Moreover, the processes of acculturation have become more complex. In particular, for the broad range of Spanish-speaking immigrants, there is a powerful attachment to the home country which operates against the acculturation of immigrants into the larger society.

Democratic states are not particularly effective in civic education. However, at the risk of being misunderstood, I assert that civic education and youth socialization are more important in a multiparty state than in a single-party state. Single-party states make greater use of coercion; they operate with low conceptions of the importance of persuasion.

Civic education means exposing students to central and political traditions of the nation, teaching essential knowledge about the organization and operation of modern governmental institutions, and fashioning the identification and moral sentiments required for performance as effective citizens. It is clear that civic education remains deeply intertwined with patriotism and nationalism. To teach "civics" without encouraging students to explore their sense of nationalism is to render the subject tepid.

Patriotism, as attachment [to] and love of one's country, leads to various forms of belief and behavior. While patriotism can result in performance which enhances the moral worth of a nation-state, it can also be a narrow-minded xenophobia. Given the extensive interdependence of the world community, an "update" in the form and content of patriotism is required to contribute both to national goals and to a more orderly world. As we analyze patriotism we repeatedly encounter the question whether some form of national service can operate to strengthen democratic practices and attitudes. In my view, there can be no reconstruction of patriotism without a system of national service.

I have sought to use a sociopolitical definition of citizenship. The result has been to highlight the conclusion that by legislation and judicial action the difference between citizen and noncitizen has lessened. The inherent advantages of citizenship are either not obvious or increasingly limited in consequence. These advantages in a democratic polity require repeated emphasis. As a result, classroom instruction in citizenship has grown even more important and, with increasing communalism and bilingualism, even more difficult. Some educators hold that the minimum cultural unity for democratic citizen rule in the United States has been eroded and has lost its self-generated effectiveness. I reject that view if only because of the potentials of the existing education system.

Education in the United States, despite weaknesses, produces a youth population with a high level of achievement, especially among its very numerous college graduates. College- and professional-level education remains impressive, even if cultural achievements are not effectively translated into a sounder set of political practices.

Moreover, the system of post–high school education touches an immense number of students who attend junior and community colleges. This junior college population includes large numbers of minority members who come from families with limited academic backgrounds.[1] Economic goals are very important to these students. Whether the essential balance between cultural pluralism and minimum common understandings can be achieved in the United States depends as much on the civic education of community college students as on the regular college graduate.

But it is clear to me that classroom instruction as presently organized is incapable of teaching the meaning of political obligations associated with citizenship. Economic goals appear paramount. Political obligation, especially in recent years, appears to be heavily derivative. Such an observation is incomplete for the United States. A tradition of political obligation is carried on by participation in voluntary organizations, many of which include various economic groups. Since classroom teaching is insufficient for civic education, the interesting question is whether the particular educational experience of national service with real-life content will strengthen popular understanding of civic obligations. Various types of national service are offered as a way of "teaching" citizens to perform the tasks which are part of civic obligation. National service should operate to balance the pursuit of eco-

---

1. A considerable number of young men and women learned their "trade" at private vocational and trade schools. These schools are important institutions in the U.S. economic system, but they hardly offer any civic education.

nomic self-interest against collective civic obligation and thus should have long-term positive effects on the individual involved.

For more than thirty-five years, I have advocated various forms of national service in order to improve and clarify one's sense of civic obligation. The early years of the 1980s have seen an intensification of the debate over the positive and negative consequences of national service. Can we think of national service as an institution that has a concern with the nation as a whole? Or must we plan for a disparate set of specialized agencies? I face an unsolved dilemma. The closer I examine the problems that must be solved in order to organize a meaningful national service, the more complex those problems become. I have not abandoned the desirability of some form of national service. But I shall argue that the forms of national service are likely to be different from those currently recommended. We do not now know how to administer a system of national service, and learning to administer it by a series of experimental programs is likely to alter its scope and content.

National service includes a military element, but of necessity the military and civic components will be separate. Moreover, it is doubtful if various social and community elements could be extensively integrated. The outcome may be voluntary national service composed of decentralized units and diverse programs. Even the term *decentralized* remains too bureaucratic: we are probably headed for a series of localized agencies.[2]

The Military Dimensions of National Service

Young men and women who have enlisted in the all-volunteer army reveal strong patriotic motives as contributing to their decision to enlist. In data collected by military recruitment stations, patriotic reasons were given by 20 percent of new recruits as either the first or second reason for joining. Attitudes manifested in these data reflect a much higher patriotic orientation among enlisted personnel than reported by the mass media. In fact, among new recruits 80 percent included service to country as a reason for enlisting during the years 1971, 1977, 1979, and 1980. Other data demonstrate the stability of such attitudes. For the period 1974–1980, active duty personnel were asked whether "everyone should have to serve his or her country in

2. There is an extensive body of writing on national service. For an overview see The Potomac Institute, *Youth and the Needs of the Nation.* See also, especially, Sherraden and Eberly, eds., *National Service.*

some way." About 55 percent of career personnel agreed. In essence, self-selection into the military and the impact of military environment were at work. By contrast, first-termers revealed a discernible rejection of the proposition that everyone should have to serve his or her country in some way. This negativism gradually dropped from 27 to 7 percent. Clearly, without formal instruction or indoctrination, first-termers were internalizing values of the career armed forces. The character of patriotism expressed remains to be studied.

The social composition of ground combat arms and debate about performance of the all-volunteer military set the stage for proposals for linking active duty force to a contemporary military option within national service. Under a national service military option, the armed forces might be able, if properly organized, to recruit between 100,000 and 150,000 persons annually. The rest would be recruited by present procedures, improved as feasible. The military option is designed to increase the social representativeness of the armed forces and to increase the educational qualifications of recruits. One obvious goal is to include more white middle-class Americans in the enlisted ranks. It is a program designed to increase the outlet for patriotic motives and, in turn, to strengthen the civic education of new generations.

Let us examine a hypothetical set of proposals for the military option of national service. The term of service would be two years; national service personnel would be expected to have above-average academic achievement qualifications. They would be responding to national goals and values as well as to economic incentives. They would not be assigned to specialized training programs but to run-of-the-mill assignments, especially those combat assignments that could be learned in a few weeks. A central element of such a program is that aside from nominal subsistence allocations and very limited cash payments, compensation would not come through monetary reward. Instead, educational benefits would be used. We would be dealing not with a mass GI education proposal but, rather, with a more limited program. Experimental programs of this variety have attracted superior personnel. For each year of military service, two years of college benefits (tuition plus a modest cost-of-living stipend, for a maximum of four years) would be offered. Such a program could solve the manpower needs of the second half of the 1980s. The cost would be equal to or less than the current cash bonus. The program would restore to the enlisted ranks important components of college-bound personnel, who would enrich educationally, technically, and morally the climate of units to which they were assigned. Their presence would be a contribution to restoring the effectiveness and self-esteem of military units. A unit composed of all or most recruits with limited educational background cannot have the morale and clarity of purpose of a unit with mixed educational achievement. Soldiers with heterogeneous backgrounds supply broader linkage between the military and larger society. I would even offer the observation that mixed educational units will have higher standards of morality and personal conduct.

The Frontiers of National Service

There is a sharp difference between national service organized to supply military personnel and one oriented to civilian tasks. This distinction will persist and become greater if national service develops in the United States.

There is no shortage of plans for organizing a civilian component of national service. The list of tasks to be performed continues to grow. While national service could, in theory, be either volunteer or obligatory, it is my view that obligatory national service in the years ahead is not feasible. The political support for an obligatory program does not now exist and is unlikely to develop in the next decade. Advocates of a comprehensive national service can aspire, over the short run, to the development of a series of experimental exercises. But in time, for example, a decade of effort could lead to a gradually growing number of participants that would involve at least half of the eligible youth—male and female.

Obligatory national service would mobilize a very small minority who are in blind opposition based on personal deviance or criminal-like personality. I would estimate that at least 5 percent of youth would fall into this category. Neither the armed forces nor the civilian component would want to act as a reformatory for delinquents. It does not take many deviants to wreck or severely strain a program. Administrative leaders would have to maintain a system of rules which would allow for easy withdrawal of those who had an oppositionist mentality. In fact, most current planning for national service is based on voluntary involvement. Milton Friedman's view that national service is a tax is widely accepted; the central issue is the size of the segment of society who are willing to pay the tax voluntarily.

Even limited experimental programs of national service with civilian options are difficult to organize. Advocates of voluntary national service are sensitive to the complex administrative and organizational tasks. Many proposals for national service envisage a national, central organization. This reflects, in part, the ideology of energetic leaders concerned with social integration.

In my view, organization on a state-by-state basis or even by met-ropolitan centers would simplify administration. Many plans have called for national service to be run by public, nonprofit national agen-cies. The effort is to separate the agency from the governmental struc-ture. In fact, plans generally call for a national agency to direct the operation and a series of operating subagencies to oversee specific pro-grams. I am not impressed with the potential of such decentralization efforts.

Plans for national service that point to a single agency to oversee specific operational programs are attempting to make up for existing institutional confusion. Such a direction does not excite me. Planners of national service are seeking to make up for defects in civilian soci-ety. I am more inclined toward a "loose" plan. To be effective, national service would have to be more of a youth movement than a youth or-ganization. The youth movement would seek to fill in gaps and to be fluid in its approach and organizational structure.

A voluntary national service must develop a widely based strategy of recruitment. There has been considerable debate on this point. We are looking for a strong element of diversity in the youth groups re-cruited. At stake is the question, why are the work features of national service likely to produce more effective citizens? First, national service is committed to a heterogeneous population. The mixing and social interaction is designed to enhance the self-awareness of those who par-ticipate. Second, the work program of national service should increase awareness of socio-economic realities. Third, and most important, co-operative endeavors should serve as forms of education that produce positive responses for a democratic society and lasting positive conse-quences for participants.

I am likely to be misunderstood when I emphasize that prospects for broad-scale national service opportunities are indeed limited and likely to remain so. The political support for a system of national ser-vice does not exist despite verbal support for particular programs. Pri-vate groups can organize equivalent programs, but they have failed to do so to any great extent.

My research leads me to the conclusion that national service can be defined as working at subsistence level after high school or later on one of the broad range of tasks such as conservation, health, or old age problems in order to participate in learning about the civic institutions of society. It is a device for teaching the student to balance rights against obligations. One cannot, of course, overlook the importance of prior classroom study in civic education. Because of routinized pat-terns of education one can afford to give a very broad content to national service. The goal is not the reinforcement of traditional patriotism but rather the development of an understanding of the tasks which must be performed in a democratic society.

We are a statistically minded nation; therefore, the suggestion has been made that we should tabulate annually the young people engaged in some form of national service. I am convinced that, even without governmental support, participation in some type of private national service is certain to grow year by year. Such an observation, however, fails to confront the central issue of developing a national service program—governmental or private sector—which will not be limited to the graduates of elite colleges but will include a broad pattern of participants. No national service system fills its objectives unless it includes all segments of the population.

Over the past fifty years, a variety of service programs open to young people have been created and abandoned, a process which reflects an unstable commitment to service opportunities. During the Great Depression, hundreds of thousands of young people participated each year in the programs of the Civilian Conservation Corps and the National Youth Administration. No federal programs existed from World War II through the 1950s, though small, CCC-like programs were organized at the state level. In the modern era of youth service programs, the Peace Corps began in 1961 and VISTA in 1964. The 1970s brought the revival of the conservation corps idea in the Youth Conservation Corps (1970–83) and the Young Adult Conservation Corps (1978–82). Major demonstrations of national service in urban areas occurred in Seattle (1973–74) and in Syracuse (1978–80).

However, as of 1982, the nation witnessed the decline of several youth service programs and abolition of several others. Among those eliminated as part of budgetary restrictions and retrenchment were the National Teacher Corps, the Youth Conservation Corps, and the University Year of Action. Estimates for total numbers of participants in the remaining programs for 1983 are as follows: At the federal level, the Peace Corps numbers approximately 6,000, VISTA about 3,000, and the National Health Service Corps about 3,000. Of Peace Corps volunteers, about one-half are aged 18–24, the other half 25 and older. The size of VISTA remains uncertain. In 1982 it entered a phase-out schedule, although Congress has been resisting its elimination. Altogether, one could say that federally sponsored service opportunities for teenagers and young adults in 1983 are estimated at approximately 10,000 (estimates from National Service Secretariat, Washington, D.C.).

At the state level, the conservation corps idea has been taken up by several states—most notably California, with about 1,900 year-round participants in the California Conservation Corps in 1982. Much smaller programs in Ohio and Minnesota add 300 more slots. Part-year and part-time programs in Illinois, Iowa, Kansas, Maine, and other states might add an additional 1,000 positions, for a total of about 3,200 (estimates from Human Environment Center, Washington, D.C.). Other service programs may exist at the local government level, but these are few and far between and are not systematically tracked.

In addition, there are many purely voluntary efforts in which young people participate in health, education, recreation, social welfare, religious, political, and other volunteer work. In a nationwide survey of volunteer service in 1974, 22 percent of 14–17-year-olds and 18 percent of 18–24-year-olds were engaged in part-time volunteer work of one kind or another.[3]

In plans developed or implemented in the United States, most recent national service programs involve adding one year to public school schooling. I prefer and am prepared to see the sixteen years required for a college degree gradually and selectively reduced to fifteen years. The "freedom" year would be devoted to some form of national service. Advance placement of high school students into college courses is an essential movement in this direction. The advantages of such a pattern would be immense; especially the financial saving in expenditures for education. I expect a gradual, long-term expansion in productivity of the U.S. economy. The current surplus of youthful labor will give way to increased shortage, especially of trained young workers. Given that shortage, the additional labor supply should in the decade ahead be of vital importance to the U.S. economy.

There is support for national service among both liberal and conservative political leaders. Various bills have been introduced, but the drive for either extensive programs or even small experimental ones does not command wide political support in part because of restraints on the U.S. federal budget.

Public opinion findings must be carefully assessed. An overwhelming majority of American parents want their children to receive civic education. Only a very small portion have specific ideas. Moreover,

3. Donald J. Eberly, in "Patterns of Volunteer Service by Young People: 1965 and 1974," *Volunteer Administration* 4 (winter 1976): 20–27, cites data from surveys by the Census Bureau.

there is a revival of concern with a "sound" education program in selected local communities. A "sound" local school program means an
attack on liberal trends and parental rejection of programs they believe
excessively permissive. Such agitations receive extensive media coverage, but do not generate actual widespread parental participation.
Nevertheless, it is striking that the bulk of U.S. parents—to judge by
national surveys—support the idea that young people should give one
year of national service. There is a view that a year of service would
"be good" for their children. To some extent such a reply is fashionable; but the replies also represent patriotic feelings and the belief that
national service will make their children more aware of their obligations as citizens.

The fundamental barrier to national service (including local programs of community service) is the attitude of American youth. Again,
public opinion surveys need to be read with great care. In the abstract,
there is considerable support among young people for the idea of national service; almost one-half of youth in the early 1980s expressed
favorable attitudes and interest in serving. But many responses represented conventional expressions of what were considered appropriate
attitudes. I do not doubt that there is considerable genuine desire
among college students and selected young workers to demonstrate
that they are "good citizens." I cannot make an effective estimate of
the real support. Young people are caught in a bind generated by parents and the school system. They are attracted to the adventure and
moral value of national service, but also feel obliged to get on with
their careers. Many people believe—incorrectly in my view—that the
economy will get worse. There is therefore considerable pressure to get
on with education and the world of work. In addition, for some students, national service is no more than a possible alternative to service
in the infantry and ground combat arms.

Nonetheless, there is clearly enough interest in, and need for, national service for a range of programs to be launched. Priority should
be accorded to conservation work and to meeting the needs of neglected senior citizens. Programs for the elderly could be locally managed and organized, while resource conservation could be linked to
national and state governmental agencies.

It is fortunate that the United States is not about to launch a large-
scale national service program including both military and civilian options. Existing restraints mean that when programs are developed,
they will be small and thus likely to develop slowly and adequately. We
may be thus spared the typical American pattern of policy implemen-

tation which is one of shifting from extreme restraint to overexpansion. As the nation moves gradually to new forms of national service, the resultant programs could be organizationally sound.

Most important, the forms of national or community service must be seen not as welfare programs but as expressions of civic duty by those who actively participate. Those very conditions which can work to resocialize poverty youth away from a dead-end existence depend upon national service not being defined as an employer of last resort, a definition that is hard to escape unless participation is relatively representative of all American youth. National service must be structured as part of a citizen's obligation.

One idea that has received lively discussion is to make federal aid to college students dependent on national service. This formulation, initially advanced by Charles C. Moskos,[4] has attracted the attention of several political leaders. Most government loan and scholarship programs have helped young people avoid military service through college deferments. In effect, we have created a GI bill without the GI. It is not politically possible to require *military* service as a condition for a government loan. But a program requiring some community service for particular forms of governmental assistance to attend college is feasible and will most likely be introduced as legislation. Although this format does not encompass what I believe are the worthiest elements of national service, it does make sense today. It is fully compatible with the previously discussed program of education benefits in exchange for military service.

Linking government-guaranteed loans for higher education to service in the student's local community is a modified version of the old work/study idea. It involves national, political incentives as well as economic ones. The nation appears increasingly prepared to accept such a work/study program. As of 1982, more than six billion dollars annually are spent for student loans. A work/study program would add little to those expenditures. To the contrary, by making a loan dependent on community service, federal costs would be reduced by the value of the work completed.

The vitality of democratic citizenship cannot be maintained by the existing range of political forms, such as voting and political participation. Historically, citizenship and patriotism have included various forms of local self-help currently associated with the idea of commu-

4. See, for example, Charles Moskos, "Making the All-Volunteer Force Work: A National Service Approach," *Foreign Affairs* 60 (fall 1981): 27–34.

nity or national service. Participation in these activities gives the idea of obligation concrete meaning. The need to make use of this tradition has grown, ironically, with the growth of the welfare state. The first step to make is voluntary national service available to all young men and women. But there is no reason why voluntary national service should not ultimately involve older people too, as they retire from regular work.

Index

Abrams, Philip, 236
Absolutist outlook, 14
Academic achievement, 289
Accountability, 259–60, 263, 269
Adler, Mortimer, 243–44
Advanced industrial society, 22, 126, 130, 137, 152, 159, 193, 198, 201–3, 207, 217, 237, 239, 250, 298; cleavages within, 238
Advanced industrialism, 128–29, 133, 188, 205, 211, 216, 242, 245
Advertising, 240
Age of Democratic Revolutions, The (Palmer), 131
Aggregated metropolitan community, 253–54, 268–69
Aggression, 185, 243
Aggressive behavior, 243, 296
Aggressive impulses, 298
Aggressiveness, 42–43, 165–66
Air force, 294
Air power, 230
All-volunteer force. *See under* Armed forces
American Academy of Arts and Sciences, 44
American Philosophical Society, 44
American Revolution, 212, 226–27, 229, 235, 237, 302–3
American Sociological Association, 44
American thought, 277
Anatomy of Revolution, The (Brinton), 235
Ancient Regime and the French Revolution (Tocqueville), 234
Anti-Catholic bias, 184
Anti-Negro bias, 184
Anti-Semitism, 4, 34–35, 176–77, 181, 184
Antiauthoritarianism, 152
Antihistorical orientation, 278–79
Antimilitary sentiment, 300
Antiphilosophical orientation, 277–78
Applied research, 87–90, 92

Aristotle, 198–99, 218
Armed Forces and Society, 21
Armed forces, 212; all-volunteer, 164, 214, 233, 293, 300, 307; mass, 223–24, 227, 229, 233, 236–37, 292
Army, conscript, 164–65; disintegration of, 160–64; ethnic composition of, 165–66
Army, standing, 212–13, 235, 237
Assumptions, 61
Atomism. *See* Rootlessness
Authoritarian Personality, The (Adorno et al.), 10, 152
Authoritarianism, 152
Authority, 151, 157, 237; relation to, 156, 243

Bacon, Francis, 127
Barker, Ernest, 213
Barnard, Chester, 79
Basic research, 87, 89, 90
Bauer, Raymond A., 240
Belgium, 139, 231, 293
Bell, Daniel, 22
Bendix, Reinhard, 202, 225
Benedict, Ruth, 151
Berelson, Bernard, 11
Bettelheim, Bruno, 9–11, 19, 24, 34
Beyond the Pleasure Principle (Freud), 190–92
Biddle, Francis, 6
Biderman, Albert, 13
Bilingualism, 305
Bismarck, Otto von, 228
Blacks, 228
Blalock, Hubert, 11–12
Blue Collar Community (Kornblum), 46
Blumer, Herbert, 187
Boundaries, social versus socioenvironmental, 70–71
Brinton, Crane, 235
Bruner, Jerome S., 189, 284–85
Buber, Martin, 21
Bundestag, 212